Finding Ruby

*The Bright and Dark Sides of a
Family's Fervent Idealism*

First published in the United States in 2024 by
Richard Rothman, in partnership with Whitefox Publishing Ltd.

www.wearewhitefox.com

Copyright © Richard Rothman, 2024

Hardback ISBN 978-1-916797-44-4
Paperback ISBN 978-1-916797-62-8

Also available as an eBook
ISBN 978-1-916797-45-1

Richard Rothman asserts the moral right to be identified as the author of this work.

All rights reserved. No part of this publication may be reproduced, stored in a retrieval system or transmitted in any form or by any means, electronic, mechanical, photocopying, recording or otherwise, without prior written permission of the author.

While every effort has been made to trace the owners of copyright material reproduced herein, the author would like to apologise for any omissions and will be pleased to incorporate missing acknowledgements in any future editions.

All photographs and illustrations in this book © Richard Rothman, unless otherwise stated.

Edited by Drew Cullingham
Designed and typeset by Karen Lilje
Cover design by Simon Levy
Project management by Whitefox

For Carl Schwab

CONTENTS

PART I OPENING WINDOWS	1
I Could Have Asked	3
The Lost Briefcase	5
The Trailhead	6
A Somewhat False Lead	21
Ruthie	28
Taube Pearl (Schechter) Rothman	31
PART II THE MAN IN THE BRIEFCASE	37
The Elusive Briefcase	39
The Aspiring Poet	41
That Party Organizer	56
The U.S. Communist Party Circa 1933	56
Scottsboro—And Irving Schwab (Take 1)	59
Notes of a Party Operative: Ruby's Little Black Book	69
PART III THE SOLDIER	73
Diving In	75
Spain: April 1937	76
The Lincoln and Washington Brigades	82
Going—and Coming—to Spain	86
A Soldier's Life	94
The New Masses Article	100
Yearning for Battle	104
Rose and Little Toby Back "Home"	107
Under Fire at Brunete	113

Shot—Courtesy of a Mule!	124
Too Late!	129

PART IV DEATH   135

He Fought for Democracy	137
Harry Fought On: Aragon	141
The Memorial and Obituaries	145
The Yiddish Surprise	155

PART V THOSE WHO LIVED ON   161

A Window into the U.S. Communist Party	163
Scottsboro and Irving (Take 2)	170
George Charney Returns	178
It Was All in the Manual	192
Khrushchev's Bomb	206
Harry	215
Rose	222
Taube	230
Irving	242
Ruby	253
Reflections	255
Epilogue	258
Acknowledgments	261
Bibliography	265
Endnotes	270

THE FAMILY TREE

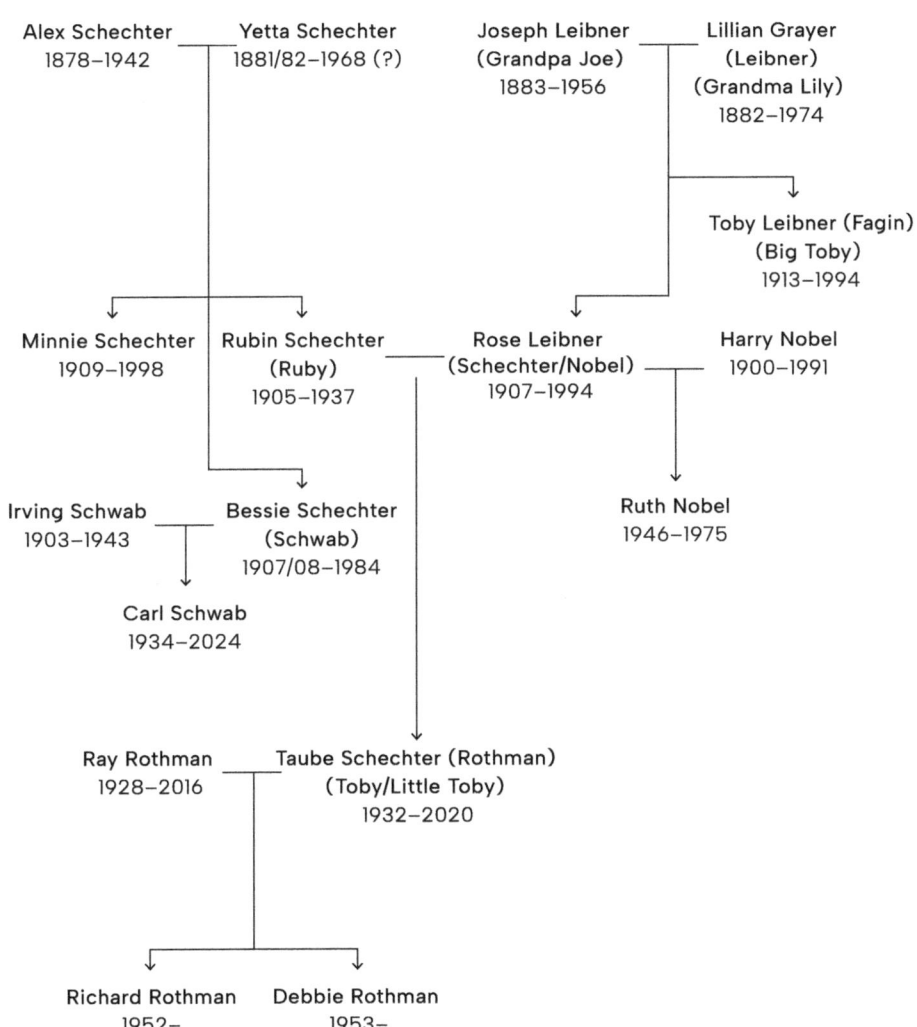

PART I
Opening Windows

I Could Have Asked

During his lifetime and most of my own, I knew more about Harry Nobel, the grandfather I grew up with, than I did about the biological grandfather for whom I was named—Rubin Schechter, known to all as Ruby. I understood that Ruby and Harry had been best friends who volunteered to join the Abraham Lincoln Brigade and, in March of 1937, went off to fight in the Spanish Civil War against Generalissimo Francisco Franco and his fascist allies, Adolf Hitler and Benito Mussolini. Ruby, who left his wife and my five-year-old mother behind, never returned from Spain, losing his life for the cause he believed in. But Harry did make it back, and several years later married Ruby's widow, my Grandma Rose. So Harry became my mother's stepfather and eventually the grandfather I knew and loved.

For most of my life, I knew little more about Ruby than that he'd been killed in Spain, that he was a Communist, and that I could thank his genes for my early balding. I was proud that he and Harry had fought in the Abraham Lincoln Brigade, which seemed to impress people I told who had heard of it. Nonetheless, and despite my interest in history, I never bothered to learn anything about the Spanish Civil War. Perhaps that's because, according to my mother, it hadn't been much of a war and Ruby's getting shot (in the hand, according to her) was a fluke. Among the things I didn't know was what had been so important to Ruby that it drove him to abandon his wife and young daughter, risking his life to fight in another country's civil war. I could easily have asked Harry, with whom I spent many afternoons talking about history and politics. But I didn't. It somehow never occurred to me during

Harry's lifetime to ask the questions that strike me as so obvious now that he's gone. And so I've been left to piece together their stories—hard for a modern-day American like me to relate to.

Like Ruby and Harry, I was a rebellious ideologue in my early days, railing against the Vietnam War and, after college, planning to devote my life to making the world a better place as a public interest lawyer. But unlike them, rather than acting on those ideals, I embarked upon a conventional, more lucrative career as a corporate lawyer, squeezing in pro bono work when I could. Although the work was interesting, often exciting, and even fun at times, I continually felt guilty for having abandoned my idealistic dreams. Having recently turned seventy, I wonder about the choices we made as young people—my grandfathers and I—that determined the courses of our lives.

This is the story of the twisted path I followed in my search to understand the burning idealism that drove my forebears to risk their lives as they participated in some of the legendary events of twentieth-century history. The kind of shining idealism, too rare in America today, that has impelled people throughout history to devote and even risk their lives for causes they passionately believe in. But to my dismay, the kaleidoscopic trail I stumbled along over the past six years also brought me face-to-face with my family's presence on the flip side of their fervent idealism: idealism gone astray or—viewed more sympathetically and perhaps more accurately—lured astray by those with less lofty aims. The ominous side of the coin looms large at home today, as millions of passionate believers blindly follow an autocratic leader down a trail that has imperiled what we naively assumed was our rock-solid democracy. The two sides of this coin can sometimes be hard to separate. They have been for me.

The Lost Briefcase

Until 2018, the only physical traces of Ruby I'd seen were contained in a black, rectangular leather briefcase I came across in the basement of my parents' Connecticut house about fifty years ago, when I was in my early twenties. One of the clasps was broken. Out of curiosity, I opened the briefcase and flipped through the mass of papers it contained. They revealed that Ruby had been an eclectic young man who wrote poetry and studied law. Particularly surprising was one of the poems—the most obscene piece of writing I'd ever read. I ran upstairs and showed it to my mother, blurting: "Did my grandfather really write this?" Evidently familiar with the poem, my mother quickly glanced at it and said, "Yes—he wrote it, and it's about your Aunt Toby" (her mother's younger sister, and Ruby's sister-in-law). I was dumbfounded.

Decades later, remembering the briefcase that the graphic poem had rendered unforgettable, I was eager to go back through Ruby's papers. But the briefcase had mysteriously vanished. My mother said she no longer had it and we assumed it had been thrown out—along with my treasured collection of rock albums—when my parents sold their house in 2001.

The Trailhead

For most of my life, the little I knew about Ruby came from my mother. Because I never had the foresight to ask any of the several family members who had known Ruby—including Rose and her two sisters, before they passed away—my mother was my only source. I can picture when she told me, in an offhand, almost dismissive manner, that my grandfather's getting shot was a fluke and that not a lot of people had died in the Spanish Civil War. It wasn't a long conversation; my mother and I didn't have long conversations. And I suspect that it may have been part of the same one in which I asked her about the obscene poem after discovering the briefcase loaded with my grandfather's papers. Nevertheless, although my mother has proved to be an inaccurate reporter in a number of instances, my memory, too, has been known to play tricks on me, so I can't be absolutely sure whether the fact that much of the information I've long attributed to my mother has turned out to be wrong is, in all instances, due to the fault of her memory or mine.

In any case, two events in 2018 opened my eyes to the reality of the Spanish Civil War and set me on the disjointed trail to Ruby—and Harry—that landed me here. The first occurred at a family dinner, when one of my cousins recommended that I read Adam Hochschild's *Spain in Our Hearts: Americans in the Spanish Civil War, 1936–1939.*

I'd known that my grandfathers' Abraham Lincoln Brigade had fought on the Republican, or "Loyalist," side of the war, in defense of the democratically elected government and against the Nationalist forces led by fascist general Francisco Franco that were seeking to overthrow the government. Hochschild describes how the Republicans were outgunned and ultimately massacred by the fascists. Republican soldiers lacked such essentials as modern weapons, shovels to dig trenches, adequate winter clothes, and experienced military leaders who could train city-dwelling novices like Harry and Ruby. Many, if not most of them, had never shot a gun before the eve of battle.[1]

Hochschild also chronicles how President Roosevelt's determination to avoid any appearance of supporting the Republicans—which, by 1939, he would acknowledge to have been a mistake—went so far as to prohibit American volunteers from sailing to Spain, forcing them to disembark in France and hike over the Pyrenees just to get to the war.[2] What they found when they arrived in Spain, as George Orwell recounted in *Homage to Catalonia*, was a chaotic, violent internal battle for control of the Republican side—a civil war within the civil war.[3]

In contrast to the Republicans, the fascist Nationalist soldiers were armed with the latest German military technology, including machine guns, bombs, and aircraft.[4] Accounts of the brutal battles ran on the front pages of the *New York Times* and newspapers around the world.[5] One of these widely reported episodes was the major Republican offensive at Brunete, where Ruby was wounded.

As I read Hochschild's account, I tried to visualize what my grandfathers would have endured: the freezing cold of the Pyrenees; the stifling heat of Brunete, where the July temperatures reached 100 degrees; the terror of watching hundreds of their comrades mowed down. And now, with more information and reflection, my question loomed larger: Why had Ruby and Harry risked their lives by venturing to Spain—with Ruby forsaking his wife and young daughter?

Hochschild pointed me to the first trail marker: the archives dedicated to the Abraham Lincoln Brigade.[6] The archives contain a brief profile of every member of the brigade—including their dates of birth and death, how and when they traveled to Spain, the battalions they served in, and the battles in which they fought. For each soldier lucky enough to have survived the war, the profile includes the date and ship on which he returned to the U.S. After learning that the brigade archives were publicly available (and online), I was excited to find brief profiles of both Harry and Ruby.

Harry's profile reveals that he sailed on the *Île de France*, destined for Le Havre, France, on February 20, 1937.[7] He didn't arrive in Spain until April 2—six weeks later. So, I speculated that Harry must have hiked over the Pyrenees in the dead of winter. He served in the "XV BDE [Brigade], Washington BN [Battalion] ... later Lincoln-Washington BN." According to the archives, Harry fought in the battles of Jarama, Brunete, and Aragon, attaining the rank of "Sargento."[8] After twenty months, he sailed home to the United States, again aboard the *Île de France*, on April 14, 1938. By then, the Republican forces in Spain had been routed and Hitler had annexed Austria.

Ruby's profile[9] indicates that he sailed to France aboard the *Washington* on March 10, 1937. Although he left the United States more than two weeks after Harry, he also arrived in Spain on April 2. Once I realized this, I wondered if the two of them had hiked the snow-covered mountains together, ill-equipped and freezing, to get to the foreign war in violation of FDR's edict. I wondered, too, whether they were afraid, and ever asked each other, or themselves: "What the hell are we doing here?" Or whether they were so excited and blinded by their idealism that they were simply propelled by surges of adrenaline.

Like Harry, Ruby served in the XV Brigade, Washington Battalion. He was the "Battalion Secretary." And he, too, fought at Brunete—where, according to the archives, he was injured in action, just three months after he got to Spain. The online record reads: "WIA Brunete July 24, 1937 while bringing ammunition up to the front lines."

The second event to unlock key pieces of the puzzle occurred during the summer of 2018, when I saw another cousin, Carl Schwab, during his annual visit to our small lake house in West Poland, Maine. Carl's mother, Bessie—now deceased—was Ruby's younger sister. Carl, who died recently at the age of eighty-nine, was a retired lobsterman in the tiny village of Port Clyde, Maine— probably the first and, until his son Bret succeeded him, perhaps the only Jewish redhead ever to haul traps on the Maine Coast.

As we sat on the screened porch looking out on the water that summer, I happened to mention to Carl that I'd been reading about the war in Spain and trying to imagine what Ruby and Harry had gone through. He told me that somewhere among his mother's papers he had a copy of a letter Ruby had written to his wife, my Grandma Rose, from the hospital in Spain after he'd been shot. He promised to find it and send me a copy.

Carl called a few days later and said that he'd found not one but two of Ruby's letters, as well as a two-page biography of Ruby. Feeling like an amateur sleuth on the brink of obtaining the missing clues that would crack the case, I anxiously awaited Carl's package.

Ruby wrote the first of the handwritten letters I received from Carl on July 25, 1937—the day after he'd been shot in the arm (not the hand, as my mother had reported). He was in good spirits under the circumstances:

> My Darling, I was shot in the right arm in battle on the 24th of July. The fact that I am writing you the very next day (using my left hand of course) will show you that it's nothing to worry about. The bullet went clean through the upper fleshy portion of the arm and did not touch the bone, which means quick healing and I ought to be back with the battalion within 15 days.
>
> My left hand will not permit me to describe the circumstances of the battle or the sensation of being hit, only this about the latter: that if one goes into a war like this one without fully knowing the possibilities he is an ostrich indeed and does not make the best fighter for the annihilation of fascist barbarism.
>
> That's all darling. A few days ago it was not easy to write because of the airplane bombings. Now it is not easy for want of the habituated right arm and because of the pain in the right arm (and hand too); the bullet shock has a special effect on the fingers—it numbs them except for fire-points of pain which suddenly pierce their deadness every few minutes.
>
> Keep writing to me c/o of the Washington Lincoln Battalion ... There is no need writing to the hospital. By the time you get this letter I shall be long back in the battalion.

My grandfather's recovery didn't proceed as expected. He wrote to Rose again on August 12, 1937, still using his left hand:

> Wounds are stubborn things.... If it were just a matter of where the bullet passed through, I would be ready to return to the front any one of these days, so well healed are the punctures. But it's the partial paralysis in the fingers ... which takes time and sometimes very painful waiting—until the torn nerves repair by themselves or if possible are repaired by the surgeon's skill.

Ruby then proceeded to give my grandmother a blow-by-blow account of how he was shot. But for the fact that he ended up dying from the wound—and even despite his demise—it struck me as hilarious:

> Because I am not certain as to whether you received my last letter I will repeat to you that I was shot through the right arm (above the elbow) on the 24th of July a little before sundown. It was on the now famous Brunete sector. How did I come to be wounded? It was on account of a mule (still one of the chief methods of transportation in this land).
>
> Our battalion was re-advancing to a position which for strategical reason we had temporarily retreated from. We had not gone 800 yards when we bumped into a fascist military patrol. Naturally, we strung out and started to go to work on the ditches. But we were short on ammunition and I started back for ammunition to our temporary base 800 yards back. I got there, loaded a dark skinned donkey with four cases of bullets and started towards our fighting

comrades. But the donkey had his own idea of how fast to go, and he deliberately proceeded to stroll leisurely down this field of whistling bullets as if it was Sunday on 5th Avenue. I spoke to the donkey in my best English (I had too much to tell him to say it in Spanish). I said to the donkey:

"See what a damn fool donkey you are. You think your dark hide will save you. You think you are camouflaged. But no one is aiming at you in particular. See how the bullets are coming in all directions. If you really had sense we could take this gap on the run. The comrades will not believe their eyes if you come tearing up with their ammunition. They will positively adore you. You will be a donkey such as never was—on sea or land. This argument does not move you because you are a typical product of the old order. You prefer to drag along at the pace of all your fathers, when some real speed would give us both a glorious lease on life. As it is you will probably be the death of both of us. That is where you conservatives always lead us to."

So I spoke to this unreasonable donkey. And you may believe me the donkey supplied me with plenty of time to say these things. Nor was he a bad listener; his only fault was that he merely listened. And so it came to pass that it was no more than thirty seconds after I delivered myself of this exhortation that one of those countless bullets swished— shot through my arm and I was forced to drop to the ground, shouting aloud for first aid. A Spanish comrade, stooping very low came quickly to me and speedily applied the first aid bandage we all carry with us. You may rest assured that I did not let go the reins of the silly donkey. I turned him over to another comrade who came stomping by, with instructions for him to lead the donkey all the way around to the right and then to the battalion, since there was no way of making him run straight there. I also took care to take all the battalion records from my knapsack. Then, assisted by the Spanish comrade, I cautiously and safely made my way back to our temporary base, where I delivered the papers to the proper authority and myself to the medical stations.

You must know darling that I am not able to write much more. I must revise my estimate of my return to the front. Perhaps it will be another month before I return.

No subsequent letters to Rose have been found. Ruby died two weeks later. His profile in the Lincoln Brigade Archives records: "d. August 24 (28, 30), 1937."[10] It seemed my family never received any information as to why Ruby died after being shot in the arm, and we were left to surmise that the cause of his death was likely an infection that would not have proved fatal today. It would be another five years before I learned that there was another possible explanation.

The last of Carl's unexpected gifts provided a revealing portrait of Ruby—and at least a hint as to what had driven him, and probably Harry, too, to wade into the foreign civil war. It was a two-page biography, single-spaced and in tiny print, entitled: "RUBIN SCHECHTER, The Chronological Biography of the Deceased." It had been published by the Lipkaner Bessarabia Progressive Society.

I couldn't imagine what the Lipkaner Bessarabia Progressive Society might have been. To my surprise, research revealed that it was one of approximately 3,000 "landsmanshafts"—mutual aid societies formed in the United States, mostly by Eastern European Jews, dedicated to the hometowns from which they had emigrated. As of 1938, there were 500,000 "landslayt"—fellow Jews who belonged to these landsmanshafts. The societies were originally formed by the immigrants to help each other acclimate to life in America.[11] After World War I, however, when new U.S. laws shut down immigration from Eastern Europe, the landsmanshafts began to focus on providing relief for residents of their former villages who were stuck in Eastern Europe. Many of the landsmanshafts, including the Lipkaner Bessarabia Progressive Society, published journals in connection with annual balls or fundraising events for relief activities.[12]

The Lipkaner Bessarabia Progressive Society appears to have been a group of Romanian Jewish immigrants from the village of Lipkani, Bessarabia. Formed in 1934, the society had a journal in which it published articles on the concept of *gmiles hesed*—a loan without interest provided to a needy person. Ruby's father, Alex Schechter, was the president of the society and the founder of the *gmiles hesed* project.[13] At Alex's initiative, the society established "The Rubin Schechter Emergency Fund" and published "The Chronological Biography of the Deceased" in January 1938, several months after Ruby died. Alex undoubtedly either had a hand in writing or heavily edited and approved this tribute to his son. The Lipkaner biography gave me my first picture, albeit sanitized, of my grandfather—and the motivation that drove him to abandon his wife and daughter.

The biography recounts that Ruby was born prematurely on July 5, 1905, in "the small town of Lipkan, Bessarabia," in what is now the Republic of Moldova. Lying on the banks of the Prut river, which forms the border with Romania, it is just a few kilometers south of the border with Ukraine.[14] Decades after Ruby's birth, in June 1941, the Nazis bombed the town, after which German and Romanian forces murdered many of the Jewish residents and sent the survivors on a death march.[15] Those who were not murdered or did not otherwise die along the way were deported to Transnistria in Ukraine, where most of them perished.[16]

The biography goes on to report that "during the first four years Rubin was reared with the greatest difficulty," and that after his sister Bessie was born in 1909, the family immigrated to America. Like so many other Eastern European Jews, the Schechter family settled "in the lower part of New York City." Referred to now as the Lower East Side of Manhattan, the neighborhood in those years was jammed with cheap tenements; today it's loaded with young professionals, expensive apartments, and trendy restaurants. Although Ruby's father, Alex, was a wealthy man by the time of Ruby's death two decades later, the hardly objective biography refers to him as a "poor worker" who sacrificed all for his only son. In 1910, having already recognized Ruby's "great aptitude in his [Hebrew] studies" at the age of five, Alex reportedly "gave his last dollar, ungrudgingly" to pay Ruby's grammar school tuition, and he and his wife "looked forward eagerly to the time when their only son would become a great scholar."

Ruby quickly began to fulfill his parents' dreams. They placed him in the "Talmud Torah, Tifereth Israel [school] under the tutelage of Mr. Petish and his principal Rabbi Aronson"—apparently a mark of distinction. Although Ruby had "experienced the bitter taste of poverty" as a child, by the time of his Bar Mitzvah in 1918, when he was thirteen, his father was well on his way to building his own lucrative rabbit-fur business, the "Alex Schechter Corporation: Fur Merchants." My grandfather's Bar Mitzvah dinner was "tendered to 400 people at the Katimsky Mansion in Brooklyn. Rubin surprised all of his guests with an address which lasted for an hour, and held his audience spell-bound." Following the Bar Mitzvah, Alex, "wishing to further his hope for his son, hired Rabbi Aronson to tutor Rubin privately," and by 1920, at the age of fifteen, Ruby was attending a teachers' seminary.

In 1922, however, Ruby took a sharp detour from the course Alex had charted for him. After entering Syracuse University, "he began to observe the oppressing conditions of the poorer students who could barely provide themselves with the sheer necessities of life. This caused him such distress and left a deep impression on him."

The Lipkaner biography goes on to fill in some of the blanks in the story of Ruby's life and sheds some light on what drove him to Spain. His "dearest" friend at Syracuse was Irving Schwab (my cousin Carl's father), and "there developed between them a faithful and intimate relationship. Rubin found in this young man that which he had long sought: a true and faithful friend who was as idealistic as himself." Ruby introduced Irving to his sister Bessie, and the two promptly fell in love. Bessie then returned the favor, introducing Ruby to Rose Leibner (later to become my maternal grandmother), "a charming and pretty young lady of the Jewish parentage residing in Brooklyn." They, too, fell in love, and Ruby, Rose, Bessie, and Irving "resolved to devote their time and energies to the betterment of the conditions of others. They entered into the Workers Movement with all the ardent fire and spirit of their young souls."

As I read this, I wondered what it meant to enter into the workers' movement—and, in particular, whether Ruby, Rose, Bessie, and Irving had all joined the Communist Party in these early years. Exactly what were they doing as they devoted "all the ardent fire and spirit of their young souls" to the cause?

The Lipkaner biography reflects that, despite their increasingly radical politics, Ruby and Rose continued to partake in the riches that Alex Schechter and Rose's father, Joseph Leibner, had by then accumulated. Alex, now "a highly esteemed businessman in the fur industry, had already offered Rubin a partnership in the business. Stocks and money were not lacking."[17]

On September 11, 1927, Ruby and Rose were married, followed by Bessie and Irving "within the hour." The extravagant double wedding took place at the renowned Hotel Astor and was attended by 600 guests.

Formal photo of Rose at the lush Hotel Astor double wedding

Following his graduation from Syracuse, Ruby worked alongside his father for a few years. But as the Lipkaner biography recounts, he was not long for the business world: "Rubin was a dreamer, an idealist and he was in sympathy with ideas which did not harmonize with business. He devoted himself, heart and soul, to the interests of the workers, gave it all his attention, neglecting himself and his family for the sake of others."

Apparently short of funds, after having left his father's business Ruby bounced back to it in 1933, but "after hours he spent all his time organizing various workman groups." It may have been around this time that Ruby met Harry Nobel. Harry was also involved in radical politics—including as an organizer for the furriers' union while he worked sewing pelts on the shop floor. It's possible that Harry worked at Alex's company. Although I've found no evidence as to whether the workers there belonged to a union, the industry was heavily unionized. Nor is there any indication in the Lipkaner biography whether Ruby and his father clashed over union-related issues, though I wouldn't be surprised if Ruby's organizing activities and ideas—which, as the biography notes, "did not harmonize with business"—put a strain on their relationship.

The biography recounts that Ruby's unbridled idealism, and altruism, drew him to the war in Spain:

> [He] sensed the dangers of Fascism and ... thought of the danger and ensuing results should Hitler and Mussolini (let their names be defaced forever) ever be able to convince the world to adopt Fascism as a form of government. This baffling question was ever uppermost in Rubin's mind. Especially was this true after the outbreak of the Spanish Civil War. Rubin's conscience was unable to rest. As a sincere

individual and a conscientious Jew, he felt the war was not a war of one Spaniard against another, but rather a conflict between righteousness and injustice, emancipating slavery. Rubin's very sensitive soul was unable to understand why others did not grasp the significance of this war.

Ruby began to work for the Spanish Republicans, the democratically elected government that Franco was seeking to overthrow. He "devoted himself wholeheartedly to this work, unwittingly neglecting his parents as well as his beloved wife and child"—my mother, born in 1932. He then proceeded to break his father's heart, and I wonder how Alex felt as he wrote, or approved for public consumption, the following passage of the biography, which describes what happened on the morning of March 10, 1937:

> [Alex] came into his office and proceeded to examine his mail. How excited and astonished he became when he opened a large envelope containing two letters from his only son. He became miserable and forlorn when he read a letter in Hebrew and another to his mother in Jewish [i.e., Yiddish].
>
> Both letters conveyed the bitter news that their only son was away and would be away for a long time on an important mission. The workers movement, which had become dearer to him than life, and to which he had devoted his life, had sent him on this mission. He must attain this goal and no one nor anything could dissuade him. He told his parents in these letters, "If you ever want to see me again don't trouble yourselves and turn to anybody; don't consult any lawyers."

He also assured them that he would not be in action in the war and that his life was not in danger.

Ruby's parents disregarded his admonition. They sent "urgent pleas by cables and letters ... that did not succeed in turning him back from his work. From the moment his parents read his letter, their lives became darkened. They were haunted day and night by frightening thoughts. They feared the worst—and the worst it was."

Whether or not Ruby ever believed it, the assurance he gave his parents that he would not be involved in the fighting was not accurate for long. As the Lipkaner biography reports, he "could not sit in an office, at a time when his comrades were fighting a desperate fight on the battlefield ... against an enemy supported by the oppressors, Hitler and Mussolini (Let their names and memories be destroyed). It is the aim of these dictators, through the medium of this and other wars, to abolish democracy of the world in order spread their poison—Fascism."

And so, on July 24, 1937, my grandfather led the stubborn, conservative mule through a storm of bullets, one of which found him.

A Somewhat False Lead

After reading Hochschild's book and then lucking into the entries for Ruby and Harry in the Lincoln Brigade Archives—followed by Ruby's letters and the Lipkaner biography—I was eager to track down the last known piece of the puzzle: the black briefcase containing Ruby's memorable poem that I'd perused in my parents' basement fifty years earlier. My mother was sure she didn't have it, so I asked my sister and, to my surprise, Debbie said she thought she had the briefcase—or at least its contents. She told me that a Talbots shopping bag in a trunk full of old family photos that she'd taken when my parents sold their Connecticut house contained a mass of letters and other documents that she (and now I) suspected were Ruby's. She brought them to my apartment for a family dinner and I tore into them early the next morning, only to be disappointed. The Talbots bag contained none of Ruby's writings. In fact, I learned very little about Ruby from its contents—but a lot about Harry.

Harry was a serious man, or at least that's how I remember him. He was about 5'4" tall, trim, and walked with a stiff gait, which may have been a remnant of his wartime experiences. To go with his narrow, angular face and protruding ears, Harry had a full head of black hair until the day he died at the age of ninety-one. He had a rather gruff voice, at least to my ear, and never shed his Eastern European accent.

Harry was born in 1900 in Galicia, Austria, in what is today southern Poland. He was the second of six children, and the oldest son. At some point in his teens, Harry's parents—sharing the same dream as Ruby's parents—sent him to Germany to study to become an Orthodox rabbi. But his radical idealism eclipsed his rabbinical career, and according to family lore—which, until I began digging into this history, I'd mostly accepted as factual—he was kicked out of the country. Regardless of the impetus, Harry and his younger brother, Max, made their way across Europe, hoping to get to America.

Harry first entered the United States in 1921. Eventually, the entire family, apart from his older sister, immigrated to the States. Due to her pregnancy, his sister was unable to get out in time and was murdered in a concentration camp along with her husband and children.

In America, Harry worked as a furrier, a common trade for Jewish immigrants.[18] He became an organizer for a radical furriers' union—probably the Fur Workers Industrial Union, formed in 1927 by a group of Communists who had been expelled from the AFL's International Fur Workers Union.[19] Apart from his years fighting in Spain and serving in the U.S. Army during World War II, Harry worked for decades on the shop floor sewing pelts into expensive coats for wealthy women, while refusing to become part of management.

But in my eyes Harry was, above all, an intellectual. He taught at the Jefferson School—an adult education institute formed by the Communist Party in 1943 to advance the teachings of Marxism. And Harry's knowledge was by no means limited to radical political theory. He and Rose were probably the most literate people I've ever known. They seemed to have read virtually every major work of fiction, drama, and poetry, and beyond those "basics" they each had their own areas of expertise in which the other was not supposed to trespass if a question arose (although Rose would often transgress). Rose's domains were art and psychology, while Harry was in charge of history, physics, philosophy, and math. I can picture him sitting on the couch of my childhood living room, with book, pencil, and papers strewn about, working out physics problems for pleasure while he babysat my sister Debbie and me, an opera blasting to accommodate his faded hearing. Harry received a bachelor's degree from NYU and had all his credits toward a Ph.D.—I believe in philosophy. I'd never been able to understand why he continued stitching furs together for virtually his entire adult life. He retired from the shop at seventy, at which point he became a bookkeeper and worked for another decade before retiring again, ultimately to a dreary nursing home on East 72nd Street, where he died in 1991.

By the time I was old enough to have a clear memory of Rose, when she would have been in her fifties, she had a rather squat build and wavy, light reddish-brown hair, cut fairly short. What I recall most about my grandmother is her unusual manner of speaking—a singsong cadence combined with a pensive tone of voice. She used it most often to pontificate about painting and art history—displaying extraordinary knowledge with no regard for whether anyone was listening. And Rose, herself, was a talented artist. But one subject my grandmother never talked about was her political past. I knew only what my mother had told me, which was that Rose occasionally had things thrown at her while making feminist speeches.

I have few memories of Harry laughing or seeming joyous. One relates to the first time he and Rose met my future wife, Melissa. Over dinner at Paul & Jimmy's, a neighborhood Italian restaurant near Gramercy Park in Manhattan, Harry and Melissa engaged in a lively discussion of literature. They first talked about poetry (Alexander Pope, I believe) and then essays. The highlight occurred when Harry couldn't remember the name of a publication and Melissa asked if he might be referring to Addison and Steele's *The Spectator* (an eighteenth-century English publication I'd never heard of). Harry squeezed Melissa's cheeks between his fingers, stared into her eyes, and then proclaimed, "She's smart!" while beaming at Rose and me.

I visited Harry from time to time after I graduated from law school in 1977 and joined the law firm in Manhattan where I would spend the next forty years. Representing the corporate titans Harry had railed against, I often felt embarrassed in his presence—ashamed that I'd "sold out" after having gone to law school intending to become a public interest lawyer. But for reasons I didn't understand, Harry seemed to be proud of me, and I could feel that he treasured my visits to their small apartment on 14th Street and Avenue C. He would greet me by grasping both my arms with his strong furrier's hands, and then shoo Rose away so the two of us could talk without interruption.

Harry and I would discuss current politics and history—which he continued to study, reading primary sources such as the diaries of Greek and Roman statesmen and generals. But we never talked about Harry's remarkable life, including his experience as a soldier. I never asked him anything at all about Spain or Ruby.

The material in the Talbots shopping bag cast Harry in a new and very different light. Most illuminating was the trove of old photographs—naturally almost all black-and-white—which fell into two groups. The first ones were pictures of Harry as a soldier—first in the Lincoln Brigade and then in the U.S. Army during World War II. While the uniforms differed, what came through in these photos of the two wars was the image of a proud soldier, in some with a wide smile—indeed, a big grin in one taken of Harry in a casual pose wearing his U.S. sergeant's uniform, and another sporting a fur-lined bomber jacket. The numerous copies of certain photos—including 8x10 prints and multiple copies of the pictures of Harry with his Lincoln Brigade comrades—echoed the sense of pride evident in the pictures themselves. What I took from these photographs—viewed against the backdrop of Hochschild's *Spain in Our Hearts*, Orwell's *Ode to Catalonia*, and the Abraham Lincoln Brigade Archives—was that Harry was not merely, or predominantly, an intellectual. He was very much a soldier.[20]

Above: *Harry (left) in Spain (1937)*
Right: *Harry in the U.S. Army during World War II*

The second cache of photos showed Harry as a doting father of my Aunt Ruthie (my mother's stepsister and Harry's only biological child), born in 1946—soon after Harry's return from the army at the end of World War II. The pictures showed a relaxed and contented Harry tenderly holding Ruthie, first as a baby and later as an adorable little girl. What was clear from both batches of pictures was that Harry had hardly been the ever-serious man I'd thought I knew. So I wondered: Were my memories of the somber Harry just wrong? Or had he undergone a seismic change somewhere along the line, between when the photos of the proud, smiling soldier and glowing father were taken, and the late seventies and early eighties, when I'd spent time talking with him about history and current affairs but not his amazing life?

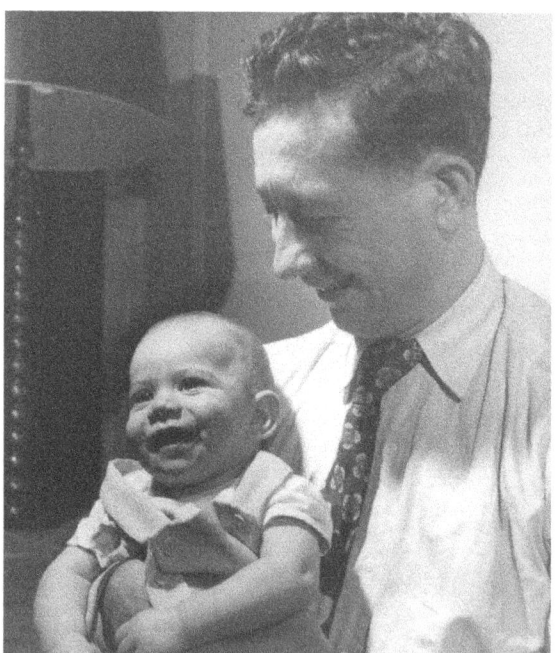

Harry and Ruthie

Even before I started investigating my family's history, I'd vaguely understood that in 1956, Joseph Stalin, the leader of the Soviet Union, had been exposed as a mass murderer by his successor, Nikita Khrushchev. It was hard to believe the revelations would not have taken a heavy toll on Harry—having sacrificed an intellectually stimulating career for a life sewing rabbit skins for rich people in apparent allegiance to the Communist Party. But he also had other, more personal reasons to grieve.

Ruthie

My Aunt Ruthie was thirteen years younger than my mother and just seven years older than me. When I was young, the seven-year gap between us seemed large. But by the time I was in college Ruthie had morphed into a wayward big sister and we were partners in crime, smoking pot at the rare family gatherings she attended. By then Ruthie was restless, rebellious, caustic, and searching—engulfed by the phases she traveled through. Astrology and Buddhism were two I recall; yet always she stuck with her genuine talent for painting. Melissa and I now have several of her works hanging on our apartment walls.

Ruthie was a beautiful young woman, with long thick brown hair, high cheekbones, generous lips, big brown eyes, and long lashes. One series of photos in the Talbots collection included romantic shots of Ruthie looking into the eyes of a handsome, strait-laced young man who was obviously a smitten boyfriend. That romance went nowhere, however, as Ruthie veered into the fast lane. Her beauty, wild spirit, and talent attracted stars: Jimi Hendrix, Joe Cocker, and Leon Russell were three I heard about. She's sitting next to Cocker and Russell in the picture on the inside cover of Cocker's *Mad Dogs & Englishmen* album jacket.

A note from Hendrix to Ruthie survives. He wrote:

> 1:30 AM
> Dear Ruth,
> You've inadvertently strung me out. I will be by at 7am Thanksgiving day to get thumb piano and drum.
> Love Jimi[21]

Ruthie

Ruthie got hooked on the drugs that permeated the world of her rock star pals. She died in her apartment on Perry Street in Greenwich Village in 1975, at the age of twenty-nine. The cause of death was a heroin overdose. I was away at law school in St. Louis and, remarkably, don't recall my reaction to Ruthie's tragic death. But talking about her still brings me to tears; her photograph sits in the corner of the mirror hanging above my dresser.

Harry surely could not have comprehended what had happened to the little girl who'd brought him such joy. He'd been raised in Poland to be an Orthodox rabbi; he'd devoted his life to improving the lot of poor workers; he'd fought against fascism in two wars. How could he understand that his beautiful daughter had thrown her life away? I imagine he was angry at first, as he witnessed her moving beyond his reach to places he couldn't fathom. And later, heartbroken.

So, my image of the rarely jovial Harry may well have been correct by the time I knew him.

Looking back over both my grandfathers' lives and the sacrifices they made as young men, I continued to wonder about the force that was so powerful as to impel them to risk their lives in a foreign civil war. Were they prescient in recognizing, as FDR failed to do, that the conflict in Spain was the front line in the existential battle against Hitler and fascism? Or were they driven by blind devotion to the Communist Party? Or was it both?

But I had no further leads. My search seemed to have come to a dead end. So, I wrote this story of my two grandfathers—it was twenty pages long—and put it to bed. Which is where it remained until my mother died in December 2020.

Taube Pearl (Schechter) Rothman

Rummaging through the Talbots bag, I found only one document pertaining to Ruby, a high school English paper entitled "Pa Pa Went Away" that my mother wrote in April 1948, eleven years after Ruby was killed, when she was sixteen. Replete with her teacher's comments, the typed paper was a thinly fictionalized account of my mother's loss of her father—and the lies she'd been told before learning that he'd been killed in Spain.

My mother began:

The sun shown brightly into the room where two people were sleeping. A woman looked down at the six year old child next to her. Today would be another day of torture, of waiting, of realizing, and of work. Today little Pearl [my mom's middle name] would ask if a letter had come from her father, and she would again say that one had not but soon would.

"Are you crying Mommy?" she asked. "Of course not. I'm just tired so my eyes are red." But Pearl didn't believe her. That Anna could see.

Why didn't Pappa write to her? Why did he have to go to Spain? She remembered sitting on the bed when Mommy had read his first letter to her. It was a nice letter and just like him.

Mommy had said, "You see there is a war in Spain. Bad men called fascists are trying to take away the people's freedom and make them slaves. So, Pappa went away to help the people." ... "That was alright," Pearl thought as she splashed water on her face. "But he hasn't written in six months. Mommy says it's because the fascists won't let the mail get through, but that's not true. I know it. I know it!

Anna was looking at the table, the tears slowly dropping on to her cheeks ... Pearl looked at her and sat down. Suddenly something hit her like a bullet would hit you.

"Suppose he is really never coming back. Suppose he is dead," she thought. She jumped up hysterically and ran to her mother. The tears were filling her eyes. Her voice was high. "He's dead, he's dead. I know he is. He's dead and you won't tell me!" she shrieked.

Anna's eyes opened wide. She stared for a moment, and gathering Pearl in her arms, she held her close. The tears were running down both of their cheeks. "Yes Pearl, he's dead. He died fighting fascism."

"Why did you let him go? Why?"

"I had to Pearl, I had to. Don't you see?"

"Why didn't you lock all the doors? Why didn't you lock all the windows? Why didn't you?"

"I couldn't Pearl."

"I would have!" shrieked the child. "I would have sat on him, scratched him. Bitten him. I wouldn't have let him go! ... He's dead," she sobbed. "He's dead. You let him go. I'll never see my Pappa again. I'll never walk with him, or talk with him. He's dead!"

Eleven years after her father was killed, my mother was struggling to understand why he had abandoned her to go fight fascism. Not surprisingly, she was still suffering, and angry at her mother. Only near the end of the trail I was following would I come to recognize that her high school paper was a remarkably accurate portrayal of the scene it dramatically depicted.

My mother had other reasons to suffer as a child, and to harbor anger at both her parents. At the age of five, after her father had left for Spain, my mother was deposited into what she later referred to as an "orphanage," where she remained for several years until her Grandma Lily—Rose's mother—took her out and raised her in Brooklyn. Considering her unusual and traumatic beginnings, she went on to lead an ostensibly normal, but also remarkably accomplished, life.

Among other talents, my mother was already a serious student of modern dance as a teenager—taking classes with the iconic Martha Graham, who demonstrated what might be described as a personal interest in her. One of Melissa's favorite stories is about my mother's experience with Graham, which she shared with us at a dinner to celebrate our engagement.

During the time that she was a student of Graham's, my mother—then age fifteen—met my father at "a Communist rally." She was immediately smitten. My mother's distractedness was readily apparent to Martha Graham, whose standards didn't allow for it. As my mother told the story, when Graham observed that my mother's attention was no longer focused on her dancing, "she dragged me across the studio floor by my hair, and snapped: 'You need to decide—it's either this [i.e., dance] or everything else.'" After a dramatic pause, my mother gave us a broad smile and said, "So I chose everything else—and here we now are."

My mother was a sophomore in high school in Brooklyn when she met my father, Ray. Four years older than my mother, he came from the same city but a world away: the Bronx. My dad grew up sleeping in the living room of a small two-bedroom apartment

Taube Pearl Schechter, dancer

along with his older sister, Gert, and his brother, Bill, while their father and his friends played pinochle, smoked cigars, and cracked jokes far into the night. My Grandpa Jack, a sheet metal worker, and Grandma Anna slept in one bedroom, and rented out the other to make ends meet. They had fled the pogroms and immigrated to the United States in about 1905. Until recently I believed and told people they were from Russia. But I now realize that, having lived near Kiev, they were probably Ukrainian.

At nineteen, when my dad met my mother he was already a senior at City College, having skipped two grades in elementary school. The Communist Party event where they met was probably about the only place their paths would have crossed. He was smart, athletic, and handsome, about 5'7" with jet black hair, bearing some facial resemblance to Joe DiMaggio. With her dancer's body and thick brown hair, my mother was beautiful. And Martha Graham was right: my mother's attention was far removed from her dancing.

She married my dad when she was eighteen and then, in addition to having moved on from her dance studies, dropped out of Queens College after one semester when she was twenty, shortly before I was born in March 1952. But my mother went back to school a decade later, initially taking one course at a time while working as a bookkeeper. She earned a bachelor's degree from Hunter College as a biology major when she was thirty-nine years old. Not content to stop there, my mother went on to receive a Ph.D. from Cornell Medical School, followed by a post-doctorate degree from the University of Pennsylvania. She joined the Columbia medical school faculty, first as a neurologist doing research, and was ultimately named a full professor some twenty years later.

Taube and Ray Rothman, newlyweds (circa 1950)

Immediately upon her retirement, my mother threw herself back into another one of her teenage passions: painting.

My parents had a stormy marriage that somehow lasted more than sixty-five years. My father died in March 2016, after a decline that robbed him of the ability to speak, and dementia that was painful to witness. A few months later, I sat down with my mother and tried to interview her about what she knew about her father and her stepfather Harry. Although her own dementia had not yet kicked in, or was not yet apparent to our family, there wasn't much of substance that she was willing or able to talk about.

By the time my mother died in December 2020, her body and mind had both failed her. Melissa, who'd had a very close relationship with her, stepped up to the enormous task of clearing out my parents' apartment. She spent months sifting through the mass of stuff my mother and father had accumulated over a lifetime of marriage, work, extensive worldwide travel, and painting. Throwing herself into the task, she found scores of my mother's paintings, along with thousands of books, including many volumes that had belonged to Harry and Rose. My mother's closets were stuffed with her academic degrees, doctoral thesis, and professional papers, as well as a huge collection of high-fashion clothes, shoes, and jewelry that I, for one, either had not realized she owned or had forgotten that she'd ever worn as she suffered, enfeebled, during her final years—the last spent largely alone during the pandemic.

Melissa's task of deciding what to throw out and what to keep, while conferring with various family members about who might want which things, was exhausting and often thankless. But then, as she neared the end of her months-long excavation, she found something that excited her. Buried at the back of the top shelf in one of the closets was an old black briefcase, with one of its buckles broken. She carried it home like a trophy.

PART II

The Man in the Briefcase

The Elusive Briefcase

When Melissa surprised me with the briefcase that night, I immediately set it down on our dining room table and opened it. All I remembered from having seen its contents once fifty years earlier was that there were some papers reflecting my grandfather's interest in an array of subjects, including law, and the obscene poem.

The lost briefcase—or "the Briefcase," as it quickly came to be known at our home—was stuffed with papers. There were several old notebooks, a slew of letters on eighty-five-year-old flaky, browned paper, and various old newspaper articles—including numerous copies and versions of Ruby's obituary. Also, several photographs.

Two of the notebooks were filled with poems. I hunted first for the obscene poem I remembered reading in my youth, recalling once again my mother's alarming remark that it had been written about my Aunt Toby. I found it and was just as shocked—perhaps even more so—than I had been upon first reading it decades before. I then did a preliminary scan of the articles and letters in the Briefcase, most of which were handwritten, but didn't take time to scrutinize them. The most noteworthy discovery I made that night was that the two letters Carl had sent me three years before, which Ruby had written to Rose shortly after being shot, had been published in a left-wing newspaper called *New Masses*.

I decided I would supplement the short piece I'd written about Ruby and Harry in 2018, but then procrastinated for several months. When I finally delved into the contents of the Briefcase again, examining the fragile pages and straining to make out the oft-faded handwriting, I felt like I was peeling back the layers of my grandfather's life; peering into his personality and picking up clues regarding some of the questions that had nagged at me. Along the way, I also discovered that many, if not most, of the few "facts" about my grandfather that I'd thought I'd known were either questionable or flat-out wrong.

The Aspiring Poet

I began my excavation of the Briefcase by turning to the two notebooks, which contained over fifty poems written between 1928 and 1933, including various working drafts and scraps of verses. The first was a faded burgundy leather 5x8-inch *1928 Year Book*. It bore the name Joseph Leibner in gold, embossed letters on the center of its cover, and "Sobel & Gray, Insurance Brokers"—from whom the yearbook was likely a holiday gift—in the lower right-hand corner. On the inside of the cover, "Rubin Schechter" was written in faded blue ink, and all of the writing in the book was his.

The introductory pages of the Year Book contained an array of rules to live by and some 1928 vital statistics. The first section, entitled "Fifteen Don'ts in Use of the Flag," included such precepts as "Do not use the flag as drapery; use bunting." And "Do not display the Flag of the United States with the Union shown down, except as a sign of distress"—which has recently taken on new meaning with America's democracy under siege. The twelve pages of statistics were a poignant reminder of a bygone era, including such nuggets as the "Number of Taxable Income by Classes," which indicated that there were 2,440,544 people in the "$1000–2000" income class (the most populous), and only twenty-one people in the "$1 million and over" income class.

Ruby evidently had appropriated the yearbook from Joseph Leibner—Rose's father, Ruby's father-in-law, and my great-grandfather. I don't remember much about Grandpa Joe, who was in his final act by the time I came onto the scene. In my eyes, his wife

Lily was the more prominent spouse, but that might not have been the case had I known Joe in his earlier years.

Family photos show Joe as a young boxer in one instance and in others as a gallant young man. And he had money—having developed a lucrative business raising carp, pike, and other freshwater fish in the Midwest, and then transporting them while still alive to New York City in some of the earliest refrigerated train cars. An article entitled "The Carp King" in the August 1940 edition of *American Business Survey* explains Grandpa Joe's innovative business:

> These live fish come to New York City in special "Pullman" cars containing nine tanks holding approximately 24,000 pounds of carp. In each car are motors attached to pressure air pumps, which force fresh oxygen through the fish tanks, keeping the fish comfortable and alive. It also requires a fish Pullman "porter" for those fish travel in grand style.[1]

The retail store, located in the Lower East Side on Sheriff Street (which no longer exists), was run by Joe's wife, Lily. Wearing boots and gloves, my great-grandmother would kill and clean the fish for customers.

One thing Grandpa Joe apparently had an aversion to was competition. As I learned several years ago, the federal government had brought a criminal antitrust case charging that Grandpa Joe and his cohorts had conspired to destroy competition—including by using threats of physical violence—from others who sought to enter the business of transporting live fish from the Midwest in refrigerated train cars. An article in the July 3, 1926, edition of the *New York Times*, entitled "Live Fish Monopoly Is Broken

By Court," reported that the case was resolved when Grandpa Joe and his co-conspirators entered into a consent decree signed by one of the country's most famous federal trial judges, United States district judge August Hand. Among other forms of relief, the decree required that two of Grandpa Joe's "specially equipped [train] cars for transporting fish alive" be sold at a public auction, "which would give competitors an opportunity to bid for the cars," and also that the government expected the divestiture "to result in lower live fish prices here."[2] So, my own career in the law can apparently be traced back to my great-grandfather's experience as a defendant in a criminal case.[3]

But there were no entries either by or about Grandpa Joe in the *1928 Year Book*. Following the introductory pages, the rest of the yearbook consisted of one page for each day of the year. Many of the pages were filled with Ruby's handwritten notes regarding the structure of different forms of poetry, fragments of verse, and more than a score of poems and drafts.

It was immediately apparent to me that Ruby had been a serious student of poetry—and that, whatever else he was doing at this point in his life, writing poetry was an important pursuit for him. The pages for January 1–4, 1928, contain his notes, in pencil, on the structures of a "Spenserian Stanza," "Shakespearean Sonnet," "Miltonic Sonnet," "Petrarchan Sonnet," and a verse form called a "terza rima." On the succeeding pages of the *Year Book* my grandfather wrote out his own sonnets and various other forms of poems, often in multiple drafts, with notations reflecting his attempts to work out the relevant meter.

Having never studied poetry, I wasn't in a position to evaluate the quality of my grandfather's poems. A more knowledgeable friend of mine who read them said he found them "pedestrian," but allowed that Ruby was only in his twenties when he wrote them and might well have developed into a great poet had he not taken his fatal detour to Spain.

I read the poems searching for clues to who Rubin Schechter had been in these formative years, and they did shed light on his personality, beliefs, and passions during that period. In particular, I found a gushy romantic young man grappling with matters of love, religion, and his identity. And in a few, I found the green stalks of the sprouting radical political beliefs that would lead him to abandon his family—and to his death. Only much later would I learn that as those stalks grew, they would leave no room for his poetry.

The pages for April 9–18 were filled with multiple drafts of a long and, in places, revealing poem. The first stanza began with a longingly romantic air:

> Listening to the song of lovers
>   meeting in secret
> From the hate of their others
> From the hate of their fathers
> They fashion the song of their love
> Oh the weakling beauty of lovers meeting
>   in secret
> Walking beside still waters
> They yearn for atonement by human hands
> And a song of acceptance from human hearts

But the third stanza contained a clue as to the radical direction in which my grandfather was headed:

> Listening to the sound of youth in
> > rebellion
> Oh the city of the enemy was
> > beautiful
> It made him weak with want
> And the wail of the hungry was
> > terrible
> It made him faint with shame
> Til desire was turned into will
> And the weakness was turned
> Into strength
> Then vengeance he took for a
> > sword—calling it Righteousness
> And he struck with his might
> against well-guarded gates

My grandfather's passionate words seemed to reveal a powerful inner struggle: fighting back with righteousness against the shameful temptation of wealth in "the city of the enemy." I wondered: Was I, the intruder, reading too much into Ruby's words, or was this "shame … turned into will" the smoldering force that led him to the Communist Party and Spain?

Only a few poems appeared in the *1928 Year Book* after June 10. The August 30 page, as well as those for October 28–November 4, had been torn out, which left me wondering what my grandfather thought was so bad or embarrassing that, unlike all his other scribblings, some of which were crossed out, he apparently didn't want these to see the light of day? Was he seeking to avert future snoops—like me, or his wife? As I would later learn, if so, his efforts were in vain. But perhaps there is no logical explanation; maybe he was just frustrated with his writing and felt like ripping out these pages.

More pages from December 25–30 were torn out, but then, on the last day of the year, I saw a draft of a letter, with various edits, that Ruby had been writing to either his or Rose's parents:

> Your Granddaughter Taube Pearl was born this morning. Rose feels fine and looks wonderful.

Although this appeared on the page for December 31, 1928, I knew it had been written on February 13, 1932—the day my mother was born (twenty years before me). The day Rubin Schechter, young romantic poet and budding revolutionary, became a father.

I turned next to an 8½x11-inch brown speckled notebook with a label pasted onto the front cover indicating that my grandfather had been studying law. The label on the cover read:

> Rubin Schechter
> Contracts

This seemed out of keeping with what I'd gathered were his radical politics, but it probably shouldn't have surprised me. Many communist activists, including Ruby's college friend and then brother-in-law, Irving Schwab, were making good use of law degrees, including to defend Black Americans against racist criminal prosecutions.

Beyond the notebook's label, the only evidence of Ruby's legal studies began on the inside of the back cover and—as reminder of

Ruby's Hebrew training—proceeded for several pages from back to front. His notes there reflect that a teacher had given the class a fairly granular outline of civil procedure law, from the pleading stage of a lawsuit through a trial, much like a summary of the Civil Procedure course that every first-year law student is traditionally required to take.

Ruby's notes included no information about contract law, and I wondered whether he'd dropped the class, speculating that he may have lost interest after joining the Communist Party. Or perhaps because he was working days in his father's rabbit fur business, organizing workers in the evening, and writing his poetry, he just didn't have time.

Except for those few back pages, the *Contracts* notebook was devoted entirely to Ruby's poetry and left no doubt as to his aspirations. On the inside of the front cover Ruby had pasted a typed list entitled "Magazines Publishing Poetry," with the names of fifteen publications, including a few with one or two asterisks beside them, such as the *Yale Series of Younger Poets*, "open to American poets under 30 who have not previously published a volume in verse." On the first page of the notebook, Ruby had pasted another typed list: "Magazines Devoted Exclusively To Poetry." This one included fourteen periodicals, again with a few of them asterisked—below which was a typed parenthetical note: "(some of the smaller ones may try to get a fee from you in their critical capacity, but you can ignore that)," suggesting to me that someone else may have typed up the list in order to provide Ruby with this advice.

The *Contracts* notebook contained a score of poems. Unlike those in the *1928 Year Book*, most of these were neatly handwritten, signed by Ruby, and dated. Quite a few were either handwritten copies or revised drafts of poems that had appeared in the *1928 Year Book*, which I therefore realized had come first.

As I read through Ruby's poems, I wondered whether he had ever submitted any of them to the publications listed at the front of the *Contracts* notebook. Had any of his poems ever been published?

The first poem in the *Contracts* notebook was entitled a "Sonnet to George." I surmised from Ruby's later correspondence that it was about George Charney, who appeared to have been one of Ruby's best friends and subsequently rose to become a senior leader of the U.S. Communist Party. The sonnet, like many of Ruby's poems, reflected my grandfather's love of literature. Dated October 1929, it began:

> Supposing George we both had never met
> You'd still do things much like you do them now—
> And I, no doubt, would be as firmly set;
> What with you feeding on Stendhal's wit
> While Hardy's steady whacks would keep me fit.
>   —Oh, we'd have gotten on quite well somehow—

And it ended:

> So we got started on some silly talk.
> I praising spit-pearls from your nimble tongue
> You going wild about my verbal dung;
>   —We'll hold fate down no matter how we hawk—

Even after I'd read through everything in the Briefcase, I never dreamed how large a role George Charney would ultimately play on my journey to understand Ruby—and Rose and Harry as well.

I obsessed about a number of poems that appeared to reflect Ruby's love for—or, at the least, fantasies about—one or more women other than Rose. A few of them stood out and left me pondering my grandfather's character. In his "Sonnet to Debbie," dated "Jan '30"—three years after Ruby married Rose—he wrote:

> Always we watched her come and smile
>   a bit
> There was a devastating sweetness there
> As if the Sweetness laid her whole heart
>   bare
> And made her weak with want.
> **It was not fit**
> **For us, because we both were deeply wed** [emphasis mine]

Another poem that raised my suspicions was an undated multipage piece that had no title but several numbered parts. Part I consisted of what had earlier been entitled the "Sonnet for Debbie," including the lines:

> It was not fit
> For us, because we both were deeply wed

Part II resuscitated verses from what had appeared as a draft in the *1928 Year Book*, including:

> A trifling with blond hair, and eyes that were
> Not like her own—but blue and smoldering
> She made him hers

As I read, I asked myself, was this blond real? I remembered that my Grandma Rose, to whom Ruby was already married by 1928, had reddish-brown, not blond, hair. Had he been having an affair of some sort—or possibly fantasizing about one? I felt like an intruder, prying into the private life of my dead grandfather.

And, finally, there was the poem that had shocked me when I'd perused the contents of the Briefcase fifty years earlier. I had recounted many times over the intervening decades that this poem was the most obscene piece of writing I'd ever read; that it made Henry Miller seem like a prude. Reading the poem again confirmed that first impression.

Dated November 19, 1932, the untitled poem was typed and pasted into the *Contracts* notebook and was one of the last poems it contained. Written from the perspective of a woman, it began:

> Come heavy cocked, short one, fill this cunt up tight
> Your mouth near my cunt has got me crazy
> Feels like your tongue is lapping too,
> Sucking inside this hot jammed hole....
>
> Filling these ass-cheeks with screaming shitting desire
> Bursting my whole great cunt

The rest of the poem continued in the same vein. So much so that I vacillated over whether or not to quote any of these lines, for fear of casting the grandfather I held in high esteem in a bad light. But what I had not remembered from my previous reading of this poem in the 1970s—and probably hadn't noticed as I was busy being stunned by the obscenity—was its last stanza, and particularly the last line:

Lift up your face and wet my lips with kisses
You are my love
Lie awhile
Nothing happened [emphasis mine]

So now I thought, hoped, that this obscene poem might depict only an unhinged fantasy, and that there was an element of love to it—not just lust.

A few other things occurred to me as I pondered the obscene poem. First, among the scores of poems in the two notebooks, there was only one laced with any obscenity. Second, going back through the *Contracts* notebook I came across another poem, dated two years earlier, ostensibly about a torrential rainstorm, that contained no explicit reference to sex and to which Ruby had appended the following note: "I have tried this same theme in direct language in the lines opening 'Come heavy cocked short one …'" (I would later learn that my grandfather was a short man.)

Finally, the obscene poem was not some casual, fleeting stream of consciousness left to be forgotten that I had just happened to find amongst a bunch of scraps. While other pages of the *Contracts* notebook, as with the *1928 Year Book*, had been ripped out, Ruby had taken the trouble to type this poem and paste it into his book, signed and dated. He obviously had not been ashamed of it.

Reflecting upon this poem together with the others that appeared to be about women other than my grandmother, it occurred to me that all of them may have involved merely the unconsummated fantasies of a young man using his poetry as a harmless, artistic outlet. Or so I hoped.

One of the last poems in the *Contracts* notebook was entitled "A Song—To Hold up the Hands of the New President." Typed and pasted into the notebook, it was dated "3/12/33"—eight days after FDR's first inauguration, on March 4, 1933. My grandfather appeared to have been writing in anticipation of what FDR would do after assuming the presidency in the midst of the Depression, when the poor, unemployed, and homeless people Ruby was dedicated to helping were suffering and desperate. But more important to me than the poem itself was the note that appeared in pencil below it. In handwriting that looked different from Ruby's were the words "*prior to joining CP.*"

The note got me thinking.

First, whose writing was this? I decided it must have been Rose's, as I couldn't imagine who else would have had the notebook, known when Ruby joined the Communist Party, and taken the liberty of adding this note. Second, if Rose read this poem at the end of the *Contracts* notebook, she must also have read those that preceded it—including the "Sonnet for Debbie," Ruby's poem about the "trifling" blond, and the obscene poem. So, I asked myself: What had *she* thought when she read those? Was she shocked, and did she feel angry and betrayed by her dead husband? Was my mother right that my grandfather had written the obscene poem about my Aunt Toby—Rose's younger sister? Toby would have been nineteen years old in 1933 and certainly not "deeply wed," as portrayed in the "Sonnet for Debbie." And if anything had been going on between Ruby and Toby, had Rose known about her husband's dalliance, or fantasy, all along? I was well aware that Rose had been a free spirit.

And finally, what was the significance of the note "prior to joining CP"? Why or how would joining the Communist Party, apparently sometime after March 1933, have made a difference to the poetry he'd been writing? And why did I find no poems dated after March 1933? Had there been some kind of conflict between Ruby's two passions?

Also included in the Briefcase was a freestanding, untitled, unsigned, theoretical thirteen-page typed academic essay. I initially had no idea who had written the paper, which was unlike, and far more militant than, any of Ruby's writings I had seen thus far. Although it had no typewritten date, someone—in handwriting that was unlike Ruby's—had written on the top right corner of the first page: "*1932 Shortly before joining the Communist Party.*" The handwriting of the note appeared to be the same as that in the "prior to joining CP" note on Ruby's March 1933 poem, and again I assumed the handwriting was Rose's.

The paper was largely inscrutable to me, even after having read it five times. The author seemed to be trying to prove an amorphous "thesis" as to the desired form and content of literature once the old "kings" were inevitably taken down and the new kings—i.e., the poor masses—had taken their place. Replete with numerous references to mythology and grandiose rhetoric that often struck me as gibberish, the paper explained how the ancient kings "at the height of their grandeur ... were cut down by convoluting lusts ... consuming vengeances, anguish and contrition from remembered sin, a small space still unconquered filling the blood with gall, eunuch loins attached to kingly sway, butchered children to keep the kingly seat, beautiful wives in the enemy's embrace ... So they were continuously and utterly destroyed."

This reference to deposed kings led me to suspect that my grandfather was probably the author of the freestanding paper, as it harked back to a typed poem pasted into his *Contracts* notebook entitled

"American Independence—Year 156." The poem, which seemed to reflect my grandfather's conflicting feelings about his country, was signed "Rubin Schechter" and dated July 4, 1932. It began:

> I love this land, and I will surely learn
> My way to be at peace with it. The land
> Is beautiful, with milky fat inside,
> And yielding greatly to man's greater hand.
> But Joy is dead. Women and men are stern

But the poem concluded with the following stanza, which had caught my attention:

> And frightened and lean; kings have risen up.
> The spreaded feasts are not for us to sup,
> Merely to gaze upon and meekly guess
> What kings may do by way of throwing men
> A bone. But for her utter hopelessness,
> But for his shame to show so little room,
> Each girl would sense in every man her groom,
> And every man could choose himself a bride;
> **When kings go down it will be so again** (emphasis mine)

The author of the thirteen-page paper proceeded to rhapsodize how the poor, once they overcame "their struggle with the three vultures appointed to destroy them, Hunger and Cold and Rooflessness," would replace the current kings—"for we know that once the monsters have been laid low, then beggars become kings at once and magically—as the bread and wine become Christ."

On page 7, the author finally broached his thesis, contemplating the form and substance that literature should take once the poor became kings. He then seemed to declare victory:

> We have shown—even if parenthetically—the importance of literature to class consciousness as the means of inducting the suffering class into the fields of bliss occupied by the oppressor....
>
> We must present a literature which shall bring pleasure, and be of use to the teeming masses of peers.

Finally, the concluding paragraph of the paper, also largely unintelligible to me, was rich in melodrama and literary allusion—including to *Oedipus*, *Hamlet*, Beethoven, Walt Whitman, and Thomas Hardy's *Jude the Obscure*—which, if nothing else, seemed to confirm my suspicion that my grandfather had written it.

So what's to be made of this zealous, often unintelligible treatise? While the logic may have been elusive and his prose melodramatic, I see here my young grandfather's blazing devotion to people living in "Hunger and Cold and Rooflessness" that, according to the Lipkaner biography, would lead him to the Communist Party, Spain, and ultimately his death five years later. And just possibly, this essay reflects an effort by my grandfather to reconcile his love of poetry and literature with the radical politics to which he was increasingly devoting his life. I can't help but imagine that he was on a precipice—trying to cling to his love of literature, and harmonize it with the radical political views he was buying into. But as he and others would discover, the Communist Party was a jealous mistress.

That Party Organizer

The U.S. Communist Party Circa 1933

It's probably difficult for most people living in the United States in the twenty-first century to understand the allure the Communist Party had for intelligent people like Ruby and Harry in the 1930s, or to appreciate the important role the Party played in America during that bygone era. The Soviet Union, the beacon of communism, collapsed in failure three decades ago; the Communist Party of the United States is now defunct; and few people living here today have anything but a negative association with either. Nevertheless, a peek at history reveals that it is hardly surprising that my grandfathers joined the Communist Party in 1933. They were in good company.

The Communist Party of the United States was born in 1919 in the wake of the Russian Revolution two years earlier. Prior to the Depression, the Communists had little success recruiting a meaningful following in the United States, as they dwelled on Marxist theory and heated rhetoric concerning the international economy. But as the Depression proceeded to devastate this country in the 1930s, the Party changed course and took a leading role in the efforts to help the millions of Americans left unemployed, homeless, and hungry—or, to put it in the words of Ruby's thirteen-page essay, those living in "Hunger and Cold and Rooflessness."[4]

For those out of work, the Party pushed for such relief as national unemployment insurance, moratoriums on mortgages, and resistance to evictions.[5] On behalf of workers who did have jobs, the Party advocated for a forty-hour work week and mounted opposition to low wages and dangerous working conditions.[6] It fought for the rights of women and pushed to get Black Americans on jury rolls.[7] Most of what the Communists advocated for in the 1930s hardly looks radical today, and much of it seems obviously righteous.[8] In important respects, they were merely ahead of the times.

Moreover, with this country's capitalistic system in shambles and tens of millions in poverty, young idealists like my grandfathers—along with many other intellectuals, writers, clergy members, and journalists—were captivated and inspired by the reports of miraculous progress emanating from the Soviet Union. Marxism was getting a trial run in the U.S.S.R. and appeared to be doing very well. In less than a decade, the world's first Marxist government was reported to have largely eliminated illiteracy and transformed the economy for the benefit of prospering workers, whose American counterparts were starving in shanty towns. The Marxists spoke with self-assurance, "breathing certitude and salvation," leading many to believe that if Marxism could work so well in the Soviet Union, it could do the same here.[9]

Finally, there were two additional causes that drew young idealists to the U.S. Communist Party, which entered the mainstream and became an important player in the Depression protest movements. One was anti-fascism. As Hitler took power in Germany in 1933, the Communist Party became this country's leading voice in the nascent anti-fascism movement—a cause that was especially compelling to American Jews. The opposition of the Party, and the Soviet Union, to the growing specter of fascism was the most powerful magnet drawing Americans to the Party.[10] The second was antiracism, another cause to which I learned Ruby had been devoted. In particular, the stature of the Party rose in the eyes of

American liberals, and its membership grew, because of the leading role it played in the legendary Scottsboro case[11]—a saga in which Ruby's college friend and now brother-in-law, Irving Schwab, was intimately involved.

Scottsboro—And Irving Schwab (Take 1)

Other than my two consecutive maternal grandfathers having fought in Spain with the Abraham Lincoln Brigade, the piece of my family history I've been most proud of over the years is the role my Uncle Irving played in the Scottsboro case. I never got to meet Irving—who, like Ruby, died young. As the Lipkaner biography recounts, the two of them bonded in college, sharing their liberal politics and a devotion to helping the downtrodden. Irving married Ruby's younger sister Bessie in 1927. He was my great-uncle, and my cousin Carl's father.

After growing up in Greenwich Village, Carl bailed for a life as a lobsterman in Maine when he was seventeen. He was a hero to me, as some of my most treasured childhood memories are of early mornings spent on the ocean "helping" Carl haul his lobster traps. Since as far back as I can remember, I visited Carl more or less annually—first with my parents as a child, later as a single adult

Author (8 years old) "helping" Cousin Carl Schwab haul lobster traps

with friends, then with my wife Melissa, and finally as a parent with our two sons.

On one of our visits, in or around 2010, I sat with Carl at his kitchen table looking out on the picturesque Port Clyde harbor dotted with colored lobster buoys. We turned the pages of a scrapbook Carl had of articles about his father and, in particular, about Irving's role in the Scottsboro case.

The name of the case still rings a bell for many Americans. Some vaguely know it involved a group of Black teenagers who were accused and, after a sham trial, convicted of raping two young white women aboard a freight train on which they had all hitched a ride, as many poor people did during the Depression. At least in my day, every law student read the Supreme Court's landmark decision in *Powell v. Alabama*, which established the right of a defendant to effective assistance of legal counsel in a capital criminal case—where the defendant could be sentenced to death if convicted. The case has occasionally resurfaced in the news, such as when one of the Scottsboro Boys was pardoned after decades, or when the last one died. But I suspect that even among those people living today who do know something about the case, most are unaware of the huge sensation it was in the 1930s, or the role it played in the development of the Civil Rights Movement. And its prominence in the public eye was due in significant part to the aggressive publicity campaign waged by the U.S. Communist Party on behalf of the Scottsboro Boys throughout the 1930s.

Here are some of the facts: The youngest of the nine Scottsboro Boys was thirteen years old and the oldest was nineteen. They didn't all know each other prior to their arrests, and not all of them were riding in the train car where the crime allegedly took place.[12] What was never disputed is that on March 25, 1931, a fight broke out between several Black and white male teenagers in the open-topped gondola car where two poor young white women, Victoria Price and Ruby Bates, were riding. They had hopped the train in Tennessee. After all but one of the white males had either jumped or been thrown off the train, one of them told the stationmaster in Stevenson, Alabama, about the fight with "a bunch of Negroes" and said he wanted to press charges. The police were notified and a posse was organized, including virtually all the white men who owned guns in Paint Rock, Alabama, the next stop on the train. The posse was ordered to arrest every Black male on the train and bring them to Scottsboro.[13] The first time the two women were asked if the boys had bothered them, they said no. They made the charge of rape only under pressure from the lynch mob awaiting them outside the jail in Scottsboro.[14]

After the boys were taken to jail, the women were examined by two local doctors. As news of the women's accusations spread, an angry mob grew to include thousands of people, most of them armed, threatening to rush the jail and thirsting to lynch the boys. Policemen beat the boys in an attempt to extract confessions.[15] In the days that followed, media stories fueled by interviews of the two women whipped the local population into a frenzy.[16] After local lawyers refused to represent the boys, and after equivocating, Stephen Roddy, a seventy-year-old lawyer from Chattanooga with a drinking problem, said he would take the case, assisted by a local lawyer.[17] Roddy reportedly showed up drunk for the first day of the trial, which began on Monday, April 6—a mere two weeks after the date of the alleged rape—with Judge Alfred Hawkins presiding.[18]

With his clients facing the death penalty, Roddy did no preparation for the trials and met with them beforehand for less than a half hour.[19] The trial of two of the boys, Clarence Norris and Charley Weems, proceeded first. Victoria Price was the star witness for the state, testifying to a vicious rape that supposedly lasted for hours.[20] Roddy conducted only a brief cross-examination of Price, during which the judge barred him from inquiring into her character or criminal history.

The prosecution also called as witnesses the two doctors who had examined Price and Bates, but much of their testimony undermined the state's case. The first, Dr. R.R. Bridges, testified that there were no bruises or tears to Victoria Price's genitals. The second doctor, Marvin Lynch, testified that he had been able to obtain only a small sample of "non-motile" semen from Price's vagina using a swab—indicating that she had had sexual intercourse, but much earlier than when the alleged rape had occurred. He told the jury that "there was nothing to indicate any violence about the vagina."[21]

The state called six additional witnesses—including Ruby Bates, who gave testimony that differed from Price's. Bates admitted on cross-examination that she had not told the posse that stopped the train about the alleged rape, and had mentioned only the fight between the Black and white teens in the gondola car.[22] The prosecution's final witness, Luther Morris, implausibly claimed that he had looked up from the loft of his barn and seen several Black men eject five white men "and take charge of two girls" in a train car just as it passed by.[23]

Having done no investigation of the facts, and lacking any evidence, defense counsel Roddy called as witnesses only the two defendants, Charley Weems and Clarence Norris. Weems steadfastly denied taking part in, or witnessing, any rape, but Norris's testimony was disastrous. On cross-examination he changed his testimony and said that all eight of the other defendants had indeed raped the two women and that he alone was innocent. It would emerge later that sheriffs had beaten him the night before he was to testify, and that Norris was either offered or sought to obtain leniency by implicating the other defendants.[24]

When it came time for closing statements, Roddy told the judge that he did not want to make a closing argument to the jury,[25] a shocking move that probably was and remains virtually unprecedented in the annals of criminal trials with defendants facing the death penalty. Two lawyers for the prosecution argued to the jury, urging that both defendants be sentenced to death.

After the judge instructed the jury on the afternoon of Tuesday, April 7, and even before it had started its deliberations, another all-white male jury was selected for the trial of Haywood Patterson, which began immediately. Victoria Price testified again, providing more detailed testimony than in the first trial. When asked on cross whether she had ever engaged in prostitution, Price stated: "I do not know what prostitution means. I have not made it a practice to have intercourse with other men.... I have not had intercourse with any white man but my husband."[26] It would later emerge that nothing could be further from the truth. Not only had both women routinely engaged in prostitution, but on the night before accusing the Scottsboro Boys of rape they had had sex with white men they knew, neither of whom was Price's husband.[27]

After deliberating for only a few hours, the first jury reached a verdict. With the second jury sitting within earshot in an adjoining room, the clerk of the court announced that the jury had found Norris and Weems guilty of rape, and sentenced them to death. The audience in the courtroom and the crowd of around 1,500 people outside erupted, with the noise drowning out the judge's attempts to gavel the courtroom to order. A witness testified that the second jury sitting in an adjacent room heard the crowd's reaction to the verdict.[28]

Roddy again declined to make a closing statement to the jury in Haywood Patterson's trial, and a half hour after his case was submitted to the jury at 11am on Wednesday, April 8, the trial of the next five boys began. Victoria Price's testimony became more lurid with each succeeding trial, as she now told the jury what each defendant had supposedly done and said to her, including that several of the boys had yelled, "Pour it to her, pour it to her!" as Willie Roberson allegedly raped her.[29]

Before lunch, and after deliberating for only twenty-five minutes, the jury in Patterson's case returned another guilty verdict and sentenced him to death.[30] After lunch, Willie Roberson testified in his defense. Like three of the accused boys who followed him to the witness stand, Roberson claimed that he had not even been in the train car where the alleged rape occurred. He also testified that he was suffering from syphilis and gonorrhea, with his genitals swollen and sore. He said he had been riding alone in a boxcar, hoping to reach Atlanta's Grady Hospital to get treatment for his painful condition.[31]

After Roddy again declined to make a closing argument, the case was submitted to the jury, and a fourth jury was impaneled for the trial of the last defendant, thirteen-year-old Roy Wright. Not surprisingly, both juries reached a guilty verdict by the following morning, April 9, although the Wright jury was divided as to whether he should be given life in prison, rather than death, given his young age. On that afternoon—sixteen days after the alleged rape—Judge Hawkins, apparently with tears in his eyes, pronounced the death sentence on all eight of the other boys.[32] But this marked merely the first of many chapters in the Scottsboro Boys' tortuous ride through the criminal justice system.

Two days before the eight youths were sentenced to death, Judge Hawkins had received a telegram from the International Labor Defense (ILD)—the legal arm of the Communist Party of the United States, based in New York City—charging that the Scottsboro Boys were being tried on trumped-up charges.[33] Formed in 1925, the ILD had participated in numerous high-profile lawsuits, beginning with the Sacco and Vanzetti case.[34] The ILD's letter to Hawkins was followed by a statement issued by the U.S. Communist Party claiming that "the Southern Ruling class" had misused the legal system to perpetrate an "illegal lynching."[35] The ILD and the Communist Party proceeded on two fronts: (1) waging a bitter struggle with the NAACP to control the defense of the cases;[36] and (2) conducting an aggressive publicity campaign to broadcast to the American public, and the rest of the world, the virulent racism that had produced the sham trial and convictions of nine innocent teenagers.

The ILD sent several lawyers from New York City to Alabama to work on the case. My Uncle Irving was one of the first.[37] According to our family lore, Irving was the lead lawyer for the Scottsboro Boys as they appealed their convictions through the Alabama court system until the case got to the Supreme Court. My mother told me that at that point Samuel Leibowitz, a prominent New York lawyer who was not a Communist, was brought in to argue the case so that it would not be associated with the Communist Party. A high point of Irving's involvement in Scottsboro was that he smuggled Ruby Bates out of the South in the rumble seat of his car, and brought her to a church in New York City where she recanted her accusations and admitted that neither she nor

Victoria Price had been raped. I related this story countless times over the decades, proudly demonstrating that my dead uncle had been an early warrior in the fight against racism.

Only after turning seventy, at the very end of my investigation into the radical past of my idealistic forebears, would I discover that here, as elsewhere, much of the family lore I'd cherished was wrong. Much, but not all: Ruby Bates did recant at a church in New York City and did go on to testify in Alabama at the new trial ordered by the United States Supreme Court. And she did indeed testify that there had been no rape, and that the testimony she and Victoria Price had given at the four earlier trials was totally false. As I would later learn, however, her testimony did not prevent the Scottsboro Boys from being convicted or sentenced to death by the white racist juries in Alabama; to the contrary, her testimony—and the role played by the Communists in securing it—may have facilitated the injustice.

Scottsboro quickly became the most sensational case since Sacco and Vanzetti, and remained one of the most high-profile media stories throughout the 1930s. It produced not one but two Supreme Court decisions, and almost a dozen separate trials.

And so, with their youthful passions inflamed by the ravages of the Depression highlighting the failure of U.S. capitalism, the blatant racism exemplified by the Scottsboro case, and the frightening rise of Hitler in Europe, idealistic Americans—especially liberal American Jews like Ruby, Harry, and Irving—flocked to the U.S. Communist Party.[38]

In fact, most of the approximately 30,000 Party members as of 1935 had joined in the two years prior.[39] The membership continued to grow dramatically, more than doubling to approximately 75,000 members by 1938.[40]

Reviewing the worthwhile causes the U.S. Communist Party was championing in those years, including the defense of the Scottsboro Boys, I initially thought to myself that had I been alive in 1933 I would almost certainly have joined the Party along with my grandparents. It would be a while before I would understand what joining the Party entailed—or why Rose's "prior to joining the CP" notes on Ruby's FDR poem and the thirteen-page paper were indeed significant. Joining the Communist Party was nothing like registering as a Democrat or a Republican today.

One surprising aspect of my experience researching and writing this book is that, in addition to finding that my thoughts and feelings about my grandparents and their motivations changed repeatedly as I stumbled upon new sources, I've also had shifting perspectives on myself. A case in point: reading Kai Bird and Martin Sherwin's biography of Robert Oppenheimer after seeing the 2023 movie based upon it, I found myself reassessing what I would have done had I been alive in the 1930s.

Like Ruby and many other young American intellectuals, Oppenheimer, the brilliant physicist selected in 1942 to head the country's massive effort to develop the atomic bomb, was attracted to the U.S. Communist Party because of its place at the forefront of such worthy progressive causes as the opposition to poverty, racism, and fascism. Beginning in 1936, Oppenheimer had a "smoldering fury" about the Nazis' treatment of Jews in Germany and the plight of migrant workers ravaged by the Depression—and he felt the need to do something about it.[41] Like Ruby and Rose, Oppenheimer participated in a discussion group that met regularly to discuss radical politics. He read *Das Kapital* cover to cover, and helped Communist Party intellectuals write papers. After the outbreak of the Spanish Civil War he made significant financial contributions to the Communist Party, attended meetings sponsored by the Party, joined organizations later deemed to be affiliated with the Party, and had friends and lovers who were members of the Party, as was his brother Frank. And some of those friends, and others in the Party with whom Oppenheimer interacted, believed that Oppenheimer was one of them.[42] But when interrogated later about his affiliation with the Party, Oppenheimer steadfastly denied that he had ever actually joined or been a member of the Communist Party.[43]

Oppenheimer acknowledged that for a brief period of time he may have thought of himself as "an unaffiliated communist," and he was clearly a "fellow traveler" who sympathized with and supported the Party's causes.[44] And many Americans in the 1930s who were concerned with economic justice, fascism, and racism, but either never joined the Party or remained members only briefly, fell into the "fellow traveler" bucket.[45] There seems to be no definitive proof as to whether Oppenheimer was ever a member of the Communist Party. In light of what I've come to learn about the Party I tend to doubt that he was, although several historians, pointing to recently-discovered evidence, believe his denials were false.[46]

Reading about Oppenheimer caused me to wonder: Had I lived in the 1930s, would I have been a fellow traveler? An independent thinker attracted to the worthy causes championed by the Party but never a member? Or would I have taken the plunge and joined the Party like Ruby, Rose, Harry, and Irving? While I'd like to think I would have been in Oppenheimer's camp, the honest answer is that I don't and cannot know. What I do know for certain is that my forebears were neither fellow travelers nor unaffiliated Communists. They were all in.

Notes of a Party Operative: Ruby's Little Black Book

I found a third notebook in the Briefcase: a 4x6-inch black leather-bound loose-leaf with rings on the top. It contained my grandfather's contemporaneous notes reflecting that he held a leadership role in the Queens County District of the U.S. Communist Party. Although the fourteen pages of notes were undated, given that Ruby joined the Party no earlier than March 1933, I assumed he made these notes sometime between March 1933 and March 1937, when he left for Spain. More specifically, given that the substance of all the notes indicated that they were written after Ruby had assumed a leadership role, I suspected they were written no earlier than 1934. In any event, the little black notebook helped me bridge the void between Ruby's period of prolific poetry-writing, which—as far as the evidence he left behind indicated—ended in 1933, and his departure for Spain in March 1937.

Other than one page of typed notes, all of them were neatly handwritten in the same outline format that I use for developing legal briefs. The first page—"Reports on Division of work"—began with point I, "Literature," calling to mind the thirteen-page paper I'd seen. It proceeded to list an array of subtopics, with detailed points below each, including:

Political Aspects
1. Education of comrades
2. Popularization....
Distribution....
3. Newsstands and Stores

The only typed page in the notebook was entitled "Weekend Training Class for Functionaries and Actives." It began with a list of subjects to be covered, including "The Negro Question," and went on to detail an onerous schedule that included all-day sessions on Saturdays and Sundays for four weeks.[47]

Another page of my grandfather's notes revealed him to have been an exacting leader, although I would later find reason to wonder about that. Titled "Weakness in Nuclei," he began:

1. Political—poor quality of work
a) Not consolidating factions
b) No political leaders
c) No Negro work

Causes
1. Lack of Leadership
2. No conscious policy of developing the shop comrades....
3. Plenty of activity and influence but no real recruiting

The last three pages were filled with notes in pencil that appeared to relate to the tense relations between the Communist Party and other left-wing factions. One page, entitled "Program for the United Front," included ten points as to which my grandfather apparently hoped the various groups could agree. These included:

1. Strike against every wage cut & worsening conditions....
6. Complete equality for the Negroes & the Negro people....
8. Civil Rights and Worker Self Defense Groups
9. Against war and fascism

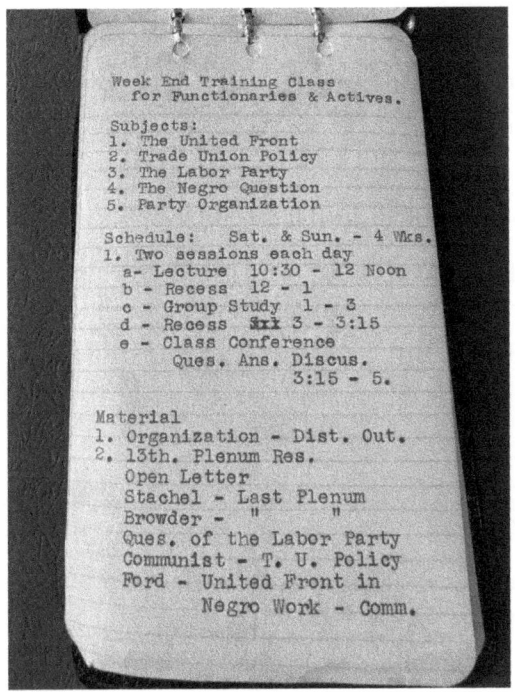

Agenda for Ruby's Weekend Training Class

Knowing virtually nothing about the history of the Communist Party when I discovered the little black book, many of the notes in it made little sense to me at that point, apart from showing that my grandfather was deeply immersed in the left-wing campaign to lift up downtrodden workers and combat racial discrimination. But even in the midst of this account of his political work, with his career as an aspiring poet apparently lying fallow, I found evidence of Ruby's romantic core.

Tucked into a flap on the inside of the back cover of the little black notebook was a sheet of fragile browned paper folded into a square. I unfolded the paper so I could read it, hoping it wouldn't rip apart, and was surprised to find a lock of light reddish-brown hair. The color I remember my Grandma Rose's hair had been. And on the paper were the following words, written in what I later came to know as her handwriting:

> I've cut off the end that I pasted down to my forehead in a little semi-circle sweeping into my eye the night we want to the opera. Here sweetheart there is all warmth and tenderness in this bundle of hair. If you look at it under a soft light it looks nice Darling. Here is a kiss for you.

I teared up as I read my grandmother's loving words and gently rubbed a small piece of her hair between my thumb and forefinger. I just sat staring at it for a minute, reflecting on how my grandfather had tucked the lock and note away in his Communist organizer's notebook almost ninety years before, when he and my grandmother were less than half my age. Then I called to my wife to come take a look.

PART III

The Soldier

Diving In

Other than the three notebooks of Ruby's poetry and Communist Party organizing work, most of the papers that filled the Briefcase pertained to my grandfather's fatal stint as a soldier. They included more than fifty letters to, from, and about him, along with a smattering of newspaper articles, most of which were variations of his obituary. Not surprisingly, a lot of the eighty-five-year-old paper was fragile.

Before delving into the Briefcase, the only traces I'd seen of my grandfather Ruby were the snippets about him in the Lincoln Brigade Archives, the two-page Lipkaner biography, and the copies of the two remarkable letters that my cousin Carl had sent me. Now I was staring at scores of my grandfather's letters, which had been crammed into the Briefcase in no particular order. My initial reaction upon skimming through the contents of the Briefcase had been one of excitement. Realizing that I now had the task of deciphering and making sense of the morass, it felt daunting. I procrastinated for almost six months before opening the Briefcase again.

When I finally dove into the trove of letters and articles, I realized I'd been given a front-row seat from which to watch my grandfather in action: to see his personality, character, and wartime experience in an unfiltered display. The Briefcase also yielded new insights into my Grandma Rose and what she had been up to while Ruby was away, as well as clues to help answer the question that had nagged me for years: What force had been so powerful as to lead Ruby to defy his government and abandon his wife and young daughter, in order to fight in a civil war in Spain—a foreign country with which he had no connection?

Spain: April 1937

The Spanish Civil War that Ruby and Harry waded into in 1937 was a bloodbath. By the time my grandfathers arrived in Spain on April 2 after hiking over the Pyrenees, Hitler and Mussolini were fully invested in Franco's success while the Western governments were locked into their near-sighted policy of non-intervention and appeasement of the fascists. As a result, the democratically elected Republican government of Spain was essentially doomed. Ninety years later, with Western governments—and particularly the United States—again struggling with how to respond to a brutal dictator bent on quashing a democracy, the lessons of the Spanish Civil War have assumed fresh relevance.

Had the civil war in Spain remained only the violent internal clash that had raged since 1931 (and even well before then), the story could have had a different ending[1], and Ruby and Harry would never have taken part in it. For the five years preceding the war's outbreak in July 1936, an assortment of groups seeking reforms of the Spanish economy and social structure had engaged in an often violent struggle with reactionary forces determined to either maintain the existing order or roll back the clock. The factions pushing for reforms—involving land ownership, redistribution of wealth, and the rights of women, among other matters—included urban workers, farm laborers, many in the educated middle class, socialists, communists, and anarchists. The reactionary players included wealthy landowners, industrialists, the Catholic establishment, and the army.[2]

In the 1936 election, the left-wing factions banded together to support the socialist Republicans, who won and proceeded to institute various reforms. Enraged, the reactionary forces, backed by a powerful contingent of military generals, were determined to take the government back by force. Francisco Franco, one of the younger generals, initially was not the chosen leader of the military uprising that began on July 17, 1936.[3] Moreover, he and his Army of Africa were stuck in Morocco with no way to get to Spain, as the Republican navy controlled the seas.[4] But things changed dramatically after Franco succeeded in persuading first Mussolini and then Hitler to throw the weight of their military arsenals behind their fellow fascist.

The two dictators each had their own reasons for inserting themselves into Spain's civil war. One motivation they shared was the desire to test the new military technologies they would soon unleash on the rest of Europe. Paul Preston, probably the leading living historian on the Spanish Civil War, quotes testimony given by Hermann Göring, Reich Commissioner for Air and head of the Luftwaffe, at the Nuremberg trials:

> When civil war broke out in Spain, Franco sent a call for help to Germany and asked for support, particularly in the air.... The Fuhrer thought the matter over. I urged him to give support in all circumstances, firstly, in order to prevent the further spread of communism in that theater and, secondly, to test my young Luftwaffe at this opportunity in this or that technical respect. With the permission of the Fuhrer I sent a large part of my transport fleet and a number of experimental fighter units, bombers, and anti-aircraft guns; and in that way I had an opportunity to ascertain, under combat conditions, whether the material was equal to the task. In order that the personnel, too, might gather a certain

amount of experience, I saw to it that there was a continuous flow, that is, that new people were constantly being sent and others recalled.[5]

Hitler's aircraft flew 15,000 of Franco's soldiers from Morocco to Spain. Without this rescue by the German air force—as well as Mussolini's—the Spanish fascists' best troops would not have been able to get to the mainland of Spain.[6]

For a few reasons, the Western democracies were content to sit back and do nothing to oppose Hitler's and Mussolini's aggression in Spain. The English and French governments, with their massive casualties in World War I still fresh in their minds, desperately feared becoming embroiled in another international war and were determined to avoid doing anything to trigger one. In addition, the Western democracies were increasingly suspicious of the Soviet Union and feared the spread of communism. Accordingly, they were not unhappy to watch Hitler and Mussolini join in the assault on Spain's democratically elected socialist government.[7] Although public opinion in England was heavily on the side of the Republican government, the policy of British Prime Minister Neville Chamberlain's Conservative government was "appeasement at virtually any price."[8]

In August 1936, France proposed an agreement providing for non-intervention in the Spanish Civil War. Twenty-seven European nations, including Germany and Italy, became parties to the agreement.[9] In the United States, where public opinion as to the war was divided, Roosevelt bowed to isolationist pressure from the right. On August 7, 1936, he announced that the United States would "scrupulously refrain from any interference whatsoever in the unfortunate Spanish Civil situation." A week later he imposed a "moral" embargo on arms sales to Spain.[10]

Finally, the Soviet Union also signed on to the Non-Intervention Agreement. Although Stalin supported Spain's socialist government, his primary goal was to safeguard his own country from the threat that Hitler would turn east—as he later did—and make good on his rabidly anti-communist rhetoric. Accordingly, Stalin sought to cooperate with Britain and France. On August 23, 1936, the Soviet Union signed the agreement and six days later pledged that it would not export arms to the Spanish Republic.[11]

The Non-Intervention Agreement quickly proved to be a sham, aptly described by Pandit Nehru as "the supreme farce of our time."[12] Hitler and Mussolini violated it with impunity while the Western democracies sat on the sidelines. In September 1936, Stalin warned Britain and France that he would have no alternative but to break the agreement if the flagrant violations by the Germans and Italians continued. With his pleas for help ignored, on October 7, 1938, the Soviet Union began shipping weapons to Spain's Republican government.[13] Two weeks later, the Soviets announced that the U.S.S.R. could no more consider itself bound by the Non-Intervention Agreement than others who were violating it. Hugh Thomas has written that at that point—with Mussolini referring to his partnership with Hitler as the "Berlin-Rome Axis"—"in more ways than one, the Spanish Civil War would be more even than a European civil war: it would be a world war in miniature."[14]

In his assessment of the Non-Intervention Agreement, Paul Preston has observed that by appeasing Hitler in Spain, the ineffectual pact emboldened the fascists and "thereby passed a death sentence on the Spanish Republic and dramatically weakened the

Western powers."[15] Roosevelt later acknowledged that his arms embargo had been a "grave mistake," and his Under Secretary of State, Sumner Welles, put it even more bluntly: "Of all our blind isolationist policies, the most disastrous was our attitude on the Spanish Civil War."[16]

As the Western powers turned their backs on the democratically elected Spanish government, the Italians and Germans unleashed their latest bomber aircraft, fighter planes, and motorized ground weapons on the Republican army and civilians alike. The casualties and atrocities were hard for me to read about. Franco and his fascist allies were intent not merely on capturing territory, but on terrorizing and exterminating the population in Republican-held areas. In Granada, for example, 5,000 civilians were shot.[17] Hundreds of civilians were lined up and executed in small villages such as Lora del Río and Palma del Río.[18] Rapes and murder of even pregnant women were rampant. One of the most horrific episodes involved the German aerial bombardment that totally destroyed the defenseless village of Guernica in April 1937, shortly after Ruby and Harry arrived in Spain. The subject of Picasso's iconic painting, thousands of civilians were killed in Guernica—a harbinger of the Nazi blitzkriegs that would soon obliterate cities throughout Europe.[19]

So the picture was objectively bleak when Ruby and Harry got to Spain in April. The Republican army they joined had two fatal problems. First, thanks to the Non-Intervention Agreement, it was starved for weapons and completely outgunned.[20] The second problem was that the various groups that made up the Republican "coalition" were at war with each other.[21] A prime example was the violent conflict between the Soviet-controlled Communist Party and groups accused of being Trotskyists, most notably the Partido

Obrero de Unificación Marxista (POUM). A civil war within the civil war erupted in Barcelona in May 1937, with Communists and Trotskyists erecting barricades and battling each other in the streets.[22] The Communists declared the POUM illegal and, in June 1937, its leader, Andreu Nin, was captured by Russian agents, tortured, and executed. Many other POUM members were killed or imprisoned.[23] As I later learned, Trotskyists may have exacted revenge on my grandfather.

The Lincoln and Washington Brigades

It's difficult for an American like me living today to envision violating the law and leaving my family in order to voluntarily risk my life fighting in a foreign civil war. But the Americans who went to Spain believed, presciently, that the fate of the world was on the line there, and that they had to do something about it. Ruby was not the only young man who left a letter for his parents telling them that he'd left for Spain and warning them not to try to get him back.[24] Some, like Ruby and Harry, had been devoted Communists before volunteering, but many others were recent converts who joined the Party due to its stand on fascism, not Marxism. Others belonged to no political party. What most of them shared was the fear that fascism posed an existential threat to the world, including to American democracy, and that time was running out. And most remarkably, they shared a willingness to risk their very lives to stop it.[25]

Ruby and Harry fit the demographic profile of many of the young American volunteers who left home to fight in Spain. Comprising approximately 3,000 Americans, what became known as the Abraham Lincoln Brigade was amalgamated with five international units from other countries to form the XV International Brigade.[26] Altogether, the International Brigades included upward of 35,000 volunteers from more than fifty countries worldwide.[27]

The first 100 American recruits to join the International Brigades—mainly political cadres of the U.S. Communist Party—left New York bound for Spain on the SS *Normandie* on December 26, 1936.[28] Initially, the American volunteers were grouped into two battalions, the Abraham Lincoln and the George Washington, the latter comprising those like Ruby and Harry who did not leave for Spain until a few months after the Lincoln Brigade had been formed.[29] On July 14, 1937, ten days before Ruby was shot, the two American battalions were merged to form the Lincoln-Washington Brigade. The combined brigade is popularly referred to today (and in this book) as the Abraham Lincoln Brigade.[30]

New Yorkers made up the largest share of the American contingent of Republican volunteers, with about one-third coming from the New York City area.[31] Likewise, most of the other volunteers were city dwellers coming from eleven states that accounted for over 80 percent of the total American contingent force.[32] Roughly four out of ten men were younger than twenty-five, with another quarter aged between twenty-six and thirty.[33] Ruby, thirty-two years old in 1937, was an outlier in another respect: only 189 of the 1,249 American Communists in Spain were married upon their departure.[34] Even fewer had children. Like Ruby (and also Harry), however, many of the American volunteers had direct familial ties to Europe, with one in three born there before migrating to America.[35] Overall, 80 percent of the Americans had at least one parent born abroad.[36]

Understanding better than most other Americans the terrors of fascism as they witnessed Hitler's rise to power in Germany, nearly a third of the American volunteers were Jewish.[37] Young Jewish men from throughout Europe also came to fight and die in Spain, merging with their American compatriots in the International Brigades.[38] Milton Wolff, the last commander of the Lincoln Battalion and a Jewish Brooklynite by birth, explained this movement when testifying before Congress in 1939: "Knowing that as a Jew, we are the first to suffer when fascism does come, I went to Spain to fight against it."[39]

Two-thirds to three-quarters of the American volunteers identified as members of the Communist Party. Nevertheless, the Party sought to downplay its Marxist revolutionary goals and emphasized its American nature. For example, the George Washington Battalion was initially named for Tom Mooney, an imprisoned Communist labor leader; it was renamed for America's first president after Party leaders in New York objected that the association with Mooney would be too inflammatory.[40] In any event, most Americans ventured to Spain not to hasten a communist revolution, but to stem the tide of fascism. About 25 percent of the American recruits claimed no political affiliation.[41]

The American casualties were horrific, and Ruby's getting shot was anything but the fluke I had misunderstood it to have been for most of my life. In the Jarama valley, where the Lincoln Brigade first took the battlefield in February 1937, the Americans were rushed into battle with little training and ordered to mount a senseless attack, armed with rifles most had never loaded or fired and that jammed in the field. They were ordered to dig trenches but lacked picks and shovels, and were forced to dig with their helmets and bayonets.[42] Some were still in civilian clothes and sneakers.[43] According to the Lincoln Brigade Archives, Harry fought at Jarama after arriving in Spain in April. He was among the lucky survivors. Of the 450 Americans who fought at Jarama, 120 were killed and another 175 were wounded.[44] According to the brigade archives, by the time the International Brigades were withdrawn from Spain in 1939, 800 of them had been killed;[45] many more were wounded.

I wondered how much Ruby and Harry had known or anticipated about the horror show they had volunteered for, or how much accurate information they received even after they got to Spain. By some accounts, the American new arrivals were not told of the massive casualties the Republicans had already suffered.[46] Another commentator reported, however, that "only the illiterate would not have known the news that all daily newspapers carried, that Spain was a brutal, dangerous place where thousands of soldiers were being killed weekly."[47]

I also wondered whether Ruby ever really believed, as he'd promised his parents, that he would not be in danger because he was slated to have only a desk job. Did he know the war was going downhill and that thousands of captured soldiers and civilians were being brutally murdered each week? If so, one would never know it from the letters my grandfather sent home. They painted a very different picture.

Going—and Coming—to Spain

Other than my grandfather's elusive poems, written in his twenties before joining the Communist Party, and his cryptic organizer's notes, the letters he sent home from Spain in 1937 provided the only firsthand account of what he was thinking and feeling—who he was and what was motivating him in what proved to be the last chapter of his abbreviated life.

The fragile and faded letters had been stuffed into the Briefcase in no discernable order. I began by attempting to put them in chronological order, guessing at where to place the random letters that were undated. I then selected those that, upon a preliminary review, seemed most important, and put them in plastic sheaths in order to preserve them as I worked.

None of the letters chronicled my grandfather's decision to volunteer for the war—or how he was recruited (I would get a glimpse of that much later, courtesy of George Charney, the subject of my grandfather's "Sonnet for George"). Nevertheless, what I found in the letters was eye-opening: an intimate, rich, and vivid picture of my grandfather as he defied his government and left his wife and young daughter behind, in order to first reach and then plunge headlong into the epicenter of a bloody, foreign civil war.

The earliest surviving letter was one that my grandfather wrote to my mother to explain that he was leaving to pursue a political cause for the "working class." Although undated, its content revealed it had to have been written in February or March of 1937, just as she was turning five and he was leaving. I speculated that he might have left it for her to read after he was gone. In the conflict between my grandfather's devotion to the Communist Party and his love for his daughter, the Party had won out:

> Little Darling Toby
>
> I told you I would write you letters. You see I keep my promise.
>
> I am going to write you more letters. Do you know why? Because I am going away for a long time. I have something very important to do for the working class. It will take a long, long time. When it is finished I will come back and we will be able to have a good time together with mama. While I am away you will be growing up. You will learn many things if you listen more than you talk. Tell me in your letters how much you are growing and how much you are learning. In each letter I will send you a big kiss. Here it is X Good-bye darling

Although Ruby broke his promise to come back, he was true to his word in one respect: in the many letters he wrote to Rose in the coming days, he almost always included the big X for his daughter.

The sparse entry for Ruby in the Lincoln Brigade Archives records that he traveled from New York to Europe on March 10, 1937, aboard the SS *Washington*. The ship was destined not for Spain but France, because the Spanish Embargo Act, passed in January 1937, barred U.S. citizens from travelling to Spain. U.S. passports were stamped "Not Valid for Travel to Spain."[48] There were 137 volunteers headed for Spain on the *Washington*; Ruby was a group leader for some unknown subset of them.

My grandfather wrote a few letters from the ship, including one to Rose and one to my mother, both dated March 15, 1937. The closing to his long letter to Rose was my first hint that, rather than having been deserted, my grandmother seemed to have been a partner in his Spanish escapade:

> We are now passing thru the Irish Sea. It is a fearful sea. The rising, heavy waters heave this ship as if she did not weigh tens of thousands of tons. Many are sick from the sea. The stewards expect this and prepare in many ways. Tomorrow it will be calm. The sick people will rise from their beds and look relieved. The craggy shores of Ireland will be visible. The trip will be nearly over and for many the beginning of more, vastly more, dangerous days. Now darling I love you. And what we are doing is also part of our love. That is why it is not hard to be brave. That is why we work so improvingly in a movement vastly broader than our love.
>
> Good night, and here is also a letter for the child

My grandfather's reference to my mother as "the child" struck me as cold and impersonal. It seemed like "the child" was merely a footnote in her parents' lives.

As Ruby's letter to my mother reported, the SS *Washington* carrying him and his fellow Communists was a luxury liner:

> I'm on a very big ship. It is bigger than a hotel. It has a lot of restaurants and a swimming pool and many playrooms for children…. I have been sailing for six days and all I see is big waves of water and sky, so much sky.

And indeed, the SS *Washington* was one of the largest luxury liners in the world at the time. Ironically, in 1941, four years after FDR appeased Hitler in Spain and prohibited U.S. citizens from going to fight the fascists there, the U.S. government requisitioned the ship to carry our troops to do just that in World War II.[49]

From his perch on the *Washington*, my grandfather told my mother:

> I have with me the picture I took where you were in the country in Nellie's place at Carmel. You and Mama are in the picture. Every single day I take it out and look at it. It is only a little picture, you are on this big ship too. I talk to you a little because you are not always good. After I scold you I laugh and we are friends again. It's all make-believe. Can you make-believe like that?
>
> In a few days the ship will come to the land. When I get on the land I will write you and mama another letter. Now here is the big kiss I promised you in every letter. X

The letter seemed to reflect that, despite his actions and callous reference to "the child," Ruby did have a genuine emotional attachment to his daughter. He spent time thinking about her and, in his own way, even attempted to play make-believe with her, albeit from a distance. His love for her was just not as powerful as the force that had beckoned him to Spain. I wonder how much thought my grandfather gave to the prospect that he could be killed there and never see his daughter again—that he could be leaving her without a father. My guess is not very much.

The Americans unlawfully headed for Spain pretended to be tourists or students, but they rarely fooled anyone.[50] Upon arriving in

France, authorities threatened that anyone who went on to Spain would forfeit their American citizenship, and pressed them to turn back.[51] But as Ruby proudly recounted in a letter to Rose from the hotel in Le Havre, his cohort defiantly pressed on:

> It was tough getting off the boat. We almost didn't. Free passage back was offered. Everyone stood his ground—not singly, collectively. 137 and not a murmur, a wonderful sight and a wonderful promise.

Subsequent letters described the journey south through France to get to Spain. The final leg of the journey—a harrowing hike over the Pyrenees to get over the French border into Spain—left a deep impression on my grandfather. By this time the French government, seeking to enforce the Non-Intervention Agreement, had closed the border to Spain, and patrols armed with machine guns, searchlights, and dogs were hunting and shooting volunteers like Ruby who were attempting to sneak across the mountains at night in order to join the war.[52]

As the six-page letter Ruby wrote to Rose on March 28, after arriving in Spain, reflected, he apparently felt it would not be safe to include a description of his trip over the mountains from wherever he was writing:

> I'm settled here.... The last push was terrific, tough as all hell. It all but floored me and the rest of the outfit. But it was a marvelous experience and of the greatest importance for our development.
>
> You see I'm not writing concretely. Soon we shall be quartered in the headquarters of the International brigade at Albacete

(southeast of Madrid, look for it on the map). From there I'll be able to tell you much more.

I suspect that Ruby was afraid to disclose the route they had taken for fear that the information could be used to target volunteers coming after him if the letter fell into the wrong hands.

My grandfather never did get around to describing the "last push" over the Pyrenees, but a colleague of his later did. A letter Rose received from a man named John Smith in May 1939, almost two years after Ruby's death, provided a glimpse of how Ruby got from France to Spain in March 1937:

> Ruby was my group leader on the SS Washington and thru France from Le Havre, Paris and Beziers to the Spanish frontier. Our group of boys climbed the Pyrenees to the Spanish side in five and one half hours … Ruby was a wonderful lad, always smiling and sociable. He sure suffered hardships lugging a shoulder pack up the mountain five and one half hours from France to Spain. Just threw himself on the ground and all in. We had five minute rest periods only twice and one fifteen minute period to smoke, rest and eat our bread and sausage. Walked through three ice cold streams above our knees almost knocking us down by its force.

Smith's description is consistent with those of other volunteers who hiked over the mountains after France closed the border. They took cabs or buses up into the foothills just after dark and then trudged up the mountains, still in civilian clothes (though some were given rope-soled Spanish sandals that skidded less than their city-bought shoes). The trails Ruby and Harry would have hiked in the cold dark of winter were steep and slippery. As Smith described it, in order to get over the border by morning they made only a few brief stops, during which men sprawled on the ground, with some having trouble getting up when the call to resume climbing came after just a few minutes.[53] It's clear that the overnight journey was a severe test of physical and mental endurance that left an indelible imprint on Ruby and many other American volunteers who managed to make it over the mountains.

I had previously wondered if my Grandpa Harry had been in the group that Ruby led over the mountains given that, according to the Lincoln Brigade Archives, they both arrived in Spain on April 2.[54] But I was now doubtful, because John Smith's letter recounted that Ruby's group was a subset of the 137 men who traveled from New York on the SS *Washington*, and I knew Harry had traveled on a different ship. In fact, as yet I'd seen no trace of Harry in any of Ruby's poems or letters.

Ruby's March 28 letter sounded a theme that would recur throughout his time in Spain. He longed to hear from his wife, who was not cooperating:

> But you could write me much more.... I would like so much to know how the folks [i.e., Ruby's parents] took things and how you and the kid get along (depending on how they took it).

Consistent with his penchant for outlining his ideas, Ruby proceeded to provide Rose with a numbered list of six subjects he wanted her to write about, including: her health "and the kid's health," her "relations with parents," and her "work for the Party." Ruby ended his letter on page 6:

Now I will finish.

Every moment of this experience I have shared with you. In trying hours I have spoken with you. I have never gone to bed differently than our last night together. I love you. I love you my darling.

I had a few thoughts after reading this letter. I was getting the clear impression that my grandfather was *not* a guy who didn't care about a wife he had abandoned, or a man who was focused solely on the movement or the Communist Party. He was constantly expressing what seemed to be his genuine love for Rose. Whatever else he was, Rubin Schechter remained a romantic.

A Soldier's Life

Romantic or no, by early April, Ruby and his fellow novices were in training to become soldiers, and beginning to get a small taste of the reality in Spain. His April 5 letter painted a grim picture:

> The cities of Spain are dark at night. The street lamps are painted dark blue.... Everyone talks in low tones. The fascist bombers must not see or hear these cities. Trains ride slowly in Spain. Sometimes they crawl. The fascists may have torn up the rails. They want to wreck the trains. On the railroad stations the miserable refugees huddle with their children and their bundles of rags. They come from the cities which the fascists have already bombarded. Therefore the fascists are hated in Spain. There is only one kind of child in Spain. The anti-fascist child.

Ruby then wondered out loud how he would fare as a soldier, and tried to reassure himself, in part based on his having led his troop over the Pyrenees:

> We are now in training. We pick up our stuff quickly. In fact, we sometimes think we are taught too slowly. The life is healthy, the food is good, and we are toughening into shape. As a soldier I am not the most convincing sight in Spain. But the crossing into Spain and the seriousness, the determination that I'm putting into my training convinces me that I will fit honorably in the Brigade.

As I read this, I thought back to the assurance Ruby had given his parents that he would have only a desk job and would not be in any danger. My grandfather already seemed to have forgotten his promise—if he'd ever believed it.

Ruby continued to pine for Rose as his training proceeded throughout April. Although he was writing to her almost daily, he had yet to hear from his wife, who was apparently preoccupied with her own work for the Communist Party.[55] Nevertheless, Ruby was upbeat when he wrote to Rose on April 25 to report that it had been a wonderful week because his friend Sidney was now with him, and that he'd heard from his friends "Bill and B ... with news of you. The first news of you (I haven't received a letter yet). Such good news. You were well, and the kid too ... Then came the *Daily Worker* of April 9 confirming your work."

Ruby went on:

> You want to know about me Darling? I'm quite happy. And growing hard and strong. We walked and carried on maneuvers a few days over a distance of 22 kilometers-20 miles. And it no more bothered me than a walk from Jackson Heights to Corona.... One of these days, my darling, I'll be writing to you from the front.
> Give the little Toby her big kiss
> X
> Send me a few more snaps of you & the kid & big Toby (send her my love) & send some more of our friends

The reference to "big Toby"—Rose's younger sister—caught my attention, as I immediately thought back to my mother's quip that Ruby had written the stunning poem about her. And I now realized that the fact that Ruby referred to my mother as "little Toby" was meant to distinguish the two Tobys, both of whom were important to him.

In the midst of his training, Ruby was inspired to write a poem, which he enclosed with his May 3 letter to Rose, noting that it was "the first actual poem since my entry into the revolutionary movement." This seemed to answer the question I'd had as to whether there was another batch of poems that he'd written after the last one in the *Contracts Notebook*—that one dated April 1933, and written in Hebrew. There wasn't. But it didn't answer the question of *why* Ruby believed that partaking in the "revolutionary movement" was inconsistent with continuing to write the poetry that had clearly been so important to him. Was it just that he did not have time in the years before he left for Spain, as he continued to work at his father's business and devoted evenings to his organizing work as he rose in the Party? Or had he come to the view—either on his own or at someone else's urging—that writing poems was a frivolous pursuit that should not divert the energies of a true revolutionary?

As for the new poem, Ruby said: "Darling, I dedicate this first effort to our daughter, little Toby. If you and our friends think the poem is good, give it to the *Daily Worker*. Sign it with my citizenship name." The new poem was entitled "IF THESE SONGS WERE WITH YOU, COMRADES." Perhaps not surprisingly, it was an openly polemic appeal, which struck me as unimpressive. It began:

> Knowing the million-throated thunder
> Of May Day in America

> I'll echo a little lilting song
> Of May Day
> Sung in Alto
> Sung by four hundred children
> In our Spanish town
> Hopeful song of Spanish children
> Red-ribboned, Republican-starred infants
> Shouting songs of freedom
> Children pledging loyalty to arms

I wondered if Rose and any friends to whom she may have shown the new poem thought it was any good, and whether it was ever given to or published by the *Daily Worker*. I discovered much later that it probably wasn't.

Ruby's May 3 letter also reported that Rose still hadn't written to him, and I found myself growing angry at my grandmother. Here was my grandfather heading into war, constantly sending her long letters, begging her to write—and she was too busy to drop him a line! I wondered what she was thinking, and feeling, about her husband training for combat in a bloody war. Why wasn't she writing to him? Or *was* she writing, with her letters just not reaching him?

Ruby continued to take pride in his development as a soldier. After professing his love for Rose, in a letter to Rose dated only "Sunday" that I deduced was written sometime between April 5 and May 12, my grandfather reported:

> Next I will tell you about my health. I'm really toughening. Some of our maneuvers take us over great distances and across every manner of field and hill.... It's trudging, dragging, lunging, dallying, dropping. It's one tough grind

learning to get to a given place effectively, yet safely. Yet because all this has a purpose, it suits me better than walking or hiking.

And, ever the meticulous leader, Ruby offered packing and sartorial advice, through Rose, to those who would be coming after him to fight in Spain:

Most of my clothing is stored away. They're of no use. Only the underwear, wool, khaki and dark colored shirts are good and these I have ... Here is something to bring to the attention of the commission. Except for the boat, when a fellow wants a white shirt and a decent looking suit, the men should avoid loaded suitcases. The suit one wears is sufficient. No bathrobes, extra sweaters, high boots, pajamas or any other trappings. An ideal wardrobe would be 1/ the suit you have on 2/ six suits of underwear at the most 3/ six pairs of socks, low and woolen preferred . . . 6/ a few toothbrushes, tooth paste, ½ kg bars of soap ... 7/ some needles and thread 8/ a good pocket knife if possible. That's all. If a fellow plays an instrument let him take it by all means (unless, of course, it's a tuba).

Ruby was also a forgiving soul. His seven-page handwritten May 12 letter began:

On Tuesday May 10, exactly two months after I left you, your letter came. I will not say much sweetheart, only this, that I walked alone a bit that night along the outskirts of our town and spoke quietly to you. Much as if you were walking by my side. As if we had been seeing each other often and had some time to spend together; so we decided to walk a bit and talk.

After recounting their imagined conversation, Ruby went on:

A few times we bent over towards each other and kissed. And when I returned alone to the lighted streets of the town I was satisfied and very happy.

I thought as I read my grandfather's words that while his penchant for poetry may have dissipated, he remained a hopeless romantic, with a literary flair and quite an imagination. I wonder how my grandmother had felt as she read his passionate words.

The New Masses Article

Upon first leafing through the documents in the Briefcase, I'd been surprised to discover several fragile broadsheet newspaper pages containing an article consisting of typed versions of four letters Ruby had written to Rose from Spain, including the two that my cousin Carl had sent to me. The article appeared in the October 1937 edition of *New Masses* magazine—two months after Ruby died.

New Masses was a Marxist publication closely associated with the Communist Party that ran from 1926 until 1948. It was named for a predecessor Marxist magazine, *The Masses*, which was published from 1911 until 1917, when it was shut down by the U.S. government for opposing World War I.[56] *New Masses* was launched by a group of artists along with the Communist Party as a magazine "dedicated to a radical perspective on art and literature"[57]—right in tune with Ruby's thirteen-page manifesto.

The article in the October 1937 edition was entitled:

> FOUR LETTERS FROM SPAIN
> What an American in the fighting forces there thinks about is clearly shown in what a seasoned revolutionist wrote to his wife

What I realized after reading Ruby's handwritten May 12 letter to Rose was that the first of the four letters printed in the article was a slightly edited version of pages 3–4 of this letter. Either Rose or the publisher had omitted the mushy beginning pages.

Preceding the excerpt of the published letter was a biographical paragraph that began:

> Rubin Schechter, who wrote these letters to his wife, died on August 28, 1937 of the wound he describes. Schechter was section organizer of the Communist Party in the Third Assembly District of Queens County, N.Y. when he went to Spain.... One of his outstanding pieces of party work in Queens was with the Committee for Equal Opportunity, which fought through to a successful conclusion its campaign to end the Queens County General Hospital's discrimination against Negro Doctors.

It's no wonder that of all the letters Ruby wrote to Rose from Spain, his May 12 letter was one of the four she or the publisher chose to print. I found it not only revealing but funny, in a tragic way, as my grandfather extolled the superiority of the soon-to-be decimated Republican army:

> Our training has taken on a spurt in the past week. We are rapidly shaping into a competent battalion under the marvelous leadership of a "Mexican" brand of commander. We are being trained not in the bourgeois ways—their way is to work away at a man until they have turned a thinking human being into a blind, brutal mechanism. Our way is to develop military understanding through open discussion and lectures. Every soldier is taught in such a way that he is able to understand and think alongside of his officers. We never say "Do this!" We always say, "The following is our purpose today. In order to achieve this, you can do it best

in the following manner. Of course this takes longer, but your soldier remains a dignified, thinking person. He grows in understanding and flexibility. A dangerous situation is something for him to think about and solve to the disadvantage of the fascist enemy.... Our army is superior to the fascist armies because its man-power is free. It follows, of course, that victory must be ours.

I chuckled to myself as I envisioned the "comrades" having a group discussion debating whether to stand their ground or retreat while the Fascist soldiers were following orders to mow them down. I would come to realize, however, that this was no laughing matter, and there was a disconnect between Ruby's glowing, optimistic portrait of his "superior" battalion, and reality. In fact, the American brigade was rife with problems. For one thing, the American volunteers were younger than their counterparts in the European brigades, and very few had had experience fighting in World War I—or any military training. They also suffered from poor leadership. There were virtually no American leaders with significant military experience in Spain, and the military commander of the American XV Brigade was János Gálicz, a Red Army officer known as "General Gal" who was widely viewed as vain, egotistical, brutal, and the worst of the International Brigade generals. And, rather than the cohesive troop of comrades collectively deciding upon military strategy described by my grandfather, dissension and disciplinary problems were common.[58]

The *New Masses* article did not include pages 5–6 of Ruby's May 12 letter, much of which concerned Communist Party politics. Nor did it include this passage, which revealed that Ruby wasn't writing his letters for Rose alone:

> I want to close with these few observations with my dearest regards to you, my love to you, wonderful comrades. What goes on in Queens is very close to me, it being my birthplace in the revolutionary movement and the place where I have formed such close and lasting friendships. I cannot address each and every one of you. But as this is read to you say to yourselves that I am speaking to you alone at the same time that I am speaking to all the others. You will get a picture of my feelings and I of yours. Salud comrades!

Thinking about this message now, I've started to wonder if my grandfather was actually as optimistic as this and his other letters indicated—or whether, knowing he was writing for a broader audience, his letters were, at least in part, instruments of the propaganda surrounding the Lincoln Brigade.[59]

Ruby's next paragraph likewise reflected his understanding that Rose was showing friends back home his missives from Spain:

> Darling, I suppose George [Charney] and Hattie will read this letter but you must tell them in addition how grateful I was for their writing.... And Hattie is a wow. Not only was I amused by her writing but I even developed some carnivorous and ungodly yearnings for her in this land of chastity and double-standard.

Reading Ruby's open admission of his lust for another woman also led me to think that Rose either knew about, or wouldn't have been surprised or disturbed to learn about, the other women featured in his poems with whom he had relations, whether real or imagined.

Yearning for Battle

Coming closer to the actual fighting, Ruby seemed neither unhappy nor afraid, and exuded confidence. As he wrote to Rose on May 30:

> We are not afraid. We know our jobs. We are well trained; by the best teachers in the entire world. Our equipment is absolutely unmatchable.... Our hatred of the enemy grows with each passing hour and with every moment of waiting.... It has been my fate since I am in the movement to be on the inside, formulating, directing, teaching. It is still so even in these twilight hours, where death shall seek its rendezvous, among us. It will find a few. But we are certain that it shall reap abundantly among the blind trembling soldiers of our enemy. We shall absolutely defeat fascism. Let there be no doubt about that.

Ruby was not alone among the fresh American recruits in yearning to join the fighting at this point.[60] Once again, however, my grandfather's confidence—whether feigned or sincere—was at odds with the reality of the war as of May 30, 1937. And sadly, his crowing that their equipment was "absolutely unmatchable" was pure fiction.

In his letters home, my grandfather also tried to put a good face on the Republican army's setbacks, and he continued to ooze optimism—probably for his own benefit as well as for Rose and those beyond her whom he expected would be reading his letters. His June 23 letter to Rose was a prime example:

Yesterday I finished in a hurry. I was anxious to get the letter out, not knowing what day I would write again. I told you that we have heard that Bilbao had fallen. It was time. But history never heard of such a fall. The entire city was successfully evacuated by our military, and with the civilians, all the valuable goods and wares. No doubt the Daily Worker will carry the miracle of Bilbao before you get this letter.

In fact, "the miracle of Bilbao" was just one in a chain of defeats following the massacre at Guernica, and preceding the battle at Brunete—where Ruby was shot. But while his exuberant sense of victory may have been delusional, my grandfather's gritty description of wartime life on the ground—including the psychological aspect—was vividly realistic:

> Last night it began to pour. In a few hours we were plodding around in a sea of mud. Right through the pour and the mud, the wet and the cold, the enemy kept up a steady artillery fire and our artillery thundered back. Every moment an attack might commence. But nothing came.
>
> Today is being spent getting dry—and the ingenious invention of rumors. My, what rumors we invent. Our news is always a few days behind, so we supplement with all kinds of "news" we invent. The thing about a rumor is that it sounds a whole lot more plausible than some real stuff, and it always originates from some "impeccable" source. Very often these rumors express the lack of something keenly desired. The most frequent rumors concern themselves with all sorts of shipments of cigarettes, chocolate and soap …

Still, the rumors sound very real sometimes, it does not mean that we do not make immediate adjustments when we are faced with realities. We are not a bunch of Brownings or Prousts.

I chuckled at my grandfather's references to Browning and Proust—a reminder of the love of literature that had not been in evidence since he'd joined the Communist Party four years earlier.

Rose and Little Toby Back "Home"

In addition to his own situation, Ruby's letters shed new and surprising light on what Rose was up to back in Queens while he was preparing for battle in Spain. She was a far cry from the spacy artist I had known.

Ruby's March 15 letter to Rose, written from the SS *Washington*, had hinted that my grandmother was hardly an abandoned, heartbroken wife. His subsequent letters confirmed that she was a full partner in Ruby's decision to go to Spain, conspiring to keep his parents in the dark regarding the peril he was in and consumed by her own work for the Communist Party. Decades later, one of my aunts remarked that Rose had not only approved of Ruby's going to Spain, but that she had pushed him to go and was responsible for his death.

Although Ruby's parents were apparently not happy with Rose's political activity, as far as he was concerned, her work for the Party had to be her highest priority. As he wrote to her on June 7:

> My darling—
> The way I wrote to my father, he will either disown you or take better care of you (giving you greater independence etc.). I believe the latter will prevail. But no matter what he does, your first relationship is with the labor movement, with the very flower of it. If you can accommodate them to this relationship—very well, but if not, close them out—utterly and completely.

Once again, in the conflict between Ruby's devotion to the Party and his love for his family—in this case his parents—the Party prevailed, just as it did in the conflicts that Rose experienced.

Ruby regarded Rose as an umbilical cord, sustaining his connection to the Party back home. As he wrote on May 30:

> Be a wire of living energy connecting me always to the movement at home—directly with the factories, the railroad, the homeowners, the Negro masses, the women and youth…. This live concrete definite connection will give me strength and direction, and I will surely communicate this strength and clarity to all my comrades-in-arms.
>
> So far Piggy, I have written only to you. Of course most of what I wrote and will continue to write is not for you alone. I am sure that you have read whole portions of these letters to our comrades and friends. Still, when we hit the front (very, very shortly) I will begin writing directly to our friends.

And Ruby's May 30 letter contained three additional sentences that caught my attention:

> And what about big Toby. Do you read these letters to her—as if she is part of them. She always will be; you know that and I do.

I immediately thought back to my mother's stunning remark fifty years earlier that Ruby had written his obscene poem about my Aunt Toby. And as I now read these three lines I wondered: What was there for Rose to know about Rose's younger sister, big Toby? Whatever it was, Ruby wasn't concealing it. I pondered again huge family affair. The children who came to board were from broken homes or couldn't stand the air in New York (asthma, allergies, and the like)... Nearly all were of working-class parents, who came out on weekends to see them.[64]

According to Nellie, they were one big happy family in which there was no such thing as punishment.[65] And Paul Avrich, the leading historian on the Modern School movement, has written that "a great majority of the former pupils ... have pleasant and enthusiastic memories of the time they spent at the school."[66]

My mother's memory of her experience there was very different. I don't remember ever talking to her about her years at Lakewood, but she did speak with Melissa about it. She told Melissa that she hated the place and had been beaten with a switch there. My mother's claim was antithetical to the Modern Schools' core precept that there was to be no punishment, much less corporal punishment. Nevertheless, Melissa's impression was that my mother's memory seemed clear and that this had not been an isolated incident.[67] While I don't know what to make of my mother's report to Melissa, on one point my mother's memory was undoubtedly accurate: she hated the Lakewood Modern School and the fact she was stuck there for several years until her grandmother took her out and proceeded to raise her in Brooklyn.[68]

As I thought about Rose's apparent disregard for both my mother and Ruby, who had been constantly begging her to write to him since arriving in Spain in late March, I found one consolation. In his June 7 letter, Ruby told Rose: "I have two letters which you wrote before the one of May 11." This got me thinking that perhaps I had been too quick to judge my grandmother for not writing to Ruby; maybe she had written a bunch of amorous letters that hadn't gotten through to him. It served as a caution about the danger of jumping to conclusions when piecing together fragments that make up only a tiny fraction of the complex picture of a person's life. Speculating as to what other people were feeling and thinking, and why they did what they did or didn't do, is a risky proposition. But that's exactly what I'm doing.

Under Fire at Brunete

The battle at Brunete was one of the most ferocious of the Spanish Civil War.[69] This major—and secret—offensive mounted by the Republican forces began at dawn on July 6, 1937. Brunete was apparently the first, and certainly the last, battle in which Ruby took part.

The Brunete offensive was merely a diversionary effort. Its goal was to temporarily take the strategically meaningless village of Brunete, population 1,500, and thereby cut off the Nationalist army's path to Madrid before Franco's reinforcements could arrive.[70] Estimates of the size of the Republican army at Brunete vary.[71] According to Hugh Thomas, author of one of the most authoritative accounts of the Spanish Civil War, there were 85,000 Republican soldiers, including those in Ruby and Harry's XV International Brigade, which was used as a shock force.[72]

The battle was raging when Ruby wrote to Rose on July 15. His account was illuminating with respect to both the war and Ruby's indomitable personality.

> We have been on this glorious offensive for one week. We drive the rats before us. I imagine how you must follow the papers. My letters have constantly indicated how planned and equipped we were for the grand opening. And what an opening.... During the fire of the victorious battle a new resolution was rising and has now taken final form—the merger of the Lincoln and Washington Battalions into one single battalion of the American people.

The fascists do not differentiate between stretcher bearers and soldiers. No one will hand you anymore baloney about the fact that we invent the horrors of the fascists. I have seen them shoot stretcher bearers. I have been crunched low watching their bombs break around first aid and ambulance stations. I can't go into any more now. Another time.

As for myself, darling. I have been under fire, even under aerial and artillery bombardment, and I am well able to stand it. As far as I'm concerned, the greatest instrument of torture the fascists have here in Spain is the merciless sun. But in time I shall find the best adjustments for that too …

Darling you cannot know the rigors, the stamina, the sacrifice and ability that an offensive such as ours requires. We are living thru it all and learning marvelously.

Look darling, I must stop this second. I'll pick up again the very next moment I have. Kiss Toby X for me

July 15 was an important day in the Republicans' Brunete campaign. It might fairly be thought of as the beginning of the end of what my grandfather described as the "glorious offensive."

The Nationalist forces had been surprised by the attack, which was itself surprising, since the planned offensive had been talked about in the cafés for months (not to mention in letters that soldiers like Ruby were writing about the upcoming secret offensive).[73] The campaign to take this arid village, located fifteen miles west of Madrid, was initially successful, as the Republicans broke through the Nationalist line, advanced nearly ten miles within a few hours, and surrounded Brunete.[74] By the following day, however, the Nationalists had brought in heavy reinforcements and began to push back.[75]

By July 13, the offensive stage of the "great offensive" was over and the Republicans were attempting to defend their initial gains. On the day Ruby wrote his letter, July 15, the Republican command ordered its soldiers to dig trenches in order to defend against the Nationalists' counterattack.[76] By July 18, the Nationalists had launched a massive counteroffensive and gained control of the skies, thanks in significant part to the introduction of the new German Messerschmitt Bf 109 fighters, which made their first appearance at Brunette and would soon play a huge role in World War II. They bombed the Republican soldiers relentlessly.[77] Trucks could not get to the battlefields and ammunition and food could only reach the American volunteers on the backs of mules—which helps explain Ruby's fatal ammunition run with the "donkey."[78] The Lincolns were massacred as the offensive crumbled, fighting during the day and sent on forced marches at night.[79] A far cry from the picture painted by my grandfather.

As I read about the disarray, I thought back to Ruby's May 12 letter trumpeting the superiority of his brigade due to the collaborative manner in which the comrades got together to contemplate their strategic moves, rather than simply following orders as the unthinking fascist soldiers did. In fact, to compound their logistical problems, there was dissension within the Republican ranks.[80] Moreover, throughout the battle, the heat was brutal, often exceeding 100 degrees Fahrenheit. Thus, Ruby's lament that "the greatest instrument of torture the fascists have here in Spain is the merciless sun" was probably shared by many.[81] And to make matters even worse, the soldiers lacked water. The contest has been referred to as the "battle against thirst."[82]

Although I had read about the intense heat and casualties at Brunete, it was only when I stumbled upon a grainy, black-and-white film—"The Battle of Brunete"—that I could begin to picture the horror that Ruby and Harry had faced. The thirty-minute program—episode 8 in a series entitled *Great Battles of the Spanish Civil War*—was narrated in Spanish with English subtitles. I found it on YouTube.

The account of the battle narrated in the film didn't seem particularly biased in favor of either side. It was generally consistent with the histories I'd read, and contained nothing of importance that was new to me. The narrator began by noting that Spain had become "the testing ground for World War II"—a contest of "fascism vs. communism." He introduced the Battle of Brunete as "the great distraction maneuver," explaining that there was nothing strategically significant about Brunete and that the only goal was to distract the Nationalists from their drive to Madrid.

What *was* new, and jarring, was watching actual footage—real-time moving pictures that brought this vicious 1930s battle to life, chronicled day-by-day, for the three weeks that it raged. What stood out to me first were the soldiers' attire and weapons. Few of the Republican soldiers had helmets or boots; the guns they fired looked more like muskets than modern rifles; and the cannons were antiques. The movie showed Republican soldiers with no protective equipment and many without uniforms, running across open terrain with machine-gun fire coming at them. They looked like a bunch of civilians playing war, but getting killed in the process, and the scene was more akin to what we associate with the Battle of Gettysburg in the American Civil War than modern warfare as we know it today—or even World War II as depicted in movies like *Saving Private Ryan*.[83]

The terrain was barren and dusty. Attesting to the heat and drought, the narrator reported that "due to the lack of water both sides drink wine ... making the fighters go even crazier," and that available "water was used to cool down the guns or clean the wounded." In some scenes, it was hard to see amidst the dust and smoke of the bombardment. As I watched the film, I could picture Ruby traipsing through the frightening hail of bullets with his slow-moving donkey laden with ammunition. And I thought of him, too, as I watched the clip of soldiers loading a wounded soldier onto an antique stretcher and hustling to carry him off the battlefield.

The narrator reported that on July 15 the Republicans "stop[ped] the offensive" even though "everything [was] on their side." The subtitles and the film clips showed that Brunete was rubble after the Republican front collapsed and the Nationalists occupied the village on July 25.[84] The trenches, like those from which Ruby wrote his letters to Rose, were "filled with dead bodies."

Both sides claimed they won the Battle of Brunete. The Republicans' attack delayed the Nationalists' drive toward Madrid by about five weeks, which was one of their goals, but they suffered 20,000 casualties and lost about 100 aircraft (the Nationalists had 17,000 casualties and lost 23 aircraft).[85]

The Republican casualties were particularly horrific in the International Brigades.[86] The Americans lost so many men at Brunete that the Lincoln and Washington Brigades had to be combined during the battle (Ruby was made secretary of the combined Lincoln-Washington Brigade).[87] Nevertheless, until he was shot on July 24—and even afterwards—my grandfather was ever upbeat and optimistic, as evident not only from his letters to Rose, but from what others wrote about him in the moment, including his friend Sidney.

Until much later, I didn't know Sidney's last name, but it was obvious from numerous letters that he was a very close friend of Ruby's. On July 18 Sidney wrote to their mutual friend George Charney. What's striking about this letter is how much of it was devoted to Ruby, including Sidney's statement reflecting that the sincerity of Ruby's promise to his parents that he'd be nowhere near the actual fighting was fleeting—at best.

> Ruby is ok, a happy, encouraging spirit in the battalion. He couldn't be kept off the front lines. After five days he had to be ordered back to battalion headquarters where his job lies. He sent me a note from which I quote: "The going is swell. I think we'll make Madrid according to schedule."
>
> But anyhow, I've this to say—I'm so proud of our friend Ruby, his courage, his spirit. He's a shining light is Ruby. There's a wounded comrade who cried when he heard his friend had been killed. But he, like everyone else, broke into smiles when I asked about Ruby. He's a good soldier, studied his military tactics, and the maneuvers, how to crawl, fall and jump, and, as ever, the theory of the thing. A grand comrade and a Bolshevik.

As I read Sidney's letter I thought to myself that perhaps the misplaced optimism and confidence in Ruby's letters was not mere propaganda intended for the broader audience back home reading his letters. Maybe he was just a die-hard, albeit somewhat delusional, optimist—and a brave one at that.

As the battle continued and the Republican casualties soared, Ruby's letters continued to combine his optimistic fantasies with a brutally realistic depiction of the war. His July 21 letter to Rose was the second of the four letters published in *New Masses* magazine two months after his death. Written from the trenches four days before he was shot, my grandfather's letter struck me as rather extraordinary:

> Darling/Sweetheart You have heard of our attack. The Lincoln and Washington Brigades took decisive parts in the great offensive. Right now we are participating in a few defensive actions. But not defensive in the old sense, the sense of stopping a fascist advance. We are holding and fortifying positions which we have already captured. We are fortifying our offensive. On other fronts, of course, we keep advancing.... We have struck deep into the vitals of the despoilers of humanity. Soon fascism will be in flames.

My grandfather's statement that his brigade's defensive actions were "not defensive in the old sense, the sense of stopping a fascist advance"—and that they were "fortifying our offensive"—might have been technically accurate at that moment, as the Republicans probably were still attempting to cling to their initial gains. But not for long, as the Nationalists and their Nazi allies bombarded the Republicans with massive air and artillery attacks. Ruby's letter proceeded to vividly capture the experience of being bombed and strafed:

> I write these general lines during these moments when everything is far from general. Twice during the course of these few sentences I have had to stop and quickly flatten out to keep out of the sight of planes. (In this case they

proved to be our own planes.) Everywhere the bullets are whistling and crackling.

Right now our artillery is raising hell with fascist lines. But almost daily we have experienced the crashing and smashing of their artillery. And as they have tasted of our serial bombardments, so have we of theirs. I can say with all pride I can summon up that our battalions have been subjected to two of the severest and most dreadful bombings from the air, and that we came out of them with flying colors; not a scratch on our morale.

After finishing an early draft of this book, I read Ernest Hemingway's *For Whom the Bell Tolls*. I thought I'd already read it decades ago, but quickly realized that I hadn't. That's because, had I read Hemingway's riveting story of the horrors of the Spanish Civil War, I would not have labored under the misconception that it wasn't much of a war. In any case, about the bombings in particular, Hemingway's protagonist, Robert Jordan, has this to say: "The damned planes scare you to death but they don't kill you ... Those things never kill anybody."[88]

My grandfather's July 21 letter provided a similar assessment of the aerial bombings in Spain, which were making their first warfare appearance long before targets could be spotted with precision. As with his earlier observation on the impact of rumors, my grandfather focused, in particular, on the psychological dimension of the bombings and their effect on morale:

As for loss of life, there is this to say about artillery and aerial bombardment: there must be a direct hit in order to do real damage. Aerial bombardment rarely gets many. It is successful if it manages to shatter the nerves and morale of those who are subjected to the bombardment. Strafing by planes is also of the same nature.

The greatest loss of life still comes from the machine gun and the rifle; it still comes from men who face each other almost within sight of each other and shoot one another. In the final analysis, planes, artillery and tanks too are auxiliaries to the soldier with his rifle and to the machine gun crew. They are peculiar auxiliaries in that they seem to dwarf the man with the rifle and even the machine gun crew. The most fearful electric storms with bolts of lightning, crashes of thunder, and sheets of rain do not give such a feeling of man's helplessness and tininess as the smashing and crashing and tearing and earth ripping and deafening rips of thunder from which all silence has been torn out of the aerial bombardment.

Darling, the last sentence I finished one hour after I started it. During this time we were subjected to a terrific aerial bombardment plus strafing. Again the damage is almost unmentionable. But how can you fight this horror? In no way at all. You lie prone, your face buried in the dirt, your body elongated, you clutch onto something. You wait. When it is over, comrades begin to raise their heads toward each other and a smile begins to flicker and spread. The curse words begin to be heard and they also spread. Then the tension snaps. Some begin to look around for the hurt. Others begin to tell their feelings and, of course, how very close they were from a bursting bomb.

You can see, darling, from what I have just said (and even from the slant of my writing) that it is extremely difficult to write under our present conditions. However, I must write just as often as possible so that you can see my writing and know that I am well.

Permit me to finish off. Perhaps some other time (when I can recollect many emotions in tranquility) I shall be able to tell you how often and beautifully you appeared in my thoughts in these hours of trial. I can only tell you this thing to make you happy—I have never once been afraid.

Here is my kiss for Toby X. My love. Salud!

Ruby

Ruby's proclamation that "I have never once been afraid" may well have been accurate. A study of Lincoln survivors conducted by Yale sociologist John Dollard published in 1943 found a strong connection between their political convictions and their personal feelings during military action; strong identification with the cause for which the Republicans were fighting in Spain improved their "battlefield reliability." As Dollard explained: "If a man knows what he's fighting for and has an intense personal need to win, his zeal in battle will tend to triumph over his fear. Hatred and anger also solidified morale."[89]

Dollard's account seemed to describe my grandfather perfectly: Ruby's hatred of the fascists and his fervent belief in the cause for which he was fighting oozed from the letters he wrote from Spain. Indeed, it was probably a lack of fear, or his ability to disregard it, that led him to recklessly volunteer for the suicidal ammunition run that got him killed.

As I reflected on the fact that Ruby had written these letters hurriedly, in a single draft, while in the midst of being strafed by Hitler's bombers, I thought to myself that my grandfather was a gifted writer (if not necessarily an exceptional poet) and a rather remarkable character. All the positive things Sidney said about Ruby in his July 18 letter to George Charney three days earlier seemed accurate. At the same time, my grandfather was hardly a realist, and the vaunted Brunete offensive was on death's doorstep as he wrote his letter on July 21.

Moreover, at Brunete as elsewhere, Franco was not content merely to win the strategically irrelevant real estate being fought over there. As Paul Preston has written: "Franco's notion of a war of moral redemption by terror did not permit him to give up an inch of once captured territory nor to turn aside from any opportunity to hammer home the message of his invincibility in Republican blood—whatever the human cost to his own side. Brunete offered an irresistible temptation to annihilate large numbers of Republican troops."[90]

And he did, killing over 20,000 Republican soldiers—including my grandfather.

Shot—Courtesy of a Mule!

Ruby was wounded on July 24—the day the Nationalists took control of Brunete. He wrote to Rose the next day from the hospital, assuring her that there was "nothing to worry about" because "the bullet went clean through the upper fleshy portion of the arm and did not touch the bone, which means quick healing and I ought to be back with the Battalion within 15 days."

A typeset version of this letter (a portion of which was quoted at the beginning of this book) was the third of the four letters published in the October 1937 edition of *New Masses*. The original handwritten letter was surprisingly legible given that Ruby, a righty, was writing with his left hand. Getting shot had not dampened his spirits, as was evident from the final paragraphs:

> And now I will end with a burst of praise for the beautiful and loving and thoroughly scientific succor which the Spanish masses have organized for their wounded fighters. The very best places in Spain have been turned into hospitals and sanatoriums. See where I am—in what was formerly one of the greatest hotels in Europe. I occupy a gorgeous, big, up-to-date room together with two more comrades. We have our tremendous closet (for which we have no special use), our three-mirrored vanity table (good for writing and eating) and a large bathroom (including the usual ladies' douche with running water—excellent for washing the loins and feet). We are served no differently from a private patient at Mount Sinai....

That's all darling. Keep writing to me care of the Washington-Lincoln Battalion.... There is no need writing to the hospital. By the time you get this letter and answer it, I shall be back in the battalion. Of course, there is no need tell the folks or our daughter, who talks in all directions. It has taken much effort to write this letter, but it is a special kind of love letter—one which we have never had need or growth enough to write. You will therefore surely forgive me if I do not write again until I can use my right hand again, which ought to be in about ten days.

Now knowing more about the carnage at Brunete and, more generally, about the massive casualties on the Republican side, I found Ruby's intention, and impatience, to get back to the bloody front—while others were close to rebellion[91]—hard to fathom. A selfless and courageous, but patently foolhardy, death wish.

It's not clear how and when Ruby's parents learned that he'd been shot. They obviously didn't know by August 4, when a relative or friend of the family named Herb wrote to Ruby with news of "the folks" and to relay a request from Ruby's father:

> It was good to read your letter of July 14th and also other communications in the hands of Irving and Rose....
>
> I am glad to say that your father is feeling pretty well although he must be very strict with his medical attention—diet and injections, etc. Naturally he still longs for you and cannot lose his constant anxiety over your welfare—the same goes for your mother....

> Papa plans to go to London and Paris late next month and as he has written you, it would be wonderful for you to meet him if you could arrange a leave of absence. Let us know as soon as possible.
>
> I am taking Taube [my mother] up to the country this weekend. I will write to you all about it in my next letter.

By the time of the meeting his father longed to have, Ruby was dead. In the meantime, however, other family members had conflicting feelings about what Ruby was doing in Spain.

Ruby's younger sister Minnie wrote to him on August 10. Her letter reflected both fear for his safety and admiration for the cause for which he was risking his life:

> Several times I have sat down to write you but each time I found I was at a loss for words. Shall I lecture you? That would hardly do, since my very words would jump back at me with the accusation of "liar." For aside from my anxiety for your safety, I cannot say that I disapprove of what you are doing. I feel badly about the grief it causes the folks but someone must be the target.
>
> Tomorrow I'm taking your daughter to the beach. You see I have a locker at Manhattan Beach and I think she will enjoy it.[92]

As Minnie's letter, like Herb's on August 4, also revealed, a number of people seemed to be tag-teaming to periodically collect my mother from the Lakewood Modern School so she could have a little fun while her father was away and Rose was preoccupied with her political work for the Queens chapter of the Communist Party.

The Man in the Briefcase

It was on August 12 that Ruby wrote his remarkable letter to Rose explaining that he had been shot "on account of a mule," and providing her (and the others he knew were reading his letters) with a verbatim account of his exhortation to "the donkey" in the minutes before he was wounded.

At this point, having read a lot about the Battle of Brunete, and especially having seen the film depicting it, I could picture my grandfather as he spoke to the mule that, by his account, got him killed. There was no cover for Ruby as the animal "deliberately proceeded to stroll leisurely down this field of whistling bullets as if it was Sunday on 5th Avenue." Ruby's beseeching the mule with the warning that "the bullets are coming in all directions" described their peril well. I tried to imagine what my grandfather was thinking—whether he was finally afraid as he wandered through the hail of bullets with comrades all around him being mowed down in the 100-degree heat. How frustrated he must have been as the mule ignored his final plea:

> If you really had sense we could take this gap on the run. The comrades will not believe their eyes if you come tearing up with their ammunition. They will positively adore you. You will be a donkey such as never was—on sea or land. This argument does not move you because you are a typical product of the old order. You prefer to drag along at the pace of all your fathers, when some real speed would give us both a glorious lease of life. As it is you will probably be the death of both of us. That is where you conservatives always lead us to.[93]

This was the last of the four letters published in *New Masses* after Ruby's death, and it put my grandfather's personality on full display: his blind idealism and optimism, his sense of humor, and his flair for writing. As I reflected upon Ruby's account, however—now with the visual images from the Battle of Brunette film in mind—it also struck me as ridiculous that he, the battalion secretary, who was not even supposed to be in combat, had been chosen, or more likely volunteered, for such a perilous mission.[94] While it speaks to his bravery, my grandfather certainly wasn't thinking of his young daughter—or his promise to his parents that he wouldn't be near the fighting—when he risked and ultimately lost his life attempting to salvage a diversionary maneuver in a battle for strategically worthless terrain.

Ruby concluded his letter with instructions for Rose about breaking the news to his parents and my mother:

> You know darling that I am not able to write much more. I must revise my estimate of my return to the front. Perhaps it will be another month before I return. I cannot handle Jewish with my right hand, so I propose you read this letter to the folks.[95] Meet everything head on.... Kiss little Toby. She will probably enjoy hearing the story of how her father was hit, and you darling have no worry at all. Here is my love. Write me often, lovely darling.
> Ruby

My grandfather wrote no further letters that survive.

Too Late!

The Briefcase also contained a number of letters written to Ruby, rather than by or about him. They were in small envelopes addressed to him with the word "MORT" written across them in large, bold letters—some in red, blue, or black crayon. They were returned or given by others to Rose after Ruby died. The first was a letter dated August 16 from George Charney that didn't arrive in Spain until August 23—the day my grandfather died. He never saw it.

> Dear Ruby
>
> I read your letter this morning addressed to Rose. That is Mary and I read it together. Mary, the darling, gathered tears in her eyes and couldn't read after your first blunt statement describing the wound. I explained the nature of it and she brightened up in a few moments. I told her how in the World War, such a wound was called "cushy" and actually welcomed by the soldiers in order to get out of the fighting which they hated and revolted against. I contrasted this attitude with the one expressed in your letter—remarks about hospital care and the love and tenderness of the Republic—your determination to return to the front as soon as possible, giving vent to an unconquerable spirit that Hitler and Franco fear most of all and with reason.[96]

As I read this letter it occurred to me that although it had at first seemed odd that Ruby's letters to Rose were being passed around for others to read—and that he had anticipated and desired this—it was very much akin to how we send and forward emails to friends in today's vastly different world. Then, my attention was piqued by a passage in which Charney referred to Ruby and Rose in proclaiming his love for his future wife, Hattie, who was also a Party operative:

> Hattie, my darling, is in Schenectady on party work for a month ... So I am a bachelor again and a little miserable, although I am proud of her. What a change—I am in love, deeply in love with her. Ruby—everything you taught me directly—thru your own relationship with Rose—finds reflection in ours.

So, here was someone who knew Ruby and Rose well, attesting to their deep love for each other, casting further doubt on my idle speculation based on his youthful poems that my grandfather was a philanderer.

The next letter that came back in an envelope with "MORT" written across it was from Rose. Dated August 19, it was eight pages on stationery of the Lakeside Motel in South Fallsburg, New York. While not explicitly, the letter provided yet further confirmation that Rose was a full partner in Ruby's plan to sneak off to war without telling his parents. For her part, Rose tried to explain why she had written to Ruby so rarely, and highlighted his parents' suspicion of her:

> My Darling Sweetheart

I received your letter of July 25. Mary brought it to me at George's before I left for here (Lakeside Hotel) with Taube.

Darling—I love you so and miss you so. One thing—when I don't write often know two things—either I don't get physical time or what is more—I miss you and feel sad—and when I feel sad—I do not want to write to you.

You know the week of July 21–26—I suffered each night—the newspapers gave accounts of American volunteers being trapped by fascists, etc. Your folks of course know nothing of your wound—and do not write to them about it.

I am here in the mountains for one week with your mother and the child. Your aunt Clara and your mother and father feel keenly that you should not be away of course. I suspect they think I have no feeling for you. There is debate whether or not I knew you were going to Spain—those who say I love you in the family say I couldn't possibly have known it. Those who hold I knew you were going away say I can't possibly love you.

I am resting here. I needed this—we have tremendous tasks ahead of us in the Party. The child is here with me. Slowly she is coming back to herself.

Rose then went on to focus on her work for the Party. She urged her husband to write letters to "the Corona Branch" and "the Italians in Crown Heights," who, she said, "are essential at this point—for the going of our Comrades to Spain is a bit dimmed in the past now." Rose then gave Ruby detailed instructions on *what* to write to them.

What stood out to me as I read my grandmother go on at length about internecine Party politics was what she did *not* talk about:

she gave Ruby no news and expressed no worries about her young daughter beyond her note that "the child" "slowly ... is coming back to herself"—the child who, not surprisingly, was having a hard time after having been abandoned by her parents and dumped at an anarchist-run boarding school at the age of five, with only occasional visits, mostly from people other than her mother.

Rose did provide what seemed to be a genuine expression of love for Ruby:

> You know, sometimes when I ride tired on the train I dream of you—on the subway I fall asleep and dream of you. I wake up startled because I have seen your laughing charming face ahead of me.... Good bye Darling one. Now I can write often—I'm on my vacation for 10 days. Write me about your arm & everything. Here's a kiss beloved—I'll think about you long after I stop writing this. Rose

It struck me as sad that, after having spent many of his days in Spain lamenting Rose's failure to write to him, this expression of her love didn't reach my grandfather in time.

Giving meaning to the phrase "too little too late," on August 23, Rose wrote another letter that later came back with "MORT" scrawled across the envelope. Here again, we see a revealing and, in some respects, remarkable jumble of my grandmother's obsession with her political work, the tension with Ruby's parents, and her love for her husband and what he was doing in Spain:

> My sweet Darling—How are you? I wonder how you are progressing. Did the arm heal or any complications set in? Maybe, sweet one, it concerns you that I should worry—Well,

I do not worry in the literal sense of getting hysterical over it. But I am away in Fallsburg with your folks. Here I am supposed to be resting from Queens activity to get back fresh for the most intensive work our Party has yet known—work to build us up from the bottom.

Well, not having any activity except reading the NY Times and playing the role of Mr. Schechter's daughter-in-law—my mind dwells so much more on you. Not that it matters to our cause whether you suffer less or more—but since I love you I would feel happier if you didn't suffer ...

Your father I feel is beginning to look upon me with hate. He begins to see I do not carry on as a wife disapproving of her husband's act. He begins to place responsibility on me. Well—it cannot be helped. However you should write to them even more than me. I am only looking how to get away from this God-damned place back to my work.

Well Baby—I love you. I hope it's not too tough on you. At night—I talk to you and talk to you without words—with kisses—with loneliness—with pride over your heroism—with love—for all our grand people—Our great army—of anti-fascists throughout the world—on whom the hope of beauty & life lie. Good bye Sweetheart—I'll write to you again this week. Rose

I found Rose's observation "not that it matters to our cause whether you suffer less or more" to be rather callous—and a reminder of her priorities. Her perception that Ruby's father was "beginning to look upon me with hate" was probably accurate, if he hadn't reached that point before then.

PART IV
Death

He Fought for Democracy

News of Ruby's death began to circulate in September, no doubt in part due to a typed letter "To the Comrades of Queens," probably issued by the Queens division of the Communist Party. I was struck by the emphasis in the letter on the lofty quest to preserve democracy that had driven Ruby and his comrades to rush headlong into the foreign civil war—when the Soviet Union, the beacon of the Communist Party, was anything but a democracy:

> We address ourselves to you in this hour of mourning the loss of a comrade beloved by us and by you—comrade Ruby Schechter.
>
> He died on August 23rd ... from a wound inflicted during the Loyalist offensive at Brunete....
>
> The people of Spain are facing a formidable enemy of treacherous generals and foreign fascist invaders supplied with all the modern weapons of destruction. They are fighting an enemy that aims to destroy all that humanity has built for centuries.
>
> We came to Spain to help the people of this land in this struggle—for the peace and democracy of the entire world. It is in this spirit that Ruby came to Spain as did 2500 other Americans. His work in Spain showed the mettle he was made of. Life could have been comparatively easy for him. Comfort, culture, health were all available to him. But being of that mold that rings true like the best tempered steel, his life could not be a happy one away from the realities of the world. He chose the path of struggle, and proved himself to

be a true and worthy son of the toiling masses—a Bolshevik in heart and in action.

From his Battalion Commander we get the following:

"Ruby was our battalion secretary, who when using the pen in his daily tasks would have close by his side the rifle. Although out of his sphere of work, he would take his place on the front lines by the side of his comrades, fighting alongside them. He was wounded while leading up a mule loaded with ammunition to a dangerous point of the battle. Even when the deadly bullet struck him, he held on to the mule until another comrade came up so as to make sure that the ammunition would reach his comrades"

We all loved Ruby. In the training camp and in battle he was like a fresh tonic cheering up and rousing the morale of the tired and exhausted comrades.

Condolence letters flowed in. It's unclear when Rose learned her husband was dead. On September 12, a letter was written to Rose by someone who had been in Spain with Ruby and had also known him before the war. I couldn't make out the name or initials with which he signed the letter. Whoever the author, he didn't mail his letter to Rose. He sent it instead to an unnamed person with a note written upside down on the top left-hand corner of the first of two pages: "PS. I am sending a letter to Rose through you. If she knows of Ruby's death, send it to her."

The letter shed some light on the mystery of how Ruby had died due to what had appeared to be a flesh wound from a bullet that went through his arm. And I was struck by the consistency in the

Death

descriptions of my grandfather in these postmortem letters with those that had been written about him during his lifetime:

> Darling,
>
> I haven't written to you much in the last few weeks, after I received a number of letters from you. The real reason for it was that I was very much shaken up by the sudden death of Ruby, and just couldn't get down to writing. Ruby's death was sudden. I saw him and talked to him about a week before the tragic occurrence. He was cheerful, happy, and getting along well. But he developed Pneumonia and his weakened system could not hold out.
>
> You know that I always liked Ruby. His gay approach to life, the cheerfulness with which he did things. I grew to like him even more in Spain. In the most difficult moments Ruby would find something to break the tensions…. Under the most terrific aviation and artillery bombardments his nerves held up strong. He would not hesitate to carry through his missions in the most dangerous spots. He proved himself to be a Bolshevik.

At least until 1956, the author's concluding observation that Ruby had "proved himself to be a Bolshevik" was the highest form of compliment. Like Ruby, the author was either delusional or trying to put a good face on the Republican cause in Spain as he turned to the offensive at Aragon that began several weeks after Brunete:

> We have been scoring victories in the recent months at the Madrid and Aragon fronts. These events have shown that the Spanish people "have just begun to fight." It may be a

prolonged struggle, and the cost may be heavy—but that Fascism will be defeated—this is the conviction of all ... Lots of Love

In fact, Aragon was another Republican bloodbath.

Harry Fought On: Aragon

While Ruby was laid up at the hospital, the surviving Lincoln volunteers spent three weeks relaxing and recovering after Brunete before being sent to Aragon—the site of the second major Republican offensive of the war.[1] According to the Lincoln Brigade Archives, my step-grandfather Harry, who I always considered to be my grandfather, was among them.

Unlike the lead-up to Brunete, when Ruby and other Lincolns had been eager to join the fighting, the mood on the eve of the Aragon offensive was grim.[2] The Aragon region of Spain was one of the driest, most arid areas of the country, with virtually nothing growing. The first target of the offensive was the village of Quinto. Like the Brunete offensive, the attack was supposed to be a surprise, and like Brunete, Aragon was another diversionary campaign that was initially successful. On August 24, 1937, the Republicans attacked, and by August 27 they had taken control of Quinto. Other towns were falling as well, with the Republicans destined for the capital of Aragon.[3]

The Lincolns were sent next to Belchite, where they were hit with heavy machine-gun fire. As one commentator reported: "They had to lie motionless through the dragging hours of the September day as the sun burned slowly across the sky, while machine guns raked the earth around them and the dust of Aragon filled their eyes and mouths."[4]

After intense house-to-house fighting, the Republicans took the village, but it was completely destroyed, and half of the Americans who took part in the battle were killed or wounded in the process.[5] Those who survived had by then become real, hardened soldiers.

As Ernest Hemingway, reporting as a journalist from Spain at the time, wrote: "Those that were left were tough, with blackened, matter-of fact faces, and after seven months they knew their trade."[6]

As I read about the brutal street fighting and massive casualties, I thought about Harry. My wife and I have two black-and-white photographs of Harry in Spain that have hung in a prominent spot in our apartment for thirty years. In these, Harry looks like a real soldier. I imagine that one of these photos—showing Harry in uniform, standing with his hands on his hips gazing out from the top of an arid hill—was taken during a respite in the early days of the Aragon offensive. Still, it remained hard for me to picture the scholarly grandfather I thought I knew firing his rifle or killing men with a bayonet in the vicious street fighting.

Harry in Spain (1937)

One thing did not change during Harry's tenure in Spain following Ruby's death: the Americans continued to be completely outgunned, as the Western powers' Non-Intervention Agreement deprived the Republican soldiers of the heavy machine guns, artillery, and aircraft they desperately needed to combat the fascist onslaught supplied by Hitler and Mussolini. In a last-ditch effort to reactivate the Aragon offensive, on October 13 the Republicans attempted to seize the town of Fuentes del Ebro. The assault was a failure, with hundreds killed, and it marked the end of the Aragon offensive.[7]

From then on, the surviving Lincolns were on the run as winter set in. Survivors scrounged for rugs and blankets as they desperately tried to keep warm. Many broke down under the pressure and threw away their weapons as they marched from one town to another, all the while being bombed from above and pursued by modern, motorized forces on the ground. The casualties were massive.[8] By the time they reached the town of Caspe in March, only 100 of the 500 Lincolns who had fought at Belchite were still together. Many of the survivors wandered the hills of Aragon, lost and alone; others were taken prisoner and then murdered.[9]

As I read about the horrific debacle, I again tried, without success, to picture Harry and to imagine his mindset. Was he one of the resolute warriors who remained in the fold? Or one of the wanderers who threw away his rifle and just tried to stay alive? I would stumble upon an answer only as this book was going to print. In the meantime, it struck me as rather amazing that this quiet and altogether understated intellectual somehow managed to survive all three of the bloody battles he took part in—Jarama, Brunete, *and* Aragon. And I thought, too, about Ruby. Given how gung-ho and seemingly reckless he'd been, including his volunteering for the suicidal ammunition run at Brunete, it occurred to me that even if he'd survived the wound to his arm and returned to the front as he'd intended, the odds were heavy that Ruby would have gotten himself killed at Aragon.

The Memorial and Obituaries

While the Aragon offensive was disintegrating, a memorial meeting for Ruby was held on Sunday, October 10 at the Woodside Labor Temple in Woodside, Long Island. The flyer announcing the meeting provided that admission was "25 cents." It had "Rubin Schechter" written across the top, with a banner running down the side of the page that proclaimed "HE DIED FOR YOU." The description of Ruby focused on his civil rights work and analogized his service in Spain to the famous Europeans who had aided the fight for freedom in the American Revolution:

> He went to aid the Spanish people just as Lafayette, Pulaski, and Von Steuben came to the aid of the American people when our country was still very young—and fighting to free itself from British tyranny.
>
> His life was given to a cause which knows no national boundaries. A Loyalist victory in Spain would be a major victory for the freedom loving people all over the world. It would stop the drive of Hitler and Mussolini for world domination.

At the bottom of the page was the following note: "Auspices: Communist Party—Queens County." Although the flyer indicated that "Israel Amter, District Organizer, New York, will be the principal speaker," I learned from a letter written a few days after the meeting that Rose also spoke and may have stolen the show.

Although I have no evidence as to how Rose took Ruby's death, regardless of how she felt there was no interruption in her work

Flyer for Ruby's memorial meeting

for the Party. Within a month of learning that Ruby was dead, she ran for office on the Communist Party ticket, seeking election as an assemblywoman in Queens. And she gave a number of the letters her dead husband had written to her from Spain to *New Masses*, which published its "Four Letters from Spain" article in the

October edition. All the while, she continued to leave my mother at the Lakewood Modern School.

Thanks to a copy of the *New Masses* article that included a photo of Ruby, I discovered that yet another tidbit from our family lore—and one of the very few "facts" I'd thought I'd always known about my grandfather—was simply fiction: he wasn't bald. I've since seen this confirmed by a few other pictures of Ruby I found in the Briefcase, including one with my mother that, given her apparent age, must have been taken shortly before he left for Spain.

Ruby and my mother

Although my grandfather's hairline had receded around the temples, he had thick black hair that came to a point at the front and was combed back. His eyes were deep set and his nose sharp. He struck me as rather handsome. My grandfather had a pipe in his mouth—probably one of the pipes in the collection I inherited and smoked for several years when I was the same age he was in this photograph. His pipes were apparently constant companions. And I still keep them.

The Briefcase contained obituaries printed in various unnamed newspapers—several of which were clearly Queens publications ("Jackson Heights Man Is Killed In Spanish Fighting"). Like the flyer for the memorial, all of them focused on Ruby's role in fighting racial discrimination, with one noting: "He was especially active as a representative of the Communist Party on the Committee of Equal Opportunities, a group of allied organizations centering around a program of equal opportunities for the Negroes of Queens. He played an important role in the fight for Negro doctors at Queens General Hospital."

Another obituary—"Rubin Schechter, Queens Communist Leader Killed Near Brunete During Loyalist Push"—extolled my grandfather as "one of the most promising leaders of the Party," and noted that "he had played an outstanding role in building the Queens section of the Party." But what struck me most about this article was the portion about Rose, entitled "His Wife Carries On As Communist Nominee":

> The lesson of the death of such heroes of democracy as Schechter—and Oliver Law, a Negro machine-gun captain

in the Lincoln Brigade—is not one of empty mourning. It is the lesson of the carrying on of the struggle until fascism is exterminated throughout the world—the lesson of building the forces of peace and democracy.

Mrs. Schechter, Rubin's wife, has set the example. Left with a child she is nevertheless carrying on for democracy—and socialism—in America by running as Assemblywoman in the Third Assembly District on the Communist Party Ticket.

A friend of Ruby and Rose, who signed a letter as "A," also lauded how Rose had thrown herself even more deeply, and prominently, into Party politics and had assumed a leadership role in Queens. Dated "Wednesday," the letter appears to have been written on October 13, referencing the memorial meeting held on Sunday, October 10:

Dear Rose

I have time for only a few words but I feel impelled to state my reaction to the meeting. Rose, Ruby has certainly not died in vain. I think somehow that one of the reasons he was so sure in his strength and determination to go to Spain and sacrifice himself is that in you, his wife, and comrade, he saw and felt that the Party had a Bolshevik who would contribute a great deal to the Revolution; who, far from breaking down would come forward with the strength of 2 Rubys and 2 Roses to make up for him. I feel that your days of doubt are over—that you will come forward as the natural leader of Queens. Everyone who listened to you Sunday felt that way. I cannot tell you how strong you made me feel—how sure and confident and how proud I was to be in the same Party with you—and to know you as a friend.

A few other letters stood out as people sought to make sense of my grandfather's death and attempted to tell Rose, and themselves, that he hadn't died in vain. One was an October 12 letter to Rose from Kenneth Hayes Miller, the legendary artist who taught at the Art Students League in Manhattan for forty years, from 1911 to 1951. Among Miller's students were such renowned American painters as Rockwell Kent, George Bellows, Edward Hopper, Isabel Bishop, Reginald Marsh, and, when she wasn't rabble-rousing, Rose.[10]

Perhaps not surprisingly, Miller's short letter captured the tragedy poignantly:

Dear Mrs. Schechter,

On returning from Zurich I was shocked to find the news of your husband's death, killed in action in the International Brigade fighting in Spain.

How much this scholar and gentle humanist must have been moved by forces opposite to his ideals to have taken up mortal weapons against those forces to give even his life for a cause in a distant land.

What words of comfort can be spoken to you, his widow? I do not know of any. But you will always have the knowledge of the nobility of his character and the memory of it, and of his courage in going out and giving his life for his belief.

Miller's apt reference to Ruby as a "scholar and gentle humanist" who was "moved by forces opposite to his ideals ... to give even his life for a cause in a distant land" seemed to describe Ruby's evolution through the three phases of his brief adult life—from poet, to organizer, to soldier. Miller would later resurface in a surprising twist to this story, shining a piercing light on Rose's dedication to the Communist Party in the decades after Ruby died.

A friend named Lou Perlman wrote to Rose on October 21. His letter expounded on a point that I'd been hoping was true. Namely, that regardless of the role the Communist Party had played in encouraging young men like Ruby to go to Spain, the cause for which they were fighting—and willing to sacrifice their lives—was democracy and the defeat of fascists, including Hitler, whose evil and ambitions they recognized while the rest of the country stuck their heads in the sand. I wanted to believe that my grandfathers had not been risking their lives merely as part of a Marxist campaign to *replace* democracies—including ours—with the Soviet model of government.

> Dear Rose,
> Please forgive me for not having written sooner.... I still am unable to grasp the reality of Ruby's sacrifice.... There are very few of us who can so completely sacrifice ourselves as he did.... In his convictions along with his love of democracy, equality, and his self trust are to be found the essence of heroism.
> Historically, the progress of democracy seems irresistible despite occasional "setbacks," because it is unquestionably the most ancient and most permanent tendency forward in history. It is men like Ruby who drag us out of the dark, abysmal "set-backs"; it is men like Ruby who will finally bring about a universal change from the delusive to the real,

and will bring about an ultimate worldly peace and true democracy. Ruby died for the world. No man can pay a greater tribute than he paid himself—

But in the midst of all the letters and obituaries seeking to find some redeeming value in Ruby's death—and the deaths of other soldiers who had fought and perished in Spain—there was a dissenter: a man name Ernest Meyer, who wrote a column in the *New York Post* arguing that it had been "a waste to sacrifice" the life of Max Krauthamer, another American killed in Spain. Although the *Post*'s archive does not contain Meyer's article, included in the Briefcase was the October 5, 1937, letter that Rose wrote in response. My grandmother excoriated Meyer, driving home the theme that the Americans like Ruby who had gone to Spain were fighting for democracy, and likening them to the heroes of the American Revolution, including those who had come to our aid from abroad:

My Dear Mr. Meyer:

As the wife of Rubin Schechter, aged 32, who died in Spain fighting for democracy, August 23rd, I feel it is my duty to criticize the conclusion you reached last week in discussing the waste of Max Krauthamer's sacrifice in laying down his life in defense of the People of Spain's fight against World Fascism.

Your conclusion leads to the error of reproving our heroic American boys who are making the supreme sacrifice for all of us to stop the menace of Fascism at its most crucial point, Spain.... We, who love and are left behind, grieve for our dead.... We, the mourners of our dead in Spain, raise our heads with hope and say: "Max Krauthamer's life and Rubin Schechter's life and the life of every other American boy who died in Spain was a contribution to the cause of democracy in our native land. They did all they could to check the advance of world Fascism."

Would you say that young Nathan Hale wasted his life when he died at the hands of the British Tories fighting for democracy? Would you say that the great Garibaldi and his battalion of Italian Democrats who came to fight in the ranks of the north during the Civil War for democracy, against slavery, were wasting their lives?

My grandmother had a point—to a point. But one big difference between Ruby's death and the historical examples she cited is that in her examples the young men laid down their lives in furtherance of a winning cause: good triumphed over evil. Ruby had sacrificed his life fighting for a lost cause, as the Nazi-backed fascists proceeded to decimate the Republican army in Spain before embarking on the quest for world domination that Ruby and his comrades who ventured to Spain had foreseen.

And so I've wondered: Has someone who risked his life for a worthy cause—and gotten killed—died "in vain" unless their team goes on to win? What about the American soldiers in Vietnam and Afghanistan who died, lost limbs, suffered trauma, and lost comrades? Is this the inevitable risk of war in which there are no guarantees of who will win? Finally, going back to one of my first questions, what is a worthy cause? Does the determination as to whether soldiers on the losing side died in vain depend on the merits of the cause for which they sacrificed their lives? And who is the judge of that?

I know of at least two people who believed that Ruby *had* died in vain: his parents. And they undoubtedly blamed Rose for having sent him off on the Spanish crusade. The "folks," as Ruby referred to them, had been living in a state of raw misery since receiving Ruby's letters informing them that he'd gone to Spain, promising that he'd have a desk job and would take no part in the fighting. I was about to learn more about that.

The Yiddish Surprise

Having finished reading the letters, articles, and other documents in the Briefcase, I paused to consider the question I'd been pondering when I set out: What force had been so powerful as to impel Ruby—and Harry—to leave home; for Ruby to leave a five-year-old daughter with a mother who would then park her at an anarchist-run boarding school in New Jersey? Was it a prescient understanding of the existential risk posed by fascism and a burning desire to forestall it? Or was it a matter of fealty to the Communist Party? Rightly or wrongly I felt fairly sanguine at this point: I had a new appreciation for the Communist Party that Ruby and Harry had joined in the early 1930s, as it stood in the vanguard of the opposition to not only fascism, but racism and poverty as well. In one way or another, I would have been with them had I lived then. And, as the postmortem tributes to Ruby attested, it appeared that he, Harry, and their comrades were, indeed, fighting to preserve democracy and freedom. The esteem I'd always had for my grandfathers remained intact.

One piece of unfinished business that remained concerned five letters I had found in the Briefcase that appeared to have been written in Hebrew, which I couldn't read. An Orthodox Jewish friend agreed to translate them for me, but after taking a quick glance she told me that they'd been written not in Hebrew, but Yiddish—a Germanic language spoken by Eastern European Jews like Ruby's mother and my father's Ukrainian parents. In his August 12 letter explaining how he'd been shot, Ruby had referred to Yiddish as the "Jewish" language, which he was unable to write with his opposite hand. Because my friend couldn't decipher the letters, I paid to have them translated.

These letters, three written by Ruby and two by his father, highlighted his father's despair, and fury, at his son's desertion. But they also revealed a fiery, intensely radical side of Ruby that had not been in evidence in his tender letters to Rose. And they confirmed once again that when forced to navigate the conflict between his devotion to the Communist Party and his other loves, passions, and obligations, my grandfather chose the former. Indeed, his only interest now was in converting his family to his radical cause.

The first of the dated Yiddish letters was written by Ruby to his father on June 6, 1937. It was in response to a letter his father had sent him that I'd initially believed had disappeared in Spain. It was clear from Ruby's letter that his father was deeply anguished about Ruby's having abandoned the family, and may have accused his son of having deceived his parents, both before and since leaving for Spain. The love between father and son was equally apparent:

> You wrote me with love and I answer you with love.... In the long months in which I have not seen you, my wife and child I read over and over again your words not because I agree but because they are your words written from pain and deep love.

Ruby proceeded to defend the veracity of what he'd previously told his father, including, it seemed to me, by prevaricating again:

> Everything I told you when I left is true. I was in France for 17 days. I was all over France and it was impossible to meet up with the business people. I wrote you that I was not

travelling to any war. That was also true. I wrote to you that I was not in danger. That was also true.

The renewed assurance Ruby gave his father that he had not been traveling to any war was patently false—and his statement that he "was not in danger" was either untrue at the time or very soon would be.

Ruby went on to unfurl his communist colors, and seemed to conjoin fascism and capitalism as the enemy he'd gone to Spain to vanquish.

Our enemy is world Capitalism which cannot bring new life to people. It can only bring sadness and hunger....

The international movement has sent out its dearest children—and I am one of them—and with the youngest heroes did it send everything important to control the enemy. In a short time Fascism will fall on the fields of Spain. A new day will open for the world. We will come home and rebuild anew.

Finally, Ruby stressed the importance of the work Rose was doing for the Party back home:

I am completely satisfied with your help for my wife and child ... you should see that nothing should stand in the way of her work. Her work is my work. The more she has a free hand will it be better for all of us later.

I later received a translation of an undated letter written by Ruby's father that I suspected was the one to which Ruby was responding on June 6 when he wrote: "I read over and over again your words not because I agree but because they are your words written from pain and deep love." Whenever it was written, his father's letter reflected his suffering, and rage, at his son's betrayal:

> My dear and beloved son,
>
> It is very painful to me, after all I did for my son he is causing us so much pain. Fighting with the fascists will not bring you any use; how many more people's lives will be shattered.... Every party has their opinion, and everyone thinks they're right. Otherwise there wouldn't be such bitterness in this world.... My blood is boiling, my eyes are wet many nights; blow the whistle and let it be over. My child, I don't know how I'm not going crazy.

Ruby's father then went on to appeal to his son's sense of guilt by talking about my mother:

> Now I will write to you about your daughter Toba. Two weeks ago, I went to her to camp and I was very happy to see her and she was happy with me. However, the happiness was not like the previous year. It was mixed with blood. She asked me why I'm not writing to daddy that he should come already. I asked her why she is not writing. She answered me that she already wrote, but nobody is coming. I think it's a crime what you are doing against yourself and against us all.

The second of Ruby's Yiddish letters was written on June 20 to family members other than his father. Even more than in the June

Death

6 letter to his father, Ruby's fiery radicalism and determination to convert the family were on display in this one:

> Beloveds
> It is very well with me.
> Naturally I am near to the battle line but as I have written to you, you have little to worry about. It's better that you should seriously interest yourselves in the anti-Fascism movement.
> When will you recognize that the Banker Industrialists finance and plan the work for the international gangsters? When you will study why it is necessary for finance capital to ignite the world, then you will understand why the millions, masses, workers, and small business people are watchful that the capitalistic Fascism should be destroyed and Fascism will surely be conquered.

My grandfather's radical rant was unsettling. I found myself wishing I hadn't paid for the translations of the Yiddish letters, which wiped the shine off my image of Ruby as a young man drawn to Spain solely by the desire to save democracy and stem the tide of fascism.

Ruby wrote the third and final surviving Yiddish letter to his family on July 14, while the Battle of Brunete was raging and the Republican army was desperately trying to withstand the fascists' counteroffensive. The letter revealed that the family was still trying to lure Ruby back from the war, now apparently using his father's recently diagnosed diabetes as leverage. Ruby, on the other hand, remained interested only in converting his family to "the movement":

My beloveds,

I heard from Mimi [Ruby's younger sister] and today from Irving ... She informed me about father concerning his sickness. I am sure you are doing everything that's possible to combat this sickness. One thing I must say clearly to you is that my return cannot cure diabetes.

I have already repeated myself that my life's work lies with the mighty anti-Fascism workers' movement.... I have in another letter written to you that you should immediately interest yourself in this major movement and also get involved. Only with understanding and not with tears can we quiet your hearts. About my body I already informed you that I am not in any danger.

Ruby's renewed assurance that he was "not in any danger" was very obviously false, and his mother and father certainly never believed it. As the Lipkaner biography recounts: "From the moment his parents read his letter, their lives became darkened. They were haunted day and night by frightening thoughts. They feared the worst—and the worst it was."

I probably shouldn't have been surprised by the Yiddish letters, as the thirteen-page paper that I attributed to my grandfather, as well as a few of his poems, contained similarly incendiary language. And I knew he had been a Communist Party organizer. Nevertheless, I was surprised—and disappointed.

PART V

Those Who Lived On

A Window into the U.S. Communist Party

Harry was in the minority of Lincoln Brigade volunteers who managed to survive and return unscathed, at least physically. He went on to serve in the U.S. Army in World War II and then, in 1945, married Ruby's widow, my Grandma Rose. Along with thousands of other devoted souls, Harry and Rose continued as Communist Party members for over two decades after Ruby's death, going along for what proved to be a twisted and ultimately disillusioning ride. Ruby's brother-in-law, my uncle Irving Schwab, joined them for a short while until his own premature death in 1943. Although I'm not aware that my parents formally joined the Party, they certainly had some involvement in Party activities. My guess is that they belonged, at the least, in the bucket of "fellow travelers".

Before putting this story to bed, I decided to do some research into the history of the Communist Party of the United States to see if it would shed more light on the letters in the Briefcase and the Lipkaner biography of Rubin Schechter. I quickly realized I should have done so long before.

I began this phase of my research with *The Communist Party of the United States: From the Depression to World War II* by Fraser Ottanelli. This, in turn, led me on a trail that continually yielded clues, and likely answers, to questions that had nagged me regarding Ruby's passionate idealism and death, while raising new questions about what had been going on in the lives and minds of Harry and Rose as they lived on. The history became a new template against which I repeatedly needed to reconsider what I'd read—and already written—about my grandparents, as well as

Irving. And the further I went, the foggier the picture became. As I knew more, I was certain of less.

Perhaps the most glaring fact I learned was that at all times from its founding in 1919 until February 1956, the policies espoused by the Communist Party of the United States were dictated by the Soviet Union and its omnipotent leader, Joseph Stalin. That fact, which probably shouldn't have surprised me but did, was deflating as I continued to cogitate about how much of my grandparents' idealistic quest was actually due to devotion to the Stalinist regime. On the other hand, reading the history of the U.S. Communist Party in the 1930s was uplifting—at least initially—as I learned more about the leading role the Party had played in fighting on behalf of those left poor and unemployed during the Depression, and in opposing racism and fascism. I was able to tell myself that while the Party's policies may have been dictated by the Soviets, they made good sense and were entirely worthy on a human level.

The neglect of my mother became more understandable (which is not to say forgivable) in light of the Party's history. Membership was an all-consuming experience that entailed mandatory attendance at late-night meetings, leafleting, and activities such as the intensive weekend educational program Ruby had outlined in his little black organizer's loose-leaf binder; activities that left little time for anything else, such as raising children.[1] I began to understand why Rose's letters to Ruby referred to my mother as "the child"—the five-year-old whose upbringing and well-being were clearly an afterthought to her parents.

I also gained new insight into the force that had impelled young men like Ruby and Harry to put their lives on the line in a foreign civil war, defying their own government in the process. During the early 1930s, the Communists seemed to label every government or group they disliked as "fascist," refusing to acknowledge any distinction between democratic and fascist forms of government. Indeed, they referred to the leaders of the Socialist Party—a bitter enemy—as "social-fascist."[2] They were also vehement critics of FDR and the New Deal, declaring that the president's policies were "masked fascization" and that "the increasing role of the federal government in the economy was a clear move toward fascism."[3] As Hitler continued on his rise to power in Germany, however, the U.S. Communist Party reversed course—as always, commanded by Moscow—and drew an increasingly sharp line between democratic governments, however flawed, like the United States, and the aggressive fascist governments in Germany, Italy, and Japan.[4]

At the Seventh World Congress of the Comintern—the Soviet-led international organization dedicated to the advancement of communism—held in Moscow during the summer of 1935, a directive was given that there was a "need for all socialist organizations and democratic forces to join together in an anti-fascist alliance to defend bourgeois democracy."[5] This was the "United Front" referred to in Ruby's little black binder, a reference I had not previously understood. The Comintern mandated that the battle to stem the tide of fascism would take precedence over every other priority. The drive for a communist revolution was put on hold.[6]

A thaw in the U.S. Communist Party's opposition to Roosevelt ensued, as the threat of fascism accelerated. With the encouragement of Moscow, by 1936 the Party was praising FDR and his New Deal policies, especially after the Spanish Civil War broke out.[7] Earl Browder, the head of the Party in the U.S., gave speeches warning of the danger of not standing up to the fascists in Spain, trumpeting the importance of defending democracy, and disavowing that the Communist Party had any intention of supporting a violent insurrection to overthrow American democracy.[8] Browder ran for President of the United States in 1936 with the slogan "Communism is Twentieth-Century Americanism." The Party came to be viewed favorably among American liberals as the foremost opponent to fascism.[9] Membership in the U.S. Communist Party grew—from 30,000 in 1935 to 75,000 in 1938.[10]

Although a trickle of European volunteers had been going to Spain since the start of the civil war, the number increased dramatically after the Comintern called for the creation of a foreign volunteer force in the fall of 1936. The International Brigades were formed under the auspices of the Comintern and were largely directed by the Communists.[11] The Comintern launched a global recruiting drive in September, assigning quotas to the various national Communist Parties depending on their membership and potential.[12] In the United States, the Communists initially concealed their role, partly because they were aiming to recruit a broad range of anti-fascists, not just Communists. Nevertheless, in September the Party's *Daily Worker* publication acknowledged that the Party was recruiting volunteers, and Earl Browder publicly acknowledged the Party's role in December. Browder stressed the need to send a steady stream of American volunteers to Spain.[13]

The Communist Party ran the recruitment process, interviewing applicants seeking to go to Spain—and either approving or rejecting them. In some cases, prospective volunteers were rejected because the Stalin-led Party deemed them too dangerous (i.e., potential Trotskyists and thus opponents of Stalin); others were rejected because the Party determined that they were too important to be spared in Spain. The Party was also believed to have put pressure on members to volunteer, and some were allegedly ordered to go to Spain.[14] The International Brigades were formed in October and

November 1936, and the first group of American volunteers bound for Spain left in December. Their transportation to France on the SS *Normandie* was arranged by Intourist, the Soviet travel agency.[15]

In light of everything I read in the Briefcase, I'm still confident that my grandfathers were passionate idealists who believed that Hitler and his fellow fascists in Spain posed an existential threat to democracy and the world. And they were willing to risk their lives to avert the catastrophe they foresaw. In light of the history I've read more recently, however, I also have little doubt that my grandfathers would *not* have joined the Lincoln Brigade and fought in that foreign civil war if the Soviet-controlled Communist Party hadn't summoned them. Indeed, upon re-reading the Lipkaner biography just before sending this book to print, I came upon a sentence I had previously overlooked that lent credence to this: "The workers movement which had become dearer to him than life and to which he had devoted his life, had sent him on this mission." And Ruby's June 6, 1937 letter to his father said the same thing. ("The international movement has sent out its dearest children—and I am one of them.")

In one sense, and as a practical matter, this is probably true of virtually all the Lincoln volunteers, even those who were not devout members of the Communist Party, given that the Party organized the International Brigades and facilitated Americans' travel to Spain. As one commentator has explained: "Without the Soviet Comintern decision to intervene directly in the Spanish War and, as part of that intervention, create a foreign volunteer force for use in Spain, the International Brigades would never have come into existence."[16]

However, in the case of Ruby and Harry—both hardcore Communists—I suspect that the Party's call to arms carried a lot of weight. So, I believe I now know most of the somewhat depressing answer to the question I'd been pondering since setting out on my search: Why did they go? They went for noble reasons, and they went because they were lured and summoned.

I do still have lingering questions as to what impelled Ruby and Harry's individual decisions. Were either of them pressured to volunteer? As for Ruby, some in the family believe that Rose pushed him to go when he otherwise would not have left home. Nevertheless, given the unbridled enthusiasm reflected in all of Ruby's letters, my sense is that he took this leap with Rose's enthusiastic support but not at her urging. Harry's motivation remains somewhat of a mystery—thanks to my failure to ask him anything about his Spanish Civil War experience.

My exploration of the history of the U.S. Communist Party also shed new, unwanted light on whether Ruby died in vain, while raising painful questions about how Rose and Harry went about their lives as they survived him.

In 1939, Stalin did a stunning about-face and, overnight, converted from being the fascists' greatest foe to Hitler's partner. Two years after Ruby heeded Moscow's call to take up arms against the fascists, Stalin understandably lost confidence in, and grew distrustful of, the Western governments that were appeasing Hitler not only in Spain, but the Sudetenland and Czechoslovakia as well. He decided that the best way to protect the Soviet Union against Nazi aggression was to lock arms with Hitler; and so, in August 1939, the U.S.S.R. entered into the German-Soviet Non-Aggression Pact.

The U.S. Communists were dumbstruck and traumatized.[17] Earl Browder and the U.S. Party initially attempted to adhere to the anti-fascist policy that had been the Party's hallmark, and for which so many young Americans like Ruby had just given their lives, but the Soviets ordered Browder to reverse course. Rather than continuing to urge Americans to join the fight against fascism, the Soviets now insisted that World War II was merely a contest among "imperialists," not an anti-fascist war, and that the U.S. Party should not support either side. They also ordered Browder to resume attacking Roosevelt and the New Deal. After attempting to resist for a few months, the U.S. Party surrendered to Moscow's demands and defended the Non-Aggression Pact, rallying its members with the ludicrous claim that the pact was a contribution to world peace and democracy that was consistent with the Party's anti-fascist policy.[18]

The Party continued to lambast Roosevelt and the "imperialist" war until 1941, when Hitler double-crossed Stalin and attacked Russia. At that point, the Party reversed course yet again, and many U.S. members, including Harry, joined the U.S. armed forces in what the Party once again deemed an anti-fascist war.[19]

As I read about the Party's dizzying policy reversals and frivolous justifications, I tried to imagine what Rose and Harry were thinking, and how they dealt with these obvious contradictions as they thought about Ruby and the many friends who had died so recently for a lost and now abandoned cause.

Scottsboro and Irving (Take 2)

Ruby's college friend and brother-in-law, Irving Schwab, lived to witness and experience only a few rounds of the Party's gyrations. He died of a short illness in 1943 at the age of thirty-nine after devoting his life to defending the Scottsboro Boys in a saga that continued throughout the 1930s and beyond. In the course of trying to make sense of my grandfathers' histories, I vacillated over whether Irving's story—and the discussion of Scottsboro revolving around him—was part of Ruby's.

Over the decades, whenever I've regaled friends with the story about how my grandfathers volunteered to fight in the Spanish Civil War, I often managed to weave in Irving's story, proud that he had been the lead counsel in the Scottsboro case and had smuggled Ruby Bates out of the South in the rumble seat of his car. And Irving and my Grandpa Ruby were kindred spirits. They'd become lifelong friends in college as they set out together to help those suffering in "Hunger and Cold and Rooflessness." When their trail came to a fork in the early 1930s, the two brothers-in-law took different paths to rid the world of the evils they both despised and couldn't ignore. Ruby was still an aspiring poet when Irving ventured to Alabama to defend the Scottsboro Boys in 1931. But as the *New Masses* article and his obituaries highlighted, after joining the Party in 1933 Ruby shared Irving's passionate opposition to racism, serving as a member of the Equal Opportunity Commission that waged the successful campaign to end the discrimination against Black doctors at Queens General Hospital.

Having learned more about what actually occurred in Scottsboro and the unbridled racism that fueled it, I decided to continue to include the story of Irving's role—this time a more accurate story. Because, as I'd come to discover, the conduct of the U.S. Communist Party in defending the Scottsboro Boys epitomized both the admirable and the disturbing sides of the Party to which Ruby, Harry, and Rose were devoted. And Irving played a role on both sides.

I decided to do some research to see what I could learn about the actual role that Irving had played in the Scottsboro case, and began with one of the leading works on the case: Dan Carter's *Scottsboro: A Tragedy of the American South*. When I got Carter's book, I immediately turned to the index to find the references to Irving, only to be disappointed. There wasn't a single one, immediately demolishing the family lore that Irving had been the lead lawyer for the Scottsboro Boys until their case went to the Supreme Court.

Looking at the bright side of the American Communists' role in the Scottsboro saga, the U.S. Communist Party and its legal arm—the International Labor Defense, known as the ILD—were indeed the most forceful advocates among white-led organizations for the rights of African Americans in this era.[20] The ILD fought aggressively and tirelessly to defend and free the Scottsboro Boys throughout the 1930s—and well beyond. And the fact that the Party recruited Samuel Leibowitz, who was not a Communist, to serve as the actual lead trial counsel tends to belie the accusations that the Communists didn't care about the Scottsboro Boys or that they sought to provoke Alabama to kill them in order to foment the communist revolution.[21]

On the dark side, however, was the ugly turf war the Communist Party and the ILD waged with the NAACP for control of the legal defense of the Scottsboro Boys—a battle in which I learned Irving did play a significant role. The NAACP took a cautious, non-confrontational approach in its advocacy for civil rights during these early years. Led by Walter White, the NAACP was initially reluctant to take up the cause of the nine accused rapists unless and until it was convinced the Scottsboro Boys were innocent.[22] Moreover, once pressured to enter the fray, White believed that the defense of the case should be confined to the courtroom and not conducted in the public arena.[23]

For its part, the Communist Party had little confidence in the U.S. legal system, particularly in the South, and insisted on waging an all-out publicity campaign to generate public support for the Scottsboro Boys.[24] It believed—and loudly claimed—that the NAACP was a tool of the white ruling class, endlessly trumpeting such accusations as that White and the NACCP were "traitors to the Negro masses and betrayers of the Negro liberation struggle," and even that they were allies of the Ku Klux Klan.[25] For its part, the NAACP claimed that the Communists were merely using the Scottsboro Boys as pawns in furtherance of their own radical agenda.

Amidst the morass of accusations hurled back and forth, one thing was clear: the Scottsboro Boys were caught in the middle of the warring factions, as the ILD and the NAACP—refusing to work with each other—took turns persuading the boys and their parents to sign agreements retaining them as their legal counsel.[26] With the second round of trials approaching after the Supreme Court reversed the original convictions, the NAACP played what it thought was a winning hand: It announced that it had recruited Clarence Darrow, the country's most renowned trial lawyer, to take the case.[27] And that's when my Uncle Irving made an appearance.

Carter reports that a meeting took place on the evening of December 28, 1931, attended by Clarence Darrow, Roderick Beddow, and Arthur Garfield Hays for the NAACP, and three lawyers on the ILD team: Joseph Brodsky, George Chamlee,[28] and, though not referenced in the index, my Uncle Irving. The purpose of the meeting was to discuss whether the two sides could collaborate on the defense of the Scottsboro Boys. Unfortunately, they couldn't agree, most importantly because the ILD lawyers refused to work with Darrow unless he divorced himself from the NAACP. After they'd gotten nowhere for six hours, at around midnight Darrow suggested what struck me as a reasonable compromise: he proposed that he, Beddow, and Hays would separate from the NAACP if Irving Schwab and George Chamlee would separate from the ILD and the Communist Party so that the five of them could work together as private lawyers to defend the Scottsboro Boys. Speaking for his group, Irving told Darrow they needed twenty-four hours to clear his proposal with the ILD's central office in New York City. And on the following day, acting on the orders of George Maurer at Party headquarters, the ILD lawyers rejected Darrow's compromise, at which point Darrow and the NAACP withdrew from the case.[29] Thus, it seemed that my uncle's most noteworthy role was his participation in excluding the country's most famous trial lawyer from the defense of the Scottsboro Boys.

After the NAACP gave up the fight, the ILD and the Communist Party assumed control of the defense, with Samuel Leibowitz as the lead trial lawyer.[30] In one respect the Communists were successful: Their public advocacy generated widespread outrage at the injustice being perpetrated in Alabama. Prominent figures in this country and abroad, including Albert Einstein, Thomas Mann and H.G. Wells, voiced support for the Scottsboro Boys.[31]

Round two of the Scottsboro trials took place in Decatur, Alabama, after the defendants' motion for a change of venue was granted and the trial was reassigned to Judge James Horton. One of the highlights of the first of these trials—Haywood Patterson's—was the testimony of Ruby Bates. Consistent with my dilapidated family lore, Bates had indeed been shepherded out of the South to New York City, where she recanted her accusation that she and Victoria Price had been raped. She was brought to New York not by Irving, however, as I'd always understood, but by someone else who has never been identified with any certainty.[32]

Bates proceeded to give explosive testimony at the trial, confessing that the testimony she and Victoria Price had given in the first round of trials—and that Price had just reprised in this one—was totally false, and that none of the Scottsboro Boys had raped either one of them. Rather than a high point of the trial for the defense, however, Bates's testimony proved to be a debacle. Wearing a stylish outfit foolishly provided to her by the ILD, her credibility was battered on cross-examination by Alabama Attorney General Thomas Knight, who charged that Bates had been bought and paid for by the New York City Communists.[33] Consequently, some commentators looking back on the trial reasonably viewed the ILD's having taken Bates to New York as a strategic blunder.[34] This was an especially ironic twist for me given that I had taken such pride in my uncle's alleged role as the driver—a detail I had initially been disappointed to learn was untrue.

The jury voted to convict Patterson and sentenced him to death, despite not only Bates's recantation but testimony from Dr. R.R. Bridges, one of the two doctors who had examined Price and Bates, which undermined the prosecution,[35] as well as evidence showing that Price was a compulsive liar and anything but the epitome of "pure" Southern womanhood. The one Alabama resident in the courtroom convinced by Bates's testimony and of the Scottsboro Boys' innocence was apparently Judge Horton. After sentencing Patterson to death, he immediately suspended the sentence and postponed the remaining trials in light of defense counsel's motion for a new trial.[36]

On the date of the hearing set for defense counsel to argue the motion, Horton, unprompted, read aloud an astonishing seventeen-page, single-spaced decision in which he combed through the trial record and detailed the extensive evidence proving that Victoria Price had "knowingly testified falsely in many material aspects of the case;" that there had been no rape; and that the Scottsboro Boys were innocent. Judge Horton set aside the jury verdicts and ordered a new trial.[37]

But the state of Alabama was unwilling to abandon its quest to put the Scottsboro Boys to death. Responding to intense pressure, the Chief Judge of the Alabama Supreme Court removed Judge Horton from the case and appointed William Callahan, a blatant racist, to preside over round three of the Scottsboro trials.[38] Patterson was convicted and again sentenced to death, as was Clarence Norris, whose trial proceeded as the Patterson jury deliberated. The appeals followed a familiar route, as the Alabama courts affirmed the verdicts and the Scottsboro Boys were again caught in the middle of an ugly internecine battle—as the Boys' lead lawyer, Samuel Leibowitz, had fallen out with the ILD.[39]

In 1935, the Supreme Court once again agreed to hear the case and, in *Norris v. Alabama*, threw out the jury verdicts for a second time. This time the court held that African Americans had been systematically excluded from the jury pool in violation of the Equal Protection Clause of the Fourteenth Amendment, and that to avoid the defendants' judicial challenge, local officials had fraudulently forged the jury rolls so as to give the false appearance that they had included African Americans.[40]

With the cases returned to Alabama for a fourth round of trials, the State persisted, but the results were surprising. Haywood Patterson was again tried first, in January 1936, and was again convicted. This time, however, he was sentenced to seventy-five years in prison, rather than death, as one juror believed all the defendants were innocent and reluctantly went along with the conviction but would not agree to a death sentence.[41] The trials of three of the remaining defendants proceeded in July 1937 after a delay of more than a year, during which Patterson's appeals were denied and the defendants remained in prison, mostly in solitary confinement.[42] But as the trial of Ozie Powell was set to begin, a stunning compromise was unveiled.

Alabama Assistant Attorney General Thomas Lawson announced that the prosecution had dropped the rape charge against Powell and allowed him to plead guilty to assaulting an officer, for which he was sentenced to twenty years. Lawson then announced that the state was dropping *all* charges against the remaining four defendants—Willie Roberson, Olen Montgomery, Eugene Williams, and Roy Wright—who were immediately released from prison. In an explanatory statement Lawson claimed that although the prosecution believed that the defendants who had already been tried and convicted *were* guilty of raping Victoria Price, Willie Roberson and Olen Montgomery were *not* guilty, and that Price had "mistakenly" identified them.[43]

The final tragedy of Scottsboro is that after acknowledging on the record that Victoria Price's testimony could not be trusted, the state refused to drop the convictions of Haywood Patterson,

Clarence Norris, Charley Weems, and Andy Wright—or even to reduce their sentences. In the years to come, the incarcerated defendants' applications for parole were repeatedly denied as they languished in one of the country's worst prisons.[44] The bottom line is that the lives of all nine innocent young men were destroyed, in one of the greatest miscarriages of justice in American history.[45]

There is much to criticize about the Communists' handling of the Scottsboro case—particularly their unseemly years-long turf battle with the NAACP, which was detrimental to both the legal representation and the mental health of their clients. On the other hand, the Communist lawyers, including Irving Schwab, worked tirelessly on behalf of the Scottsboro Boys and, but for their efforts—including their aggressive publicity campaign—all nine almost certainly would have been put to death, probably in 1931. And beyond Scottsboro, the Communists were in the vanguard of the nascent battle to combat racism, defending other African Americans in the South at a time when, as with respect to the rising tide of fascism, most of the country was asleep. As I would later learn, my Uncle Irving played a prominent role in some of those cases.

George Charney Returns

Fraser Ottanelli's history of the U.S. Communist Party yielded a surprising new trail marker that led me further on the haphazard route I'd been following since receiving Ruby's letters and the Lipkaner biography from my cousin Carl. When I came to Chapter 5, I noticed that the introductory quote was attributed to George Charney—one of Ruby's two best friends, the subject of his "Sonnet to George," and one of the people Rose had stayed with while Ruby was in Spain. The footnote to the quote revealed that Charney had written an autobiography—*A Long Journey*—published in 1968.

I found a used copy on eBay and waited impatiently to receive it, hoping that Charney had said something about Ruby. When the book turned up a week later I immediately went to the index and saw references to both Ruby and Rose. The first was a passage on page 19 that brought me to tears:

> My other new friends were Ruby and Rose Schechter. They had married early, he barely out of Syracuse University, she a young art student, both unaffected by the prevailing bohemian influence that frowned on marriage and all such decadent institutions. Ruby was short, roly-poly, dark, cast in an ancient Hebraic mold. He had eyes that could dance with merriment and, in another moment, express brooding melancholy. He was an American Hasid, whose boundless joy of living was derived not from the old mysteries or dog-eared Commentaries but from the great poets, Shakespeare, Milton, and the Old and New Testaments and,

above all, from life itself. Those of us who knew him well, loved him as a poet and as a man.

Rose was his joy. They were completely opposite. He short and Semitic; she tall and Nordic blond. He was quick; she was slow and seemingly phlegmatic with large eyes that looked askance at the world. Each gave to the other his love of people and art, truth and beauty, in their common effort to understand this world and play their part in it.

Ruby died in Spain, a young man scarcely thirty years old, an American volunteer in the Spanish Civil War, leaving behind widow and child. He never published a line of poetry, this poet I knew as a man.

This gave me new insight into both the physical appearance and the soul of my grandfather. Charney's description of Ruby's personality and passions also confirmed my impression that, at least until joining the Party, Ruby had aspired to be a serious poet—and it answered my question as to whether any of his poems had been published: not even one saw the light of day.

Noteworthy to me, Charney's description of Rose as a blond, not a redhead as I remembered her, suggested that the romantic references in Ruby's poem to a blond woman could have been about Rose, and not the other woman with whom I had cavalierly speculated he was having or fantasizing an affair. And here, as elsewhere, Charney gave witness to the fact that my grandparents had a genuine, loving relationship. I harked back to the line in Charney's wartime letter to Ruby citing Ruby's relationship with Rose as the inspiration for his own budding love affair with Hattie.

Charney also confirmed that Rose was, indeed, an active partner in Ruby's political activities, and unveiled the role the couple had played in leading Charney, himself, to the Communist Party, as well as the passionate idealism that drove all of them:

> The depression was at its worst; unemployment was paralyzing. The signs of grinding poverty and despair were evident everywhere. Breadlines, the Hoovervilles' shacks along the Hudson, the plight of college graduates, all contributed to sharpen my awareness of the turbulent crisis and of new voices in protest.
>
> For the first time my friends and I heard, as from a distance, the challenging appeal of Marx and the Communist movement. Some had already been drawn into discussion circles. In Sunnyside, Queens, where Rose and Ruby lived, a large group was formed to hear serious debates between V.J. Jerome and Bertram Wolfe....
>
> I had a keen interest in life, and yet I was adrift with an ever more insistent yearning to become part of something, some group, some movement with a purpose. The evenings at Rose and Ruby's, in which we discussed art and literature into the early hours and expressed our contempt for the social mores, were no longer satisfying. We were overwhelmed by the pressure of a world collapsing around us. The rise of fascism sharpened our sense of a world in crisis as it made us more aware of our isolation and futility.
>
> My contact with communism and the party, initiated by Rose and Ruby in the discussion group in Sunnyside, came at a moment when I was most receptive to its eloquent and universal appeal.[46]

Reading this passage of Charney's book had me thinking once again that had I lived in Queens in the early 1930s, I would have been in this salon along with them.

I went on to locate the remaining passages of Charney's book relating to Ruby and Rose cited in the index. Equally moving, they continued to answer questions I'd had. Charney recounted that there had been a group of four close friends, all of whom volunteered to fight in Spain: Charney, Ruby, someone named Joel, and Sidney Babsky—Ruby's other best friend, whose last name I had not previously known. Babsky made it to Spain and wrote the letter to Charney discussed earlier, extolling Ruby's character as a soldier. But the Communist Party recruiting office rejected Joel and Charney's applications, Joel's due to illness and Charney's because the Party had bigger plans for him. He was assigned to run the Party's Harlem Division.

More important than divulging Sidney's last name, Charney wrote that Sidney was killed in Spain—among those brutally murdered after having been captured and suffering a lengthy period of imprisonment. As I read this, I thought back to a perplexing, undated letter I'd come across in the Briefcase that my five-year-old mother had written to Sidney, which had previously made no sense to me. In her little kid's handwriting, she had written:

Dear Sydney, How are you feeling? I am sorry you are in prison. Come back to America and have a happy time here. Bring some of the Spanish Children and see Mary and Mose and me.... Get out of prison soon.

I now understood that my mother hadn't been making it up.

In his book Charney wrote that the Party had also assigned him to tell Rose and Ruby's parents, as well as Sidney's family, that Ruby and Sidney were dead.

> I received the cable from Bill Lawrence, who was commissar of the [Lincoln] Brigade. Ruby was dead, and it was my duty to break the news to Rose and the family. From Brunete to the Ebro retreat the death toll had mounted staggeringly; there was hardly a Communist family that did not have a relative or friend on the casualty lists. We glowed over the news stories of the heroism and leadership of such men as Steve Nelson, Johnny Gates ... and so many others, and wept over the dead. The quick and the dead. But Ruby? It couldn't be true. We held a moving tribute in Queens, and a thousand people came to mourn and clench their fists. We could almost accept the cost; we had fascism to fight and we were dedicated. But what of Ruby's folks? He was their only son. The old man knew nothing of politics, of communism, or of the cultural interests of his son. He was a businessman, something of a buccaneer on Seventh Avenue, in the fur trade; and yet they were exceedingly fond of each other and spoke in a family language all their own. How could we measure or mitigate his loss?[47] Charney, himself, was broken-up over Ruby's death. Nine years later he named his daughter Ruth after Ruby.

As I prepared to read the entirety of Charney's personal account, I suspected that it would provide important insights into questions I'd failed to explore with Harry during our many talks, including how he had felt when the Party abandoned its anti-fascism policy in 1939 after he'd answered the call to risk his life in Spain and so many of his friends had been killed there. Further, rightly or wrongly I thought the path Charney had traveled was likely similar to the one Ruby would have followed had he returned from Spain. For me, Charney became a stand-in for the grandfather I'm named after. His autobiography would offer clues as to how Ruby might have reacted to the Party's dizzying policy reversals, and what he might have done had he not been killed in 1937 at the age of thirty-two. I went on to read every page of Charney's life story with that in mind.

Much of what I learned, or deduced, from Charney's book was depressing. His autobiography was a stinging indictment of the Communist Party and an unsparing, self-critical examination of his own role in the Party leadership over the course of the twenty-five-year period beginning in 1933, when he and Ruby joined, until 1958, when Charney finally abandoned the sunken ship.

Before joining the Party, Charney attended the Wharton School at the University of Pennsylvania and then went on to get a law degree. He explained that three things drew him to the Communist Party and dramatically diverted his career path: (1) the ravages of the Depression, which highlighted the gross wealth disparity in this country and the ineffectiveness of American government; (2) the rise of fascism, especially Hitler's ascension in 1933; and (3) the Scottsboro case. More than eighty years ago, Charney highlighted what many white Americans living today are only now discovering, and referring to as "structural racism" and "white privilege":

> Scottsboro was a transforming experience. It dramatically illustrated the evil institution of Jim Crow that was not only

embedded in our social structure but in the hearts of the white majority of which I was a part. I could not view it objectively as a social problem. It became a personal problem as well, which forced me to purge myself of the moral guilt of years of indifference and insensitivity and hence complicity with this immoral condition.[48]

Charney's eloquent words meshed with the description of Ruby's idealism in the Lipkaner biography and in the obituaries highlighting his role in the campaign to end racial discrimination at Queens General Hospital. Ruby had likely been drawn to the Party by the same causes that motivated his friend George—especially because, as Charney recounted, Ruby and Rose were the ones who had led him on the road to joining the Party. Once again, I was feeling encouraged about my ancestry.

But while I would have liked to think, and at one time had believed, that these humanist passions were all that had attracted Ruby to communism, Charney quickly disabused me of that notion. Making notes of key passages in his autobiography, I hesitated to write down his ensuing ode to Marxism, which spoiled my idealized belief—my hope—that my grandparents' involvement in the Communist Party was driven only by their commitment to anti-fascism, anti-racism, and elevating the poor—causes we still uphold—rather than abstract Marxist political and economic theory, now so thoroughly discredited after its perversion in the Soviet Union: "Marxism provided the key to our understanding of the social disorders of our times, as the party provided the means to overcome these disorders and lead mankind to a new form of social existence."[49]

And right from the start, the Soviet Union loomed large in Charney's mind, and thus, it seems fair to deduce, in the minds of my grandparents. He explained that standing in stark contrast to the broken capitalist system in the United States was the young U.S.S.R.:

The Soviet Union was living proof that its materialistic philosophy was laying the foundation of a new society, free of tensions and antagonisms, and of a new type of man....

We had no difficulty in dismissing contradictory accounts for they were obviously inspired by anti-Soviet prejudice.[50]

Charney was fairly typical in this regard, as Marxism—and the U.S.S.R.'s living testament to its truth—was a magnet for many young American Communists who joined the Party in the midst of the Depression. Indeed, as one former Communist explained: "I didn't join the Communist Party because of starvation or Depression. I joined because a new world was coming, and I wanted to be part of it. And if you wanted to be part of that world in 1935 you became a Communist."[51]

One of the most striking aspects of Charney's account—and, in my mind, of the history of the Communist Party in America—was that so many brilliant recruits like Charney and my grandparents cast aside and suppressed their questions and doubts about the ever-changing party line emanating from Moscow. They became addicted, impervious to facts—"dismissing contradictory accounts." As Charney explained:

> It was not long after I joined the party that I came to accept each doctrine promulgated by the party as an "article of faith," never to be questioned. Somehow, somewhere, the element of faith extricated itself from its scientific embodiment to dominate our outlook and ultimately proved our undoing.
>
> At the time, all doubts had been resolved. I had become dedicated to the movement. Not the least important was the fact that I was in the company of my dearest friends [i.e., Ruby and Rose].[52]

Here again, Charney was far from alone. Vivien Gornick, whose *Romance of American Communism* was based on her extensive interviews of former Communists, explained that the Marxist vision of the world induced people "to become not only attached but addicted. While under its influence, no reward of life, neither love nor fame nor wealth could compete."[53] As one former Communist reported to her: "There was a time in my life when the Party was everything.... I would have left my wife if necessary. I thought to myself, she can always get another husband but there's only one Party."[54]

The attitude of another former Party member toward her child brought to mind my grandparents' abandonment of my mother: "Didn't I feel I had to stay home and care for the child? No, I guess I didn't. I was on fire to go, and nothing was as real to me as that fire burning inside me. So I left my kid with his father, with my mother, with neighbors, anybody."[55]

For Charney and other American Communists, including my grandparents, the Party quickly came to dominate and encapsulate their lives. One former Communist explained that the Party "was a total world, from the schools to which I sent my children to family mores to social life to the quality of our friendships to the doctor, the dentist, and the cleaner.... No one who didn't live through it can understand what it was like or why it was so hard to give up."[56]

Their commitment to the Party left little permissible room for other pursuits or passions, as reflected in Charney's account of an incident involving Ruby: "I had met Hattie only recently.... She came at the right moment—when I had decided to give up my bohemian ways that seemed to violate my mission in the party. Only recently Ruby and I had been reprimanded for our discreditable behavior."[57] I speculated that the "bohemian ways" that violated Charney's mission to the Party, and the "discreditable behavior" for which he and Ruby were reprimanded, may have involved their devotion to, and late-night discussions of, literature and art.

My speculation was on solid ground. One former Party member recounted that he'd been criticized for reading Faulkner and going out with "non-party girls." Another was told to stop seeing his own sister because she was taking a course at NYU with a politically undesirable professor. An accomplished pianist gave up playing because of the guilt she experienced due to the conflict between her obligations to the Party and her love of the piano.[58]

It now made sense to me that Ruby had suddenly abandoned his passion for writing poetry after joining the Party. As for so many others, in the conflict between his devotion to the Party and his love of poetry, the Party won out.

Things went steadily awry for the U.S. Party in the years after Ruby died. Charney described his reaction to the Nazi-Soviet Non-Aggression Pact:

> The signing of the Nazi-Soviet pact in August of 1939 ... came as a complete shock ...
> The shock was due in large part to the fact that we had become totally committed to the anti-fascist struggle. The agony of Spain, events in Germany, the frightful anticipation of the world war, all of these had filled us with an implacable hatred of Hitlerism. The pact left us limp and confused ...
> And yet, in spite of these shattering experiences, our faith held. The Soviet Union could not be wrong. It was still the socialist fatherland, the only force that could save the world from catastrophe. **We managed to submerge our doubts.**[59] [emphasis mine]

The more I read of Charney's self-criticism and soul-searching, the more I got the sense that the Communist Party was essentially a cult, with Stalin as the cult leader. It was an autocratic organization fueled by constant proselytizing—and, as I would soon learn, one that aggressively maintained control over its subjects. But what was most striking and perplexing to me was that while I had previously assumed that cults tended to prey on the young, the uneducated, and/or the devoutly religious, many of the people indoctrinated by the Communist Party—including Charney, Ruby, Rose, and Harry—were among the smartest, most educated, and, at one time, intellectually curious people in the country. Looking back, Charney repeatedly expressed amazement that they had so blindly accepted and parroted the "party line," even when it defied reality: "How we, presumably intelligent people, persisted all these years in accepting and perpetuating this myth is beyond me."[60]

The respect and admiration I had so recently gained for the U.S. Communist Party when I first read about the great causes it had championed in the 1930s were now gone. A sense of anger for the Soviet-controlled cult was brewing within me. And yet still to come was perhaps the most disturbing part of the story: the brutal discipline the Party used to maintain control over its faithful members and to destroy anyone who dared to question the party line.

Reflecting on the post–World War II period of "Reconstitution," when Stalin was determined to reestablish a disciplined, unitary world outlook, Charney explained:

> Following reconstitution, however, no latitude was permitted. The most dangerous enemy was ideological heresy, and the party was alert to the slightest hint of deviation....

The polemics were sharp and even savage. In the new atmosphere a form of witch-hunting developed in defense of ideology that warped our approach to people and ideas.[61]

As Charney recounted, Party members stayed mum as they watched previously revered senior members of the Soviet Party put on trial and executed at Stalin's behest. And closer to home, they remained silent and loyal to the U.S. Party as friends were put on trial based on spurious charges, expelled from the Party, disgraced, and ostracized.

As one former Communist put it:

> It wasn't that we didn't feel badly when someone was expelled. We did. Very badly. But party discipline had at all costs to be upheld, defended. This was a fundamental no one questioned. And when someone was expelled it was because—and this we could always see clearly—Party discipline was being threatened.
>
> Now the thing is this: you felt badly, sometimes so badly you became nearly ill. But you got over it.[62]

Charney, who rose to become chairman of the New York County chapter, turned the lens on himself: "We all served as hatchet men in one way or another, or found willing subordinates to wield the axes while we stood aloof." The few who "ventured to utter independent ideas were soon excommunicated ... We deviated not an inch from the line of the Cominform and its tortured analysis of events."[63]

Moreover, excommunication meant not only expulsion from the Party, but banishment from the community, as the deviants were shunned by longstanding friends. One woman recalled that after she and her husband quit the Party in 1958, her former comrades crossed the street when they saw her coming. "It was as though I had some contagious disease."[64]

As I read these accounts, I thought about Harry and Rose—who, like Charney, appeared to have continued to toe the party line, with Harry teaching *Das Kapital* at the Jefferson School after its formation in 1943. And I thought about what Ruby would have done had he returned from Spain. I wondered whether he and Charney, such close friends who could probably talk about anything, might have resolved to stand up together to challenge the party line and policies. But I concluded that any such hopeful speculation was naive, and that Ruby would in all likelihood have followed the same path as Charney. Even more troubling, I feared that had I been alive and a member of the Party, I, too, could very well have gone along with the flock, lacking the courage to speak out and face the inevitable: brutal expulsion and disgrace. Now, however, having learned even more about the tortuous history of the Party, I'm not sure what Ruby, or I, would have done.

As Stalin and thus the Communist Parties in this country and elsewhere became increasingly intolerant of any hint of dissent in the postwar years, a growing number of intellectuals left the Party.[65] 1950 saw the publication in England of *The God That Failed*, a powerful collection of autobiographical essays by six world-renowned intellectuals chronicling their prior attraction and devotion to the Communist Parties in Germany, Italy, and the United States, followed by their disillusionment and break from communism. The authors included such luminaries as Arthur Koestler, André Gide, and Richard Wright, whose "I Tried to Be a Communist" article, previously published in 1944, was one of the essays in the collection.[66] *The God That Failed* sold more than

160,000 copies in English in its first four years and was published in sixteen languages.[67]

The U.S. Communist Party also suffered a decline in African American membership—which, for Charney, as it might have been for Ruby, was "perhaps the most disillusioning and heartbreaking episode of this period."[68] The persecution of suspected Communists during the McCarthy era and the criminal trials of Party leaders under the Smith Act took a further toll. Adding to these blows, the Party cannibalized itself, as it engaged in its own vicious campaign to weed out weak links.[69]

Would Ruby, the dormant poet and civil rights activist, have been among the disaffected intellectuals who abandoned the Party? It's impossible to know, but I tend to doubt it. Because through it all, many American Communists, including those Ruby was closest to—Charney and Rose, as well as Harry—remained in the fold. They continued to submerge their doubts and adhere to Moscow's dictates, dismissing all contrary facts as "anti-Soviet propaganda." As Charney explained, they worshipped Stalin, who they saw as "the central, dominating figure of our generation. He was half-man, half-myth, the soul of the revolution and socialism ... over the years Stalin provided the unfailing guide to all of us, and in each crisis we waited eagerly for him to speak."[70]

And even after Stalin's death in 1953, they remained loyal to the Party—impervious to facts; accepting and parroting the implausible party line handed down from Moscow.

It Was All in the Manual

Of all the sources I read about the history of the U.S. Communist Party, the most eye-opening was one of the very last I stumbled upon on the internet: *The Communist Party: A Manual on Organization*. Published in 1935, this 132-page tome is stunning in both its granular detail and the brazen way in which it unveils the organization, policies, and seditious goal of the U.S. Party, as well as the rules by which members were required to live. Unfortunately, much of what I'd been wondering about my grandparents fell into place as I made my way through the *Manual*.

I could find no record of the *Manual* ever having been updated, and didn't recall seeing any reference to it in the books I'd read about the Party. So I wondered whether it was actually used and, if so, for how long. But given how closely the *Manual* matched what I'd learned about the conduct of Party members, and that the Preface was signed by Jack Stachel, a senior Party official, I was inclined to believe that the *Manual* accurately reflected the Party's governance structure, policies, and requirements. Moreover, I realized that the notes in Ruby's little black organizer's loose-leaf notebook closely tracked the dictates of the *Manual*, and suspected that he—as well as Rose and, in all probability, Harry—had read it.

Stachel's preface explained that "much of the material used ... as the basis for this *Manual*, was, it is true, available, but is scattered in many documents over a period of years." He wrote that the *Manual* was needed because the majority of the U.S. Party members had joined since 1933, and there were "many new comrades with little organizational experience assum[ing] leading positions in the lower Party organizations"—i.e., comrades like Ruby. "Hence, many mistakes are made all over again by the new functionaries."[71] The preface concluded by emphasizing the need for every Party member to read the *Manual*—"especially every comrade holding a post of responsibility."[72]

The *Manual*'s first chapter—"Fundamentals of the Party Program"—openly announced that "the Communist Party of the U.S.A. leads the working class in the fight for the revolutionary overthrow of capitalism ... [and] for the establishment of a Socialist Soviet Republic in the United States." It was sobering for me to think that this is what Ruby, Rose, Harry, and Irving had signed up for. And I thought back to Ruby's fiery Yiddish letters.

The *Manual* explained that certain conditions would need to exist before the capitalist system could be "overthrown." Most importantly, a majority of the class-conscious workers would need to "understand the necessity for revolution and be ready to sacrifice their lives for it."[73] Reflecting the paternalism that pervaded the entire document, the *Manual* provided that for that to happen the workers "must have a Communist Party which leads them in their struggles ... and teaches the workers the lessons that should be learned in their struggles."[74] A far cry from Ruby's comical description of the Lincoln Brigade's collegial "training" meetings in his May 12 letter to Rose, in which he proclaimed the Republicans' superiority over the fascist army: "Our way is to develop military understanding through open discussion and lectures. Every soldier is taught in such a way that he is able to understand and think alongside of his officers. We never say 'Do this!'"

In order to achieve its revolutionary goal of overthrowing the capitalist system, the *Manual* stressed that the Party would need to mobilize not only the "workers"—the proletariat—but their "allies."[75] Along with farmers, it identified African Americans as among the most essential "allies" of the working class, and highlighted the role of the Communist Party in leading "the mass of 13,000,000 Negro People in their struggle against national oppression ... as the only Party which is courageously and resolutely carrying on a struggle against the double exploitation and national oppression of the Negro people ... [the Communist Party] can win over the great masses of Negro people as allies of the proletariat against the American bourgeoisie."[76]

As I read this, I wondered whether the Communist Party had been invested in fighting racism because of a genuine belief in the cause, or merely because it was a necessary means to obtaining the critical mass the Party needed to mount its revolution. Was that why it had jumped into the Scottsboro case and made it such a cause célèbre—as one commentator has suggested?[77]

Reading the *Manual* through my twenty-first-century eyes and thinking about my grandparents, the section entitled "International Solidarity" was chilling:

> The Soviet Union is the only fatherland of workers all over the world ... It is the most important factor for the liberation of all workers in every country. Therefore, the workers all over the world must help the Soviet Union in building socialism, and must defend it with all their power against the attacks of the capitalist powers.[78]

Chapter two, entitled "Basic Principles of Party Organization," laid bare the militaristic structure and operation of the Party. The *Manual* provided that the Party was organized on the basis of something called "democratic centralism," under which "the lower Party committees and all Party members ... have the duty of carrying out the decisions of the higher Party committees and of the Communist International."[79] As the *Manual* explained: "Party discipline is observed ... because only those who agree with the program of the Communist Party and the C.I. [Communist International] can become members of the Party."[80]

As for the "democratic" aspect of democratic centralism, the *Manual* provided assurance that "free discussion on questions of Party policy ... is the fundamental right of every Party member as a principal point of Party democracy."[81] It was immediately obvious, however, that this nod to democracy was farcical, as the *Manual* cautioned:

> It is clear, however, that basic principles and decisions, such as, for example, the Program of the Communist International cannot be questioned in the Party....
>
> We do not question the political correctness of the decisions, resolutions, etc., of the Executive Committee of the C.I. ... or of the Central Committee after they are ratified.[82]

As I read this and other sections of the *Manual*, I repeatedly told myself that they certainly hadn't been hiding the ball as to what was required—demanded—of those joining the Party. And the chapter on "Rules and Methods for Disciplinary Cases" made clear that failure to adhere to the party line would not be tolerated. It provided that charges could be made by any Party member or committee, and that "a member must submit to examination by any Party body even when no definite charges are communicated to him."[83] Reading the *Manual* confirmed my hunch that the independent-thinking Robert Oppenheimer—openly skeptical of Stalin's autocratic regime—had testified truthfully when he insisted that he had never been a member of the Communist Party.

The *Manual*'s section relating to "self-criticism" was particularly enlightening with respect to Ruby. It explained that "Self-criticism is the most important means for developing Communist consciousness and thereby strengthening discipline and democratic socialism." It emphasized that "without pointing out and exposing openly and honestly, as Bolsheviks should do, the shortcomings and mistakes in our work, we block our road to progress."[84]

I now realized that the passages in Ruby's little black organizer's loose-leaf criticizing various aspects of his Queens Section's operation were probably not, as I'd believed, merely a salutary product of his personality or personal leadership style. He was following the mandatory playbook. And once again, the *Manual* firmly circumscribed what and who could, and could not, be criticized:

> We should make it very clear that there are two kinds of criticism: one, which on the basis of the line of the Party ... analyzes mistakes and shortcomings, and offers concrete proposals for improvement in the work of the organization or individual member. This is Bolshevik self-criticism—constructive criticism.... The other is the kind of criticism which is based on distortion of the line of the Party.... This is destructive criticism.[85]

The *Manual*'s third chapter—"Structure and Functions of the Party Organization"—shed more light but also raised more questions as to what had been driving my grandparents. It began by identifying the important points where the Communist Party "must work untiringly so as to fulfill the task of winning the majority of the working class for the struggle against capitalism." After listing the big factories, mines, docks, railroads, and unions, the *Manual* pointed to the "Negro organizations," presumptuously claiming that "the Communist Party through well-functioning fractions" in Black churches, fraternal and cultural institutions "leads the fight for the special interests of Negroes (against discrimination, segregation) for the liberation struggle of the Negro people." And again, the overriding goal:

> The main strategic aim of the Communist Party is to win the majority of the working class for the proletarian revolution. In order to achieve this aim the Communist Party establishes closely knit organizations everywhere workers work for their living (factory), where they live (neighborhood) ... [and] where they are organized for satisfying their cultural desires (club, sports, and cultural organizations).[86]

Here again, my mind turned to the question of why Ruby had joined the Party: Did he enlist for humanitarian reasons and get hooked on the Marxist drive for revolution? Or was he first attracted to the Communist Party doctrine and then just went along to support the good causes the Party championed—one of which, anti-fascism, would cost him his life? I also wondered whether Ruby and Harry had joined for the same reasons.

Based on all I'd read about Ruby, I still wanted to think—and still do believe now—that he was driven, at least in the first instance, by an irrepressible humanist desire to join the fight against poverty, racism, and fascism, for which the Party was an obvious vehicle given its leadership role battling these evils. Probably unfairly, I was less sure about Harry, the Jefferson School professor and Marxist theorist. In any event, regardless of which came first—either the Communist Party's strategic agenda to pull off the revolution, or the American causes it was championing—Ruby was following, and playing an active role in the Party's game plan. The part of the *Manual* entitled "The Party Organizations" showed exactly where he fit in.

This chapter revealed the labyrinthine organizational structure of the U.S. Communist Party and how the leadership micromanaged its numerous components. The *Manual* detailed the roles, authority, and obligations of each of the various Party organizations and their leaders. They ranged from the small Shop and Street Units in each territory at the bottom of the ladder, to the Sections above them, which, in turn, were overseen by District Committees that reported to the National Convention, the Central Committee, and, of course, sitting on top of the heap, the Soviet-dominated Executive Committee of the Communist International. The *Manual* stated explicitly that the decisions of the Executive Committee were "binding for all parties belonging to the Comintern and must be promptly carried out."[87]

There seemed to be no detail too small for inclusion in the 132-page *Manual*—including, for example, how agendas for the mandatory meetings at every level of the Party were micromanaged:

> The first point should always be a well-prepared discussion on a certain actual political problem.... A well-organized, well-prepared discussion should not last longer than from one to one and a half hours.
>
> The next point on the agenda should be the checkup of the assignments of the individual members.[88]

Ruby's obituaries confirmed that he had been the Section Organizer for the Third Assembly District of Queens County. Until I read the *Manual*, I had no idea what that meant. But his role and responsibilities were specified in minute detail here. The Section Organizer was an elected officer and the head of the Section Committee, responsible for the performance of all the Shop and Street Units within the territory of the Section. As the *Manual* provided: "He is the leader not only of the Party organization in the territory of the Section, but also must be or become a leader of the masses in the territory where the Section is operating."[89] The Section Committee was charged with holding weekly meetings, with the agenda once again prescribed.

The *Manual* spelled out the authority of the leaders at each level of the Party—and the limits of their authority. The order of command could not have been clearer:

> All Party organizations may decide on local questions independently insofar as these decisions do not conflict with any decision of the higher Party organizations....
>
> The Section, District and Central Committees ... always have the right to approve or disapprove any decision of the lower organizations.[90]

In other words, Ruby had been a big fish in a relatively small pond—one of many overseen and ruled by Joseph Stalin.

In the section laying out the "conditions for membership," the *Manual* reprinted a pledge read by Earl Browder to 2,000 workers initiated to the Party in 1935:

> I now take my place in the ranks of the Communist Party ... I pledge myself to spare no effort in uniting the workers in militant struggle against fascism and war ... I solemnly pledge to take my place in the forefront of the struggle for Negro rights; against Jim Crowism and lynching, against the chauvinist lies of the ruling class. I pledge myself to rally the masses to defend the Soviet Union, the land of victorious socialism. I pledge myself to remain at all times a vigilant and firm defender of the Leninist line of the Party, the only line that insures the triumph of Soviet Power in the United States.[91]

The *Manual* also noted that "Our party application carries this declaration": "The undersigned declares his adherence to the program and statutes of the C.I. and the Communist Party of the U.S.A. and agrees to the discipline of the Party and to engage actively in its work."[92]

I wondered if Ruby, Rose, Harry, and Irving had taken this pledge or signed such a declaration. Regardless, I had little doubt that they knew, in joining the Party, that they were taking a huge step and committing their lives to the Party. I now understood the significance of Rose's handwritten notes on Ruby's "Ode to FDR" poem and thirteen-page essay recording that they were written prior to joining the Party. Ruby and Rose may have subscribed to the views espoused by the Party for a number of years before 1933 as their discussion group met in Sunnyside, but actually enlisting was a very big deal.

Indeed, the section of the *Manual* entitled "Transfers" made clear that the Party would control even where they lived: "If a member of the Party moves from one place to another, he must secure a transfer from the Party organization before he moves. No Party member has the right to leave his Unit without permission."[93]

Even more stringent obligations were placed upon the "cadres" in each Unit, which presumably included Section leaders like Ruby and Jefferson School teachers and union organizers like Harry. Such a "professional revolutionist" was a Party member who "gives his whole life to the fight ... ready to go whenever and wherever the Party sends him ... They accept Party assignments—the matter of family associations and other personal problems are considered but are not decisive. If the class struggle demands it, he will leave his family for months, even years."[94]

So, it is not surprising that Harry—and even Ruby, who had a wife and young child—heeded the Party's call to leave home to fight in Spain during the period when anti-fascism was temporarily in vogue in Moscow.

The concluding section of the *Manual*, "For the Bolshevization of the Party," carried a stark admonition: "Every Communist must know that the Party has a historic mission to fulfill ... that it has the mission of organizing and leading the masses for the revolutionary overthrow of capitalism, and for the establishment of the new world, a Soviet America."[95]

As I finished reading and reflected on the *Manual* as a whole, it occurred to me that nowhere in the *Manual*, or in anything else I'd read, was there an indication as to *how* this "overthrow" would be accomplished in the United States, or what would become of America's democracy if the revolution were successful. The otherwise explicit and exhaustive *Manual* masked a huge potential conflict looming for my grandparents and other American Communists: the glaring contradiction between the Soviet

Communist model to which they'd pledged their allegiance, and not just capitalism, but their *democracy*.

My grandparents were repeatedly forced to choose between their loyalty to the Party and their other passions, loves, and obligations. In each case they resolved the conflict by bowing to the demands of the Party: Ruby abandoned his family to heed the Party's summons to Spain, crushing his parents and leaving his five-year-old daughter fatherless; Rose, like Ruby, defaulted in her obligations as a parent, depositing my mother at the Lakewood Modern School so she could bury herself in her work for the Party; Rose also abandoned her painting, while Ruby sacrificed his passion for poetry in deference to the Party; and those who lived on after Ruby's death likely abandoned and ostracized friends who were excommunicated by the Party and, more generally, closed their otherwise intelligent minds to reality in order to accept and adhere to the ever-changing party line.

But the looming conflict between democracy and communism seems to have remained unspoken. I wondered whether my grandparents and Irving had considered and agonized over the questions that seemed obvious to me, such as: Would the "militant" struggle to ensure the "triumph of Soviet Power in the United States" take the form of a violent uprising, akin to the 1917 Russian Revolution? Would the touted "revolutionary overthrow of capitalism" to create "Soviet America" also entail the overthrow of the American democratic system, to be replaced by the U.S.S.R.'s autocratic model under the leadership of the all-knowing Communist Party?

Perhaps I'm just naive and it's obvious that Ruby, Rose, Harry, and Irving had crossed the Rubicon, having had no trouble with the prospect of discarding the American democratic system in exchange for the Soviet Union's communist utopian model. But I'm not so sure. In fact, I doubt it.

The U.S. Communist Party's success in luring young Americans like Ruby, Rose, Harry, and Irving in the early 1930s occurred only when the Party began to downplay its theoretical Marxist messaging and to instead take the lead in advocating for Americans ravaged by the Depression. Its United Front policy, launched in 1935, entailed joining together with democratic governments like FDR's United States to oppose fascist dictators intent on quashing democracies. In beckoning young men like Ruby and Harry to take up arms in Spain, the Communists heralded the icons of American democracy, naming the units in which Ruby and Harry fought the George Washington and Abraham Lincoln Brigades.[96] And, as I'd seen in their letters attempting to make sense of Ruby's death, Rose and other American Communists trumpeted that he'd died in the quest to preserve "democracy"—likening the young Americans who died in Spain to Nathan Hale and others who had sacrificed themselves for the cause of freedom and democracy in the American Revolution.

To my relief, despite the *Manual*'s repeated references to the "revolution" and the "militant overthrow of capitalism," I never saw any reference to a violent overthrow of the American government. Earl Browder, the head of the U.S. Party, repeatedly stated that the Communists did not advocate the use of force, were not conspiring to overthrow the country's democratic government, and would help to crush any group that attempted to overthrow or weaken American democracy.[97] And Vivian Gornick, who grew up among Communists and wrote *The Romance of American Communism* based on her interviews of former Party members, made a similar observation:

> Never once did I have the impression that anyone around me wanted to see the government overthrown by violence. On the contrary: I saw them working to see socialism become the norm through a change in the law; a change that would insure that with the defeat of capitalism, the American democracy would keep its broken promise of equality for all.[98]

I very much doubt that Joseph Stalin shared this view, however; he was just biding his time. I wondered what my grandparents would have done if at some point Stalin had decreed "The time for the revolution has come!" and ordered American Party members to take up arms or otherwise support campaigns of sabotage and insurrection to accomplish the "revolutionary overthrow of capitalism for the establishment ... of a Socialist Soviet Republic in the United States"?[99] Would that have been the *one time* when Ruby, Rose, Harry, and Irving—or any of them—finally said "no más" and defied the Party's command? The one conflict in which their fealty to the Party would not win out?

It never came to that. Ironically, the only plot to overthrow the U.S. government by means of an armed insurrection was mounted *not* by the Communists but by far-right white nationalists acting in league with German Nazis in 1941.[100] Nevertheless, one person who firmly believed that the Communist Party meant what it said when it spoke of taking over the U.S. government was J. Edgar Hoover. As his biographer, Beverly Gage, has written of Hoover's views in the 1940s: "Though he could not yet prove his allegations, Hoover came away from the war convinced that the Communist Party and the Soviet Union were actively seeking to undermine the U.S. government from within."[101]

Throughout the early 1940s, the FBI engaged in a surveillance campaign targeting the Communist Party, planting bugs and wiretaps in Party offices and cultivating human informants. Hoover secretly accelerated those surveillance efforts beginning in 1944, when he came to believe that a serious Soviet espionage scheme was underway.[102] Proof that the Soviets were indeed running a substantial espionage network in this country emerged, largely due to the interception and decryption of thousands of encrypted cables bound for Moscow. Codenamed "Venona," the decryption program led to the discovery that a Soviet agent, Klaus Fuchs, was embedded inside the secret Manhattan project led by Robert Oppenheimer.[103] It also revealed that, among hundreds of others, Julius Rosenberg was engaged in the Soviet espionage efforts.[104] Finally, as time went on, Hoover's FBI engaged in increasingly aggressive tactics to disrupt and sow dissent within the Communist Party, including working to instigate anger between white and Black activists.[105]

The Communist Party of the United States never achieved the critical mass necessary to mount its revolutionary overthrow of capitalism. It continued to lose members, Joseph Stalin died, and his successor, Nikita Khrushchev, proceeded to drop the bomb that decimated the Party.

Khrushchev's Bomb

For more than two decades, American Communists like Charney, Rose, and Harry continued to toe the party line—submerging their doubts, remaining impervious to facts, and dismissing all contradictory accounts as, in Charney's words, "obviously inspired by anti-Soviet prejudice."[106] Nothing could shake the Soviet-controlled Party's ironclad grip on their lives. Their illusions were shattered only by the Party itself, when Nikita Khrushchev gave what became known as the "Secret Speech" at the 20th Congress of the Communist Party of the Soviet Union on February 25, 1956, three years after Stalin's death.

I had heard about the Secret Speech from my parents, and seen references to it over the years as a cataclysmic event that caused the implosion of the Communist Party. I vaguely understood that Khrushchev had accused Stalin of being a mass murderer, but I never knew what he actually said. Although the speech was never published, I found a transcript on the Wilson Center Digital Archive.[107] Ten pages long, it was indeed explosive.

Khrushchev began by noting that Vladimir Lenin had warned that Stalin was guilty of an abuse of power and urged that he be removed as Secretary General of the Party. Khrushchev then launched into a detailed exposé of the crimes Stalin had committed. He explained that whoever disagreed with Stalin or "tried to prove his viewpoint ... was doomed to removal from the leading collective and to subsequent moral and physical annihilation." The only proof against those branded as "enemies of the people" were the confessions of the accused themselves—confessions "acquired through physical pressures against the accused."

Khrushchev then proceeded to back up his accusations with data and specific examples. He told the congress that "of the 139 members of the party's Central Committee who were elected at the 17th Congress [held in 1934], 98 persons, that is, 70 percent, were arrested and shot (mostly in 1937–38)." And, of 1,966 delegates to the 17th Party Congress 1,108 were arrested. Khrushchev castigated Stalin's "mass repressions," which had been justified by the "slogan of a fight against the Trotskyites"—when, in fact, there was no genuine threat and "there was no basis for mass terror in the country." He said that when the cases against the "so-called spies and saboteurs were examined it was found that all their cases were fabricated," and that the confessions of the accused had been "gained with the help of cruel and inhuman tortures." Khrushchev then went on to list individual cases of once-respected leaders who had been deposed and killed based on sham confessions.

Finally, Khrushchev took direct aim at Stalin's "cult of personality" that had so captivated Charney and other Communists in this country and around the world. Referring to Stalin's "mania for greatness," he asserted that Stalin had "lost consciousness of reality," a problem that had infected the Soviet Union's relations with other nations. He pledged: "We must abolish the cult of the individual decisively, once and for all."

The speech was intended to remain secret, as Khrushchev admonished his audience: "We cannot let this matter get out of the party, especially not to the press." Nevertheless, news of the explosive revelations leaked out in the months that followed. Communists in this country and around the world were shocked—and crushed. One former Party member recounted that the news of the speech "struck me like lightning." Another reported that after Khrushchev dropped the "bomb", "everybody knew nobody knew what to do, but everybody needed comfort real bad. Everybody needed to huddle and try to figure out what our lives had been all about and what we do with them from here on in."[108]

As David Ross, a Party member from 1941 to 1956, explained:

> For sixteen years ... I was suffused with the dogma of Communism. It was the air I breathed, the food I ate, the wine I drank. My studies, my marriage, my friendships were all strained through the liquid flow of Marxist thought before they entered my brain and my feelings. That flow seemed to me alive with chemical being, essential matter. It contained everything necessary to life.
>
> In 1956, after the Khrushchev Report, the flow dried up, and I found myself living in a world that for me had turned arid, barren and bitter as gall. I ceased functioning entirely.[109]

But as Charney explained, despite having long worshipped Stalin, paradoxically there was widespread "readiness" within the U.S. Party to accept Khrushchev's stunning revelations:

> Despite our glorification of Stalin, certain doubts had accumulated over the years, some of which we expressed, most of which remained unspoken. They had sunk deep into our consciousness to cause occasional disquiet and anguish—the trials of the thirties, the Nazi-Soviet pact....
>
> The revelations suddenly brought all the accumulated debris in our minds to the surface and gave them order, consistency and meaning. Perhaps the bitterest pill of all was that we grasped the truth of the revelations not only on the basis of these events in Soviet history but on the basis of our

own experience—of the authority we exercised and abused, of our own misdeeds, of the countless numbers chastised and expelled on the flimsiest evidence.[110]

Charney's blunt self-criticism got to the crux of questions I'd been pondering as I speculated about what Harry and Rose must have thought and felt as news of Khrushchev's revelations spread and the Soviet utopia to which they had devoted their entire adult lives was exposed as a fraudulent mirage: "The revelations destroyed the spirit of idealism that animated our people ... The hardships and sacrifices of the past were now bereft of meaning and this resulted in greater disillusionment and greater losses."[111]

1956 marked the death of the U.S. Communist Party as a meaningful entity. Thirty thousand Americans quit the Party within months[112]—an exodus to which the FBI's intense campaign to disrupt and discredit the Party during this period of high vulnerability probably contributed.[113]

As for Harry and Rose, who had dedicated their lives to the Party for decades, I can only imagine that they were initially in a state of disbelief, followed by despair and probably fury. Many years later, my grandmother told my cousin Donald that she and Harry joined the Italian Communist Party, which rebuked those Communists who tried to come up with rationalizations to defend Stalinism after Khrushchev's Secret Speech.[114] She referred to the Russians as "those damn Bolsheviks!"—rather amazing, as I thought back to all the letters referring to Ruby as a "Bolshevik" in order to pay him the highest tribute.

As for Charney, despite what he referred to as the "exodus" from the U.S. Party, he, like most other senior leaders, remained onboard even after news of Khrushchev's Secret Speech filtered out. Charney "found it exceedingly difficult and painful" to cast out the last twenty-five years of his life as he harked back to the ideals that had drawn him, Ruby, and Rose to the Party.

So Charney remained in the fold after being devastated by the Khrushchev revelations, even as he argued that the Party had to move beyond Stalinism and debated those who insisted on staying the Stalinist course. The internal conflicts over what direction the Party should take were intense: "Yesterday we had been united, and now there was suddenly chaos and we fought with each other with ferocity that made a mockery of the term 'comrade.'"[115]

In attempting to make sense of how and why he hung on, Charney explained:

> I stayed because of a feeling of responsibility to others in the party.... I just could not leave in a situation in which comrades looked to me for answers, demanding, arguing, pleading until the early hours, if only to be reassured that their lives had not been wasted. They were as anxious as I to arrive at some conclusion, but they needed time and help.[116]

I wondered where Harry and Rose had stood as these battle lines intensified. Given their migration to the Italian Party—which rejected Stalinism—they were probably in Charney's camp. Charney finally resigned from the Party in 1958 after losing the battle to the Stalinist faction led by William Foster. By then, the New York branch of the Party, with a heavy contingent of Jews, had been further rocked by the disclosure of antisemitism in the Soviet Union. As Charney put it: "Our whole world was falling apart."[117]

So, what would Ruby have done? Given that he'd played a leadership role in the Party before going to Spain, it's easy enough to speculate, as I originally did, that had he lived Ruby would likely have continued to rise in the Party ranks along with his friend George, and remained in the Party with Charney for some period after 1956. But I've come realize that the history of who stayed onboard and who left the flailing U.S. Communist Party—and when—is too complicated to permit intelligent speculation as to what Ruby, or I for that matter, would have done during the many-chaptered tumult of the 1940s and 1950s. In light of what I've learned of my grandfather's personality and early interests, I feel on safer ground imagining how he might have emerged from the rubble in the years after whenever he would have left the Party.

As I read through Charney's autobiography, I eagerly awaited the final chapter—"The Aftermath." I was impatient to learn what he had done after finally resigning from the Party. Had he stayed involved in politics? Was he forlorn and bitter, obsessed that his life had been wasted? I thought the answers might give me a window into how Ruby's storyline could have gone had he returned from Spain.

Writing eight years after resigning from the Party, and in his typically introspective fashion, Charney described the painful, gradual process by which he had finally wrenched himself away from the Party—then in ashes—and looked back on his life of dedication to it. He was invited to join the Socialist Party, but declined. With a group of other former Communist Party members, he considered forming an independent group, but they couldn't agree on anything.

Charney turned back to literature—much as I imagine Ruby would have done. He began to read, including Faulkner, "rekindling the love of books" that had lain fallow for the preceding twenty-five years, during which he had digested little but party polemics. Talking about the writers he was drawn to, Charney explained: "They helped to revive and nourish the spirit of idealism that was part of our history.... Many of my friends were experiencing a similar reawakening.... The party was over; now we turned to restoring the broken fragments of our lives."[118]

As friends gathered to sort through the past and think about the way forward, Charney zeroed in on the jugular question they all struggled with but had trouble answering, or admitting the answer to: "Perhaps all the memories evoked at these meetings, of the people we knew and loved, made it difficult to arrive at a simple evaluation of our life in the party—'Was it a tragic waste?'"[119]

Ultimately, Charney rejected Marxism, and communism: "I arrived finally at the belief that one had to go beyond Marxism to discover and thereby influence the course of social development.... And so I come to the end of the journey. I joined the party because of the ethical appeal of Marxism and its vision of freedom. I left because this vision was betrayed."[120]

Charney did not answer, at least directly, the question whether his life—and those of my grandparents and so many others—had been a "tragic waste." The depressing answer seems pretty clear to me. But he did emerge with his idealism and optimism relatively intact—and with an appreciation for American democracy. Writing in 1966, he reflected in his epilogue:

> We may never achieve utopia, or the utopia I dreamed of for a lifetime; but without the utopian vision life has little meaning, nor can there be hope of change ...
>
> We are in serious trouble, here and abroad, and we need the wisdom of the ages and the fortitude to withstand and overcome it. I can't be sanguine about the outcome, but neither will I despair.
>
> I see the poverty, the violence, the corruption all around me. I also see the good and the yearning for the good, the people to be trusted and the ideas that endure ... And so I remain the optimist.[121]

As I put down Charney's book, I thought about my grandparents and my Uncle Irving in light of the canvas Charney had painted. I considered what I'd read about Ruby, and what I remembered about Harry and Rose, whom I'd seen so often as an adult even though I'd never asked them about their political past. How did they experience and handle the trauma Charney described, and how would Ruby and Irving have emerged from the ashes of the Party had they lived on?

I'd come to realize by now that such speculation was precarious business—particularly because, as Vivian Gornick observed based on her interviews of former Party members, there was no "monolithic Communist experience so there is no monolithic *ex*-Communist experience." Gornick also reported, to her surprise—and mine—that she "had expected to find a great many burnt-out souls, people who had wandered in a kind of post-passion purgatory these twenty years. I found nothing of the sort. I found, for the most part, people who had remade their lives brilliantly; people who when they could no longer organize the revolution had organized themselves."[122]

With this and everything else I'd learned bouncing around my head, and with even less confidence than I'd had before I'd delved into the history of the Communist Party, I proceeded, gingerly, to imagine how my forebears had processed the extraordinary implosion that upended their lives.

Harry

Harry had to have suffered an enormous amount of anger and pain over the course of his lifetime. He'd seen the Communist Party to which he'd sacrificed his life go up in smoke, and his only child, my Aunt Ruthie, tragically die of a drug overdose.

Having read about the bloody battles at Jarama, Brunete, and Aragon in which Harry fought and saw so many of his comrades slaughtered for the Republicans' lost cause, I initially imagined that Harry would have been bitter about the experience and permanently scarred by the debacle into which the Communist Party had lured him. And understandably, some Lincoln veterans reported being haunted by nightmares or other trauma symptoms for the rest of their lives.[123]

But I may have been wrong. A Yale psychologist's study of the Lincoln vets found that relatively few of them suffered lasting psychological damage due to their wartime experience.[124] Rather, for the vast majority of the Lincoln volunteers, "the Spanish War was the highpoint of their lives. All of them looked back on it in later years as the most clean, noble, and glorious thing they had ever done."[125] And, unimpeded by any trauma suffered in Spain, just a few years later hundreds of Lincoln volunteers, including a beaming Harry, plunged back into the war against fascism, joining the U.S. armed forces in World War II.[126]

Just as this book was about to be typeset, I stumbled upon a new piece of evidence which confirmed that Harry had good reason to look back on his experience in Spain with some pride as "the most clean, noble, and glorious thing" he had ever done. In the course of my final proofreading, I looked back at the profiles of Ruby and

Harry in his U.S. Army WWII uniform

Harry in the Lincoln Brigade Archives and noticed a section of the profiles that I had previously ignored. Entitled "Sources," it appeared to contain citations to the repositories of the information in my grandfathers' profiles—and very possibly more material about them. Two citations, in particular, stood out: "RCASPI Fond 545, Opis 6, Delo 945 II, 21-23" and "USSDA 2.0804, 58.0347." I had previously skipped over the citations because the acronyms were unintelligible to me, other than that the second seemed to be some type of U.S. government document. Now, however, I was annoyed at myself for never having attempted to investigate them. More to the point, I worried that there could be information in those source documents that would reveal that what I was about to publish was not merely incomplete, but false.

I reached out to Sebastiaan Faber, Co-Chair of the Lincoln Brigade Archives, who put me in touch with their archivist, Chris Brooks. Within a few days Brooks sent me an email attaching eleven documents from the archives relating to Ruby and Harry, as well as an obituary of Harry that had appeared in *The Volunteer*—the publication founded by the veterans of the Lincoln Brigade. Only two of the documents related to Ruby, of which only one was of any significance.[127] The remaining documents all pertained to Harry, two of which were slightly different versions of the same extraordinary report. With no title, and labeled only "52, Nobel, Harry," it was a single paragraph, excerpted from a larger document concerning other Republican soldiers, that appeared to be an assessment of Harry. It stunned me.

Whoever had written the assessment described Harry as "Exceedingly trustworthy, strongly disciplined with morale and general outlook improving under stressful conditions.... Military development good, rising to rank of sgt. in Army." Those two sentences—the only written trace of Harry in Spain or as a young man anywhere that I'd seen since beginning my research six years earlier—instantly transformed my image of the grandfather I had always pictured as an intellectual, Marxist theorist, and had been unable to visualize fighting in three of the war's bloodiest battles. I was particularly uplifted by the statement about Harry's "morale and general outlook improving under stressful conditions"—indicating that, like Ruby, Harry seemed to thrive as a soldier under fire. I could begin to visualize Harry during the perilous street fighting and hand-to-hand combat of the Aragon offensive, culminating in the collapse of the Republican army. While some of Harry's comrades threw away their guns and wandered aimlessly and alone, Harry, I now believed, was not one of them.

In response to my follow-up question, Brooks told me that "RGASPI"—the source of this mysterious document—was an acronym for the "Russian State Archive of Socio-Political History."[128] Reading this, I realized that the glowing portrait of Harry was not a mere puff piece; it was an evaluation prepared by one or more of Harry's superiors in the Soviet-controlled Communist Party—people who had no ostensible incentive to provide anything other than a frank assessment of him. I felt I could rely on it, and emerged with a new, shining image of Harry in mind. At the same time, I shuddered to think how close I'd come to selling Harry short in this book, reminded once again of the precarious nature of an attempt, particularly by an amateur like me, to reconstruct history from afar.

Harry may have sought refuge in his time presciently fighting fascism in Spain as a means of salvaging the one worthy aspect of his decades-long devotion to the Communist Party. Indeed, it's hard to imagine that Harry felt anything but disgusted about how he spent the decades following his return from Spain. He had a college degree, all his credits toward his Ph.D. in philosophy, and, according to the Lincoln Brigade Archives, he was a member of the teachers' union. It was always hard for me to understand why my scholarly and intellectually curious grandfather spent his career sewing pelts of fur to make luxury coats for wealthy women.

My mother said Harry remained on the shop floor because he didn't want to become part of management—i.e., the "ruling class." But having now read the Communist Party Manual, I think there was more to it. As the *Manual* commanded, a party member had to be "ready to go whenever and wherever the Party sends him. Today he may be working in a mine ... tomorrow, if the Party so decides, he may be in a steel mill.... They accept Party assignments."[129] Consistent with this mandate, loyal Party members were sent "into industry" to work in factories and shops in order to educate workers and recruit them to join the Communist Party.[130] I now suspect that the Party "decided" that Harry would remain a furrier and continue to serve as a union organizer—and so that's what he did for more than twenty-five years.[131] It's impossible for me to believe that Harry was not bitter when the Party that had sentenced him to life on a sewing machine was exposed as a fraud. His huge sacrifice had been for naught. I'm not sure how one processes that.

Harry at his sewing machine

On top of the trauma described by Charney, Harry had to witness the disgrace of his furriers' union. In 1973, the senior leaders of the union, then known as the Furriers Joint Council, were indicted and later convicted on charges of corruption, extortion, and racketeering, including for taking bribes and using threats of physical violence.[132] I was well aware of the case because the lead defendant, George Stofsky, the CEO of the union, was the father of one of my closest high school friends in Dobbs Ferry, New York. My friend's dad was a handsome, tall, strong, and imposing man, with a deep voice and combed-back silver hair. I remember him being sent to prison, ripped away from my friend's family.

And to compound the coincidence, many years later I learned that another friend of mine, this one a fellow partner of my law firm, knew a lot about the Stofsky case, having been a prosecutor in the U.S. Attorney's Office for the Southern District of New York. He disabused me of my wishful thinking that the case against Stofsky had been merely a groundless political hit job. And Harry didn't seem to believe it was either. While I don't remember his exact words, when I asked him about the case he immediately expressed his disgust for the "crooks" who had sullied the union that was so dear to him.

During the many years I knew Harry, I never sensed that he was anything but a liberal Democrat. But having taught *Das Kapital* at the Jefferson School and having joined the Italian Communist Party after Khrushchev's Secret Speech in 1956, I wonder whether Harry ever abandoned his faith in Marxism—as Charney ultimately did after the Stalinist party crumbled.

I also doubt that Harry emerged from the rubble of the Communist Party with George Charney's optimism. He did experience enjoyment—reading primary-source history, or working out physics problems while babysitting for Debbie and me, making us eggs-in-a-hole for breakfast in the morning. He enjoyed our family dinners, and Melissa vividly remembers Harry as warm and loving, and especially devoted to me. I sensed that he cherished the afternoons we spent together discussing history, current politics, and books when I visited their apartment on East 14th Street. Nonetheless, even before he lost his daughter my Grandpa Harry never struck me as an optimistic man.

Now knowing some of the sordid history of the Communist Party, I can understand why he may have been proud of me even though I was using my legal degree to represent the capitalist titans he'd fought so long to vanquish. What I still can't understand is how, in all of the many discussions I had with Harry about history and politics, I never once asked him about his own personal history, or what he knew about Ruby. My failure is particularly noteworthy because, as a lawyer, I have extensive experience interviewing people. I've written about techniques I've used, and others have observed that I'm unusually good at asking questions and learning about people's lives—whether friends or strangers.

I think now of the many questions I could and should have asked Harry: What led you to go to Spain? Can you tell me about the hike over the Pyrenees? What do you remember of the Battle of Brunete? How did you know Ruby, and what was he like? How did you feel when Stalin entered into the Non-Aggression Pact with Hitler? When did you start to have doubts about the Communist Party? When did you leave it, and why? The list goes on, and had I asked my grandfather even a few of the questions that now run through my mind this would have been a much shorter book with much clearer answers. The one question I don't regret never having asked Harry is how he felt when his daughter Ruthie died.

Rose

Rose retreated from her political activism at some point and went back to painting, turning out large oil paintings, lithographs, and woodcuts, several of which now hang on our apartment walls. I used to think of my grandmother as a spacy, somewhat eccentric artist and passionate lover of art history. She talked endlessly about artists and was very knowledgeable, but as senility began to set in she spoke almost exclusively about Leonardo da Vinci. Whatever the subject, my grandmother would launch into a lengthy monologue to explain that Leonardo knew all that is now known, and was responsible for all the technology we have today. At the same time, however, she was a wealth of otherwise accurate information about him, including the location of certain of his more obscure paintings.

Until reading the letters in the Briefcase, I wasn't aware that my grandmother had played any role in the Communist Party. She never discussed or even alluded to her political history in my presence. How did Rose process not only the trauma Charney described, but also the death of the husband she apparently loved very much—a husband who had lost his life fighting for a lost cause that was soon abandoned by the same Soviet-controlled Communist Party that had summoned him to it? And how did she absorb and survive the death of her second daughter, which resulted from a heroin addiction that some in the family believe Rose had unwittingly financed?

I speculate that my grandmother dealt with this enormous load by denial—by retreating, self-absorbed, into her world of art. By painting and talking about it; filibustering to avoid talking or thinking about the pain of the past. One of the last surprising discoveries on my journey seemed to confirm this speculation.

In 1990, when Rose would have been eighty years old, my cousin Donald interviewed her, as well as her two sisters—big Toby and Mildred. The hour-long video interview of Rose was recorded on a VHS tape cassette. As I watched the video wide-eyed, my grandmother came back to life. Donald, who was interested in exploring the history and life of the family during the Depression, had found the interview largely worthless, as Rose talked almost entirely about herself, regardless of the questions he asked. I had a very different reaction. Although Donald never asked my grandmother about her political past, in the course of her ramblings Rose dropped a few bombs that shed new light on her—and potentially on Ruby's death.

Wearing a deep pink suit, she sat on the edge of an ottoman in the bedroom of a Brooklyn apartment during a family gathering at which children could be heard playing in the background. Rose's memory was sharp in places, though fuzzy or faulty in several others. She was fairly lucid and animated; if her dementia had begun to set in it wasn't obvious to me. Rather, it was just my rambling grandmother exactly as I remembered her.

Asked about what life in the family had been like, Rose noted that her father Joe became very rich as his fish business boomed; that they moved to a "swanky house" with "sumptuous furniture" on Madison Avenue; and that some Wall Street report pegged Joe's net worth at $20 million (an example of where her memory was almost certainly wrong, although he was undoubtedly wealthy). But Rose quickly pivoted to a tangent about how a neighbor who got into trouble for being a Bolshevik took them on Sunday mornings to the Metropolitan Museum of Art, where she fell in love with a painting of Jesus by an artist named Fra Angelico, and how Rockwell Kent gave a trove of his paintings to Russia after he'd been spurned in this country for being a Bolshevik. She went on: "So what did Kent do? He took his whole collection and sent it to Russia and it's on the top floor of the Hermitage. Look what dopes we were!"

And then, out of the blue, my grandmother talked about her dead husband. She couldn't remember Ruby's name at first, and confused his name with mine. She said, "I married a man who's just like the one outside [i.e., at the family gathering, where the interview took place] ... I got married to Richard. Richard was a very intellectual man. He went into the Lincoln Brigade." My grandmother proceeded to paint a picture of my grandfather's death that was completely at odds with what I had always understood, and in conflict with the letter in the Briefcase written by a fellow Lincoln Brigade soldier reporting that Ruby had died of pneumonia:

> His death was a horrible death. There were two groups in the war against Franco—the Trotskyites and the Communists; he was a Communist. He got hurt on the battlefield. He was killed there. He never came back. It was a horrible death. It seems that when he was on the surgical table the Trotskyites killed him on the table and threw his body down in the cellar.
>
> There were two guys from the Brigade who were given leave and went to see him in the hospital. When they got to the hospital there was a terrible odor. They went down to the basement and found him, and they got wood and made a coffin and buried him.

I was stunned, and didn't know whether to believe Rose's detailed account. I'd seen no trace that Ruby was murdered in any letter or other document I'd read, and particularly in her later years my grandmother was known to have some elaborate fantasies. Nevertheless, this would have been a bizarre story for her to make up and, in light of the violent clashes between the Communists and the POUM—including the Communists' murder of Andreu Nin, the POUM's leader[133]—the notion that Trotskyites killed Ruby did not strike me as implausible. I could also imagine that if Ruby *was* brutally murdered, a decision could have been made to withhold that information so as not to further upset a family already devastated by his death. Indeed, Rose went on to recall how her own father, not known to be an emotional man, "wept at the breakfast table" upon learning of Ruby's death. "Tears fell into his coffee cup." On balance, however, I'm skeptical of my grandmother's account.[134]

Rose's voice was winsome, somewhat distant, as she said in a flat tone: "It was quite a tragic incident in the family—in Ruby's family [she now remembered his name] and in our family." She went on to talk about the effect of Ruby's death on my mother: "My daughter Toby was his child—it was very hard. She didn't understand that he died, but she knew he wasn't there."

And then, in words that mirrored the "Papa Went Away" story my mother had written in high school sixty years before, Rose recounted that my mother had yelled at her: "Why did you let him go? Why didn't you shut the doors, shut all the windows so that he couldn't go?!"

Rose went on:

> She was just a little kid and she'd lost her father. She didn't understand....
>
> It hurt Toby a great deal as a child. And I think to this day—I don't like to say it and never say it to her—but to this day she still bears the marks of it. I notice things she does and things she gets angry at and things she says, and it's all tied up in that package and that's all.

It apparently never occurred to Rose that my mother's anger, or any scars that she bore throughout her life, might be attributable to Rose's neglect of her, both before and after Ruby was killed. And completely absent from my grandmother's reminiscing on the tragic death of her husband was any mention of whether or how she, herself, had been devastated or impacted by Ruby's death—a horribly violent death by her account. Instead, Rose seamlessly slid into a monologue about the Art Students League and Kenneth Hayes Miller, who had written a moving letter to her (quoted earlier) shortly after Ruby's death.

Rose explained to Donald that Miller had been considered to be one of the top American artists at the time, and that anyone who was anything had studied under him at the Art Students League, including such renowned artists as Reginald Marsh and Rockwell Kent. She said that Miller "considered me a very talented person" and that at one point he instructed Marsh to "stand behind me and watch me paint." According to my grandmother, Miller then told Marsh: "You see, she has six fingers. The sixth is the brush. You should learn to use the brush in the same way she does." Hard to believe, but again, not easy to make up—and my grandmother really was talented.

Until this point in the interview Rose seemed to have studiously avoided talking about her own political past, even as she made numerous references to other "Bolsheviks." But then, unprompted, she opened up, saying: "After Ruby died I became an 'actiff.'" Although I'd never heard that term, her next words clarified its meaning: "I became a speechmaker, making speeches on street corners and collecting money against Franco. I had no time to paint." In other words, just as Ruby gave up his poetry and other Party members surrendered their musical instruments, Rose and other Communist artists laid down their brushes in order to do the Party's bidding.

My grandmother then related an extraordinary anecdote involving Kenneth Hayes Miller that revealed how she felt, looking back, about her decades of blind devotion to the Party. She explained that "a very interesting thing happened" when she went to the Frick Collection to see some art loaned to the museum by the King of Italy. She ran into Miller, who was there to see the same exhibit.

> He asked me what I was doing and I told him I was a Communist working for the Communist Party, just like that.
> Well, I thought he would faint!
> And he said something very significant. He had two people who had gone to Russia. One was the cartoonist for the *Daily Worker* and the other was studying art with him. And he said: "How could you do this? How could you give up your talent for art for what is going on there? Don't you know that they're murdering people over there? Don't you know what's happening there?"

She explained:

> You see these two guys had reported to him what they had seen in Russia. And I went home—I was married to Harry Nobel then—and I said: "You know I think Kenneth Hayes Miller has become senile. He said didn't I know what terror was going on in Russia, that there's blood being spilled there?" I said, "He's senile!"
>
> Well, of course, I was senile! He was right. He got a report from the two guys who went there. I was senile!
>
> Later on, in recent times when I read the papers I would think to myself, imagine when you said he was senile. And all this was going on there, and he knew about it and he was telling you, and you made fun of it.
>
> So that's my career. I laid off and didn't paint for a long time. I used all my energy to make a better world.

Rose then changed topics and, without being asked a question, explained that at some point she went back to Hunter College, graduating in 1960 with a degree as an art teacher. From what I could tell, like most former Party members, the years of Rose and Harry's political activism were behind them by the time I was a teenager in the mid-1960s and might have been aware of her politics. But, in her own way, Rose remained an idealist. She explained that sometime after getting her art degree she decided to become a rehabilitation counselor, and that she worked at the New York Association for New Americans, helping Russian Jews who came here after the Soviet Union allowed them to emigrate.

Upon hearing this, I remembered that my grandmother also worked for a time at Mobilization for Youth, a nonprofit agency dedicated to helping reduce juvenile delinquency in the Lower East Side of Manhattan. And she was true to the mission. At some point during her tenure there she was mugged while waiting for a bus. As her assailant ran away with her pocketbook, she yelled: "Young man—come to Mobilization for Youth and I shall rehabilitate you!" That was my Grandma Rose.

Taube

My mother, little Toby (aka "the child"), pretty much abandoned by her parents and having suffered the death of her father, went on to lead a rather remarkable life as she danced, painted, raised a family, traveled the world, went back to college and medical school, and rose to become a full professor at Columbia medical school. Upon retiring, she immersed herself in art classes, regularly exhibiting and occasionally selling her work. Despite Rose's musing in her video interview, I don't remember my mom doing or saying anything in anger or otherwise that I associated with the death of her father, although she was an extremely anxious person and undoubtedly was scarred by her troubling childhood. Her "PaPa Went Away" story reflected that she had struggled as a teenager not only with her father's abandonment and death, but also with her mother's role in it.

As an adult, my mother's relationship with Rose was, not surprisingly, complicated. She complained that her mother was selfish, and I don't ever recall her expressing love, or even affection, for my grandmother. But she was dutiful, and saw Rose and Harry frequently. My sister Debbie, who has a better memory for these things than I do, says that my mother was more like a parent than a daughter to Rose, and that Rose hadn't known how to be a parent to Ruthie any more than she'd been able to be a mother to our mom. Debbie remembers that our parents were angry at Rose and Harry for continuing to bankroll Ruthie's drug habit. In my parents' view, Rose and Harry failed Ruthie by not cutting her off as she was reeling toward her premature death.

Those Who Lived On

My mother tended to worry about everything—things that had happened in the past about which nothing could be done, and future contingencies that almost certainly would never happen. Her incessant fretting was a constant source of friction between us, as I was dismissive and impatiently scoffed at her unrealistic worries. A prime example was her fear that the family's radical political history would come back to haunt me. While I was proud that my grandfathers had fought in the Abraham Lincoln Brigade, she was panicked that my law firm would fire me if the family's Red pedigree became known. She pleaded with me not to reveal it. As usual, I insisted that she was being ridiculous.

The notion that a major New York City law firm would fire me in the 1980s because my grandparents, or even my parents, had been Communists decades before was preposterous; seemingly irrational like so many of my mother's other fears. What I didn't appreciate until very recently, however—or, to be more accurate, was insensitive to—was that my mother's fear was entirely rational in light of her experience and the history she had lived through. This revelation didn't occur to me until, after having written multiple drafts of this book, I read Peter Carroll's *Odyssey of the Abraham Lincoln Brigade*.

Much of what I read in Carroll's book wasn't news to me in light of what I already knew about the McCarthy era of the late 1940s and 1950s. I knew that respected movie directors and actors were blacklisted because of their actual or suspected Communist ties. I knew that Pete Seeger refused to answer questions at a hearing before the House Un-American Activities Committee; that he was indicted for contempt (and later convicted); and that Seeger's Weavers, until then perhaps the country's most popular music group, was banned from TV, lost their recording contract, and disbanded.

But what *did* come as news, and upended my superficial understanding of my mother, was Carroll's account of how the Lincoln veterans and their families were conspicuous targets of the government campaign to rid the country of Communists during the Cold War.

With Hitler and Mussolini having been defeated, the one prominent fascist dictator left standing in Europe after World War II was Francisco Franco in Spain. And as the battle to stem the expansion of Communism intensified, Franco came to be viewed by the Truman administration not as the reviled fascist, but a valued ally—rewarded in 1950 with a substantial loan from the U.S. government.[135]

In sharp contrast, due to the link between the Communist Party and the anti-fascist Republican side in the Spanish Civil War—and the fact that many of the Lincoln Brigade veterans were, or had been, Communists—J. Edgar Hoover suspected them all of disloyalty. The Lincoln veterans' continued opposition to Franco (and their protests against his ongoing atrocities in Spain) was viewed as un-American. With the approval of the president, Hoover ordered FBI surveillance of their activities.[136]

The surveillance of the Lincoln veterans increased after the members of the U.S. Communist Party's executive committee were indicted in 1948 for violating the Smith Act, which prohibited conspiracies to overthrow the government by force or violence. The government pursued the Lincoln veterans' alumni association—the VALB—with a vengeance. In 1953, now under the Eisenhower administration, the Subversive Activities Control Board (SACB) notified the VALB that it was under investigation and, after extensive hearings, ruled in 1955 that the VALB was a Communist front. The SACB ordered the VALB to register with the federal government as an agent of a foreign power under the McCarran International Security Act of 1950.[137]

In the midst of this inquisition, Lincoln veterans were arrested, and dozens were criminally prosecuted during the 1950s. In other words, it wasn't just about the "famous" artists, as I'd previously misunderstood;[138] ordinary citizens with an actual or suspected past connection to the Communist Party—especially the Lincoln veterans and their families—were placed under surveillance, picked up and interrogated, prosecuted, and/or fired from their jobs.[139] Moreover, no one was exempt. Robert Oppenheimer, an icon revered for his service to the country, saw his career destroyed due to his flirtation with the Communist Party decades before.[140]

As I absorbed this history, I thought back to my mother's unrealistic fear that my law firm would fire me if my family's Communist pedigree became known. And I suddenly got it: Harry and Rose had been obvious targets of the government witch hunt, as illustrated by the fact that FBI agents interrogated my mother's little sister, Ruthie, about them. And, for all I knew, my mother had been questioned too. I've recently learned that, like hundreds of other public school teachers, one of my uncles lost his job because he refused to provide the government with the names of Communists he knew.[141] Moreover, in 1951—the year after my parents were married—the family's dear friend, George Charney, was arrested, prosecuted, and later went to prison for his leadership role in the Party.[142]

In short, while I was playing touch football and trading baseball cards in a well-insulated, carefree bubble, the adults in our family were living in a state of terror. I can only imagine the late-night conversations they had after my sister and I had gone to bed about the latest friend who'd been interrogated, arrested, or fired. And about who would be next.

I suspect that my mother may have been traumatized by what she'd experienced and witnessed during this tumultuous era—coming on top of having been abandoned as a child and the loss of her father. I was objectively right in insisting that there was no way my law firm would fire me in the 1980s because my grandfathers had fought in the Spanish Civil War. Indeed, by the mid-1970s the Abraham Lincoln Brigade and its veterans had again acquired an air of respectability. Their annual reunions drew crowds of over a thousand,[143] and people were impressed when I told them my grandfathers had volunteered to fight in Spain as part of the Lincoln Brigade. Nevertheless, I can now see why my mother worried about bad things that were not likely to happen. A lot of bad, surreal things *did* happen to her on account of her parents' passionate idealism and radical politics. I wish I'd been more understanding during her lifetime.

Moreover, my mother had her own political baggage that may also have scarred her—or caused her to worry that her past could come back to haunt my sister and me. I don't know that she or my dad ever joined the Communist Party, but at the very least they had been sympathizers who took part in some Party activities. I had only a glimpse of their involvement. I knew from my parents directly (although my mother eventually denied this toward the end of her life) that they first met at some sort of Communist "rally" when my mother was fifteen, and that two years later they attended the historic 1949 Paul Robeson concert in Peekskill, New York—referred to ever since as the "Peekskill riots."

Robeson was an extraordinary figure: a popular Black opera singer, actor, professional football player, and an outspoken civil rights activist who, while not a member of the U.S. Communist Party, didn't hide his Communist affiliations. Although I don't recall the context, I remember my father recounting on one occasion that their bus going to or from the concert was pelted with stones. But until I recently read the firsthand account of the Peekskill riots published by novelist Howard Fast, I didn't realize what an extraordinary event it was, or how frightening it must have been for my seventeen-year-old mother.[144]

There were two Peekskill riots—one week apart—triggered by the Robeson concert. The concert was originally scheduled for the evening of Saturday, August 27, 1949, at the Lakeland Acres picnic grounds on the outskirts of Peekskill, with the proceeds to go to the Harlem chapter of the Civil Rights Congress. This was Robeson's fourth concert in the Peekskill area; the first three had been uneventful.[145] But not this one, as a mob led by antisemitic white supremacists and anti-Communists launched a violent attack that forced the cancellation of the event.

Fast became a spokesman for those on the concert grounds in the melee that occurred before the concert was scheduled to begin. As he later wrote, the violence erupted on the road leading into the picnic grounds:

> They poured down the road and into us, swinging broken fence posts, billies, bottles, and wielding knives. Their leaders had been drinking from pocket flasks and bottles right up to the moment of the attack, and now, and now as they beat and clawed at our lines, they poured out a torrent of obscene words and slogans....

"We're Hitler's boys-Hitler's boys!"

"We'll finish his job!"

"God bless Hitler and f____ you n_____ bastards and Jew bastards!"

"Lynch Robeson! Give us Robeson! We'll string that big n_____ up! Give him to us, you bastards!"¹⁴⁶

Bloody, hand-to-hand combat ensued between the violent mob and those seeking to protect the group of about 120 people on the picnic grounds—many of them women and children.

Paul Robeson didn't make it to the concert site. According to his biographer, Martin Duberman, as the car in which Robeson was riding neared the picnic grounds:

> It was immediately apparent that a brawl was in progress. A truck was deliberately parked in the middle of the road, effectively blocking it, forcing traffic to a crawl, allowing marauding groups of young men to check the occupants of each car, yanking some passengers out while a jeering crowd on the sidelines yelled "Dirty Commie" and "Dirty kike," tossing rocks, mauling suspicious strays. Police were visible on the sidelines, some smiling, none making a move to interfere with the mob.

Robeson wanted to get out of the car but his friends would have none of it. Sydney Danis, who was driving, managed to back out of the line of cars and drove Robeson to a safe location thirty minutes from Peekskill. The concert was cancelled, as the mob proceeded to smash the stage, torch the camp chairs around it, and attack concert-goers.¹⁴⁷

In the days that followed, the riot received extensive media coverage and a rally attended by 3,000 people was held at the Golden Gate Ballroom in Harlem. Robeson gave a lengthy, fiery speech, and sang as well.[148] And Paul Robeson was not one to back away from adversity. Over the objections of some who were fearful and wanted to limit the protest to the Harlem rally, he supported a decision to reschedule the concert for the following Saturday, September 4.[149] They found a new location in Cortlandt Manor, not far from Peekskill, after the original host balked, and Robeson and Pete Seeger planned to perform.

Tension began to mount in Peekskill as news that Robeson would return got out. Two effigies of him were hanged on the night before Saturday's rescheduled concert. Anticipating that there could be a repeat of the previous week's attack, a group of labor unions, led by Leon Straus of the International Fur and Leather Workers Union—Harry's union—organized and manned a defense around the perimeter of the concert grounds.[150]

More than 20,000 people ventured to the concert. Many, like my parents, came by buses booked by the Communist Party, unions, or other left-wing groups. And unlike in round one, there was a massive police presence.[151] Despite fears that the mob of about 8,000 people that had assembled was intent on killing Paul Robeson, including with high-powered rifles that were spotted,[152] both Seeger and Robeson performed and the concert went relatively smoothly. Robeson sang "Let My People Go" and "Ol' Man River." There were no speeches, political or otherwise.[153]

Trouble erupted *after* the concert ended, as the vigilantes first blocked the exit road and then forced the cars and buses to run a gauntlet, attacking with stones, clubs, and other weapons.[154]

Moreover, rather than restraining the mob, police stood idly by and, in some cases, joined in the assault. As Fast described it:

> A small cluster of hell was at work at the entrance; cops, in a craze of hate, were beating cars, not people, with their long clubs, smashing fenders, lashing out against windshields.... Even through our closed windows we could hear the flood of insanely vile language from the police, the unprintable oaths, the race words, the slime and filth of America's underworld of race hatred compressed into these "guardians" of the law, and released now. There were about thirty of them grouped there at the entrance, and they flogged the cars as if the automobiles were living objects of their resentment.[155]

The violence continued as the cars and buses made it onto the roadways, with organized groups of rock throwers lying in wait. Fast continued:

> Never in all my life have I seen so much blood; never have I seen so many people so cruelly cut and bleeding so badly. At another service station we saw three cars parked in a great spreading pool of blood and people trying to staunch the flow of it.[156]

In addition to recounting his own experience, Fast's book includes an appendix with various eyewitness accounts. I thought of my teenage mother as I read the accounts of others traveling home by bus:

F. Charles M., Bronx: reported that his bus was "stopped at Hartsdale by police of Greenburgh. All the way down, the bus was chased by cars who tried to run them off the road. People in the bus were covered with flying glass. They were stoned all the way to Briarcliff Manor. People came out of the bars to stone them."

H. Nina P., N.Y.: "A group of hoodlums came directly in front of the bus and threw a huge boulder in. This boulder struck my left hand and when I looked down I saw that the third joint of my middle finger was barely hanging by one tendon. Witnessing this whole incident were state troopers who were laughing. As the stones kept coming, all I could think of was: This is not America. This is Nazi Germany. I don't want to live like this."[157]

Others attending the concert were dragged from buses and beaten as police stood by and, in some cases, joined in the violent attacks. More than 100 people were injured.[158]

I don't know if the windows on my parents' bus were smashed, with people screaming, bleeding, and scared for their lives. My father didn't elaborate when he told us that the bus he and my mother rode in was "stoned." Knowing him as I did, I suspect that, if anything, he would have downplayed the violence when mentioning it to his kids. In any event, I realize now that the Peekskill riots may well have been just one more traumatic experience that left my mother prone to incessant worrying—an anxiety to which I was insensitive.

Despite the friction between us, my mother and I shared a deep emotional bond. I realize now that she knew me a lot better than I knew her, and she seemed to always know when something would instantly bring me to tears—like any reference to Ruthie. But our bond was largely unspoken; with few exceptions, we never had serious talks. One of those exceptions occurred in 2018 when I interviewed her to learn more about Harry and Ruby. She had little to tell me about them other than disabusing me of my long-held understanding that Harry and Ruby had been best friends. She said they had known each other but had not been particularly close. I didn't know what to make of this revelation, totally at odds with what I had always understood, but I now realize that she was right. I had not seen a single reference to Harry in any of the letters written by or to Ruby.

My mother also told me that while others in the family (implicitly, it seemed to me, my father, as well as Harry and Rose) continued to buy the Communist party line until Khrushchev's Secret Speech leaked in 1956, she had become skeptical and soured on the Party sometime before then.

As with my many talks with Harry, what is striking as I reflect back on my interview of my mother are all the meaningful questions I failed to ask her that day, or at any other time. I asked her nothing about her childhood, such as what she remembered of life at the Lakewood Modern School. I asked her nothing about what Harry and Rose had been up to in the postwar years; or whether she, herself, was ever questioned by FBI agents. And I asked her nothing about the "rally" where she and my father met or about her experience at the infamous Peekskill riots.

Until the final chapter of her life my mother was an interesting and empathetic woman, constantly thinking of others, often excessively. She underwent a dramatic transformation after a painful abdominal surgery, and the broken hip that soon followed, put an end to her painting classes and Pilates—and accelerated her dementia. Covid made her already bad situation worse, as she lived in isolation with a changing lineup of home aides. My mother became self-centered, selfish, angry, and distrustful. Any or all of these traits—including her paranoia—may just have been symptoms of her dementia. But I wonder now whether some of them could have reflected a long overdue release of the justified anger, hurt, and resentment she had suppressed over a lifetime, after having been effectively abandoned by both her parents, followed in short order by the death of her father.

Irving

Before receiving my cousin Carl's scrapbook about his father, I knew nothing about Irving Schwab other than that he was a lawyer, the inaccurate family lore about his role in the Scottsboro case, and that he had died young. Back in 2018, Carl had opened a window to Ruby when he sent me the Lipkaner biography and the two letters Ruby wrote to Rose from Spain after he was shot. Carl's scrapbook provided me with a glimpse of Irving that quickly washed away the disappointment I'd experienced upon discovering that the family lore regarding his Scottsboro role was wrong. It resurrected Irving.

My cousin Kim, the third of Carl's five children, sent me the scrapbook, which she had prepared as a present for her father in 2009. What the two of us referred to as a "scrapbook" was actually a white loose-leaf binder entitled:

IRVING SCHWAB
1904–1943

A photograph of Irving's tombstone reflected that he was born on July 4, 1903—two years before Ruby—and that he died shortly before his fortieth birthday. There was a large, formal black-and-white photo of Irving on the cover. Wearing a tuxedo and a white-ruffled tuxedo shirt, he appeared to have been in his mid-twenties when it was taken. Although Irving had dark hair while Carl was a strawberry blond, I thought I saw a resemblance between father and son. Carl was eight years old when his father died.

The most riveting material in the scrapbook for my purposes were three obituaries. The first, an article from an unnamed, obviously left-wing newspaper, was entitled "600 Attend Funeral for Irving Schwab." It began:

> Irving Schwab was buried yesterday, nine years from the day on which Haywood Patterson, after a second "trial" in the Alabama courts, was sentenced to 75 years in prison.... Irving Schwab had been among the framed boys' attorneys employed by the International Labor Defense.
>
> Joseph Brodsky [the lead lawyer on the ILD's Scottsboro team], who was in charge of the funeral services, said that as he was entering the building a young Negro touched him on the arm and announced himself as "one of the Scottsboro Boys" who but for Irving Schwab's tireless aid would have been legally or illegally lynched years ago.
>
> Schwab died of hardening of the intestinal arteries.
>
> More than 600 persons yesterday jammed the funeral chapel. Many of them were Negroes.
>
> Brodsky, describing Schwab as a practical idealist "who felt that the world could be changed for the better and who did his part in helping to change it," pledged that the young lawyer's work on behalf of the Scottsboro Boys and other oppressed would be carried on.
>
> Martin Popper, secretary of the National Lawyers Guild, said that Schwab was among a small group of men who some 15 years ago formed the legal staff of the ILD, the group which became the nucleus of the Lawyers Guild.

From what I'd just learned about Irving, including his date of birth, I had a more accurate picture of my uncle's role in Scottsboro. He was a young lawyer in 1931—twenty-eight years old, and probably only three or four years out of law school—and he was, indeed, actively involved in the defense of the Scottsboro Boys.

Much of the material in the scrapbook consisted of articles and other documents relating to the Scottsboro case that did not refer to Irving's role, including profiles of each of the Scottsboro Boys, the two trial judges, and the lawyers. But what struck me as most important were the tidbits in the obituaries that provided a window into my uncle's work *beyond* Scottsboro.

Toward the end of the first obituary, the following note caught my eye:

> Other speakers included Leonard Lamb of the Lincoln Brigade, who spoke of Schwab's aid to the Spanish Republic and to the veterans of Spain's anti-fascist war. Lamb credited Schwab with making it possible for numerous veterans to reenter the country and again take up arms against the Axis.

As I read this, I wondered if Harry was among the Lincoln Brigade vets Irving had represented as they sought to return to the United States after having violated FDR's edict prohibiting Americans from taking part in the Spanish Civil War.

A second, lengthy obituary referred to my uncle as a "well known labor lawyer ... prominent in anti-fascist activities for many years." The article recounted that Irving had been an attorney for a number of CIO and AFL unions, including the "Fur Workers Union"—Harry's radical union.

Like the first obituary, this one reported that "Mr. Schwab was one of the most useful attorneys in the famous Scottsboro case that saved nine innocent Negro boys from the electric chair in Alabama." But this second one went on to attest to Irving's legal work on behalf of African Americans in other cases:

> He gave noteworthy services in the cause of freedom in the South also in the famous Alabama sharecropper cases, where he defended Negro farmers who had defended themselves against a mob. His opponent in this case was ex-United States Senator Tom Heflin, chief White Supremacist advocate in the South.

There was more, as the article recounted that my Uncle Irving "defended hundreds of workers arrested on picket lines in other anti-labor prosecutions." And finally this:

> Mr. Schwab was an authority on immigration cases. A member of the board of the American Committee for the protection of Foreign Born, he gave much of his time to defending men and women threatened with deportation to foreign countries, or otherwise persecuted.

The last article was entitled "Negro Leader Mourns Death of Schwab." Quoting a statement released by Benjamin Davis, Harlem leader of the Communist Party, it stated that "Mr. Schwab was particularly beloved by the Negro people, who will always remember as a part of their own history the great and selfless fight he put up for the Scottsboro Boys, for Angelo Herndon and for the Negro and white sharecroppers in Alabama."

The article noted the risk to Irving's personal safety that he disregarded as he sought to protect Black victims of racist prosecutions in the South:

> Many times when Schwab was working on court cases in Georgia and Alabama his life was in danger because of Ku Klux Klan threats, but he "could not be frightened," the statement said. "Once he barely escaped a lynch mob, but he returned again and again to oppose the poll taxers and their lynch system," Davis said.

Understanding that the testaments to my uncle were likely exaggerated, I was nevertheless impressed—amazed frankly—at how much this idealistic young lawyer had done in dedicating his brief career to worthy causes. At the same time, it occurred to me that although Irving didn't abandon his wife and young child as completely as Ruby did, he probably had scant time for his son Carl as he immersed himself in the uphill battle against racism in the 1930s South.

Several other items in the scrapbook caught my attention. One was a pamphlet that cast new light on Irving's role in the Scottsboro case. Entitled "Eight Who Lie in the Death House," it was written for the National Committee for the Defense of Political Prisoners by Paul Peters, who was billed as a playwright, author, and journalist. The pamphlet had been written after the oral argument in the Alabama Supreme Court, and before the U.S. Supreme Court issued its decision in *Powell v. Alabama* on the appeal from the original convictions.

Peters had been in the courtroom for the argument. Writing in the present tense, he began: "five lawyers from the International Labor

Defense stand up and argue that 8 young boys have been railroaded to a savage death sentence in a Southern court." He went on to discuss only three of them: George Chamlee, a distinguished lawyer from Tennessee; Joseph Brodsky, the lead ILD attorney who later presided over Irving's funeral; and, to my surprise, my uncle. After Chamlee presented the defendants' account of the facts for the court, Irving attacked the prosecution's case. This was Peters's review:

> Irving Schwab, second attorney for the International Labor Defense, now analyzes their story. Lies, perjuries, contradictions, faked testimony, one by one he rips them open. Both girls are known prostitutes. Both have been seen time and again drunk in Chattanooga brothels. One has a long police record in Huntsville, Alabama. ... But the Scottsboro court barred this information.
>
> As this earnest young ILD lawyer speaks, the whole case against the Negro lads collapses like a house of cards.

Following Irving's presentation, Brodsky made the final argument for the defense, attacking the hysteria surrounding the trials, the "exclusion of Negroes from the jury," and how some of the boys were under sixteen and "were ruthlessly raced through to death sentences in a court with no authority to try them at all."

The Alabama Supreme Court wasn't swayed by Irving and his colleagues. It was left to the U.S. Supreme Court to reverse the convictions on the grounds that the Scottsboro Boys had been unlawfully convicted in a sham trial without effective representation. Nevertheless, Peters's article confirmed that, despite the inaccuracies in my family legend, Irving Schwab had indeed been a key member of the Scottsboro defense team.

The final document in Carl's scrapbook that was of importance to me was a May 1976 edition of *Political Affairs: Journal of Marxist Thought and Analysis*, which contained an article entitled "The Real 'Nate Shaw'." Although an obvious polemic, the article included a smattering of facts that shed further light on Irving's brief but impressive career battling Southern racism.

The article dealt with a high-profile criminal prosecution brought in Tallapoosa, Alabama against Black sharecroppers who were shot and then criminally prosecuted after one—Cliff James—refused to surrender his mule and cow to white law enforcement officers seeking to seize the animals in order to satisfy a mortgage.[159] The outrageous episode was memorialized in Theodore Rosengarten's *All God's Dangers: The Life of Nate Shaw*.

According to the *Political Affairs* article, the ILD furnished the defense for the defendants. In a tribute to the organization, the author reported, at page 58:

> One can only marvel today at how the ILD was able to respond to the many cries for help which reached it. At the time of the Tallapoosa case (December 1932 to April 1933) heavy demands were being made upon its financial and personnel resources. There was also the case of the nine youths facing death in Scottsboro some 200 miles north. There was the death rap confronting young Angelo Herndon over the border in Atlanta, Georgia.

And then, at page 60, the author reported that Irving Schwab was the "chief counsel" for the Tallapoosa defendants. So I now realized that at the same time that Irving was embroiled in Scottsboro, he was also immersed in another high-stakes criminal case involving blatant racism in the South. In addition, as the "Negro Leader Mourns Death of Schwab" article recounted, Irving also participated in the defense of Angelo Herndon—the third high-profile case referenced in the *Political Affairs* piece.[160]

As I absorbed all of this, I told myself that whatever motivation the Communist Party may have had for injecting itself into the Scottsboro case and seeking to protect its African American "allies," Irving Schwab had believed, genuinely and deeply, in the cause of antiracism to which he selflessly dedicated himself.

One of the obituaries indicated that Irving died after a "short illness" at the age of thirty-nine in 1943, six years after the death of Ruby, his kindred spirit and brother-in-law. At the very back of Carl's scrapbook were two photos of Ruby. One was of him in uniform, probably taken in Spain. The other—a 6x9-inch formal portrait—was remarkably similar to the large photo of Irving on the cover of the scrapbook: both of tuxedoed young men, married in a double wedding, who would soon die and leave behind young children who would grow up sharing their loss and bonded for life. The formal photos were taken at that ill-fated double wedding.

The short inscription on Irving's tombstone aptly read "His life was his own best tribute." As I put down Carl's scrapbook, I sat in awe. Irving had begun as my hero in the debunked story I'd so often told about how he was the lead lawyer in the Scottsboro case until it went to the Supreme Court; about how he had smuggled Ruby Bates out of the South in the rumble seat of his car. Although Irving had been temporarily dethroned when I'd found holes in my family lore, he had now been restored to his pedestal. Given all the people he'd helped before his premature death in 1943, if anything, his star shone more brightly than in the tattered family lore.

Formal photo of Irving Schwab (September 11, 1927, double wedding)   *Formal photo of Ruby (September 11, 1927, double wedding)*

I wondered whether Irving, a young lawyer, had been a pure idealist, unsullied by the dark side of the Communist Party, standing apart from this story of idealists lured astray. But reflecting a few days later on two things I'd learned along the way tempered my rosy view.

First, I considered Irving's role in excluding Clarence Darrow from the Scottsboro defense team, which I had thought of as a funny anecdote. As I pondered it now, I realized that it was a serious event that had impaired the quality of the defense of the Scottsboro Boys. Granted, Irving was the junior member of the ILD team and just taking orders—and it's highly doubtful that any lawyers could have won an acquittal for Black teenagers accused of raping two Southern white women in a trial presided over by the Honorable William Callahan before an all-white Alabama jury in the 1930s. Nevertheless, the Darrow episode highlights that Irving was an active participant in the ugly battle between the Communist Party and the NAACP that did a disservice to their clients, the Scottsboro Boys.

Also sobering was something I remembered reading about Irving. Like Ruby, Irving didn't live through all the Communist Party's policy flipflops and absurd Moscow-driven explanations that Harry, Rose, and George Charney meekly accepted for almost two decades. But he did witness the shocking Soviet-German Non-Aggression Pact that Stalin entered into with Hitler just two years after Ruby was killed, having heeded the Party's call to join the war against fascism. And as I thought about whether Irving would have bolted the Party before 1956 had he lived, I remembered a passage in Charney's autobiography.

After Khrushchev exposed Stalin as a fraudulent mass murderer in 1956, Charney sought to understand why he and so many others had previously failed to challenge American Communists' sycophantic adulation of Stalin. It turned out that the one time he had dared to broach the subject was in a conversation with Irving. On page 247, Charney explained:

> I remember—many years before Khrushchev's revelations—traveling with Irving Schwab from Washington. He was an old friend and one of the first attorneys to go to Alabama in the Scottsboro case. He was a thoughtful man, rarely given to emotional expression. I could speak to Irving without reservation, and I asked him on that occasion about the unseemly adulation of Stalin. It went against the American grain—the thousands of great photos, the place names, the genuflections, the religious adoration of the masses. He smiled and simply recounted the achievements under Stalin's leadership.

His summary was impressive, and no doubt I was looking for the assurance that what appeared to be a ritual antagonistic to the spirit of Marxism and the democratic tradition, had in the minds of men its own unique, historical justification.

In short, my uncle closed the door on Charney's probe, and it appears that, as genuine as his belief in the cause of antiracism may have been, Irving was also blinded by, and in the grip of, the Soviet-controlled Communist Party. So it's not unlikely that had Irving lived, he would have stuck with the Party for some considerable period, in tandem with Harry, Rose, and Charney. At the same time, I'm certain he would have continued to devote his legal career to helping those in need. Irving Schwab would have done a lot of good—and been a role model for me. I wish I'd known him.

Ruby

Having now read Ruby's poems, his letters, and what was written about him, I feel like I've gotten to know my grandfather. Indeed, in important ways I've come to know this grandfather I never met better than I ever knew Rose or Harry, with whom I spent so much time during the first four decades of my life.

Harry and Ruby were both fervent idealists, but while Harry's youthful passions and personality remain largely a mystery to me, I've seen that Ruby was a big-hearted romantic in the early 1930s—and I continue to believe that it was compassion, not Marxist theory, that initially drew him to the Communist Party. Had the Russian Revolution not occurred in 1917, Ruby would have found another way to dedicate himself to fighting unemployment, poverty, and racism, although he would not have abandoned his five-year-old daughter to risk his life in a foreign civil war in defiance of his parents and his government.

Two other defining characteristics of Ruby help me imagine how my grandfather would have emerged from the debris of the Communist Party. Ruby was an ebullient optimist with a magnetic personality. As Rose's sister, Mildred, wistfully remarked decades after Ruby's death: "Everyone loved Ruby." Like his remarkable friend George Charney, I bet my grandfather would have emerged with his optimism and idealism intact.

Ruby would have been fifty-five in 1960, four years after Khrushchev's revelations. Whether he would have jumped into the Civil Rights Movement of that era or been politically active in some other way is obviously unknowable; Charney and many other former Party members remained on the sidelines, politically inactive.[161] But that Ruby would have found some way to pursue the compassionate causes that had motivated him as a young man—and drawn at least a few others along with him—is likely. And it's a virtual certainty that he would have either returned to his poetry or put his writing talent to some other good use. We would have heard more from Rubin Schechter than what I found in his Briefcase.

Rubin Schechter

Reflections

With my family lore in tatters, I sought to make sense of all that I'd learned since beginning this search—when I'd been proud that my two grandfathers had volunteered to fight in the Abraham Lincoln Brigade and, as I then believed, that Irving had been the lead lawyer in the Scottsboro case. I paused to consider whether I should still be—whether I still *was*—proud of them. I tried to assess the life-defining choices that they, as well as Rose, made in their youth, and whether their lives were wasted.

My understanding and feelings about what motivated my grandparents—and how to assess what they did with their lives—had changed repeatedly as I'd made my way through the letters in the Briefcase and then stumbled upon one historical source after another that caused me to reconsider my previous opinions and feelings. It had been like looking at my grandparents through a kaleidoscope.

Here's where I came to rest: I'm confident that Ruby, Harry, Rose, and Irving joined the Communist Party for good reasons in the 1930s. I'm saddened that my grandparents' legacy has been clouded by the dark history of the Party; that their motivation was not purely about fighting poverty, fascism, and racism; that my own mother was a casualty of her parents' version of idealism; and that Harry and Rose continued to blindly follow Stalin for decades, just as Ruby and Irving likely would have done.

But there was one final kaleidoscopic twist in my perspective—on Harry and Rose, in particular—that didn't occur to me until after I thought I had finished writing this book. While working to polish what I thought was the final draft, I realized that somewhere along the way I'd lost sight of the fact that while they, like George Charney and so many other American Communists, had remained under Stalin's spell for the better part of three decades, the causes they were so committed to fighting for were still virtuous and important. For example, the U.S. Communist Party had continued to vigorously oppose fascism—actively protesting against Franco's brutal dictatorship in Spain after the U.S. government embraced Franco as an ally and lavished him with generous financial support while he continued to murder hundreds of thousands of people. And the Party remained in the vanguard of the opposition to racism, at least among white-led organizations, as illustrated by its role in connection with the Paul Robeson concerts that led to the Peekskill riots.[1]

And so, in the end, I do still admire my forebears for acting upon their ideals and sacrificing the easy life in an effort to make their country and the world a better place. It's unfortunate that they chose the wrong vehicle, driven by a fraudulent murderer, to rid the world of fascism, racism, and—to use Ruby's words—"Hunger and Cold and Rooflessness." I can take some solace in the fact that there weren't a lot of other cars on the road going their way at the time.

In any event, while I may be deluding myself, I'll continue to tell their story. Because the world needs people like Rubin Schechter, Harry Nobel, Irving Schwab, and Rose Leibner, who are willing to sacrifice and risk everything for worthy causes they believe in, not knowing whether they'll be successful in battling against heavy odds. Hopefully, those people will not often be led astray by cult leaders who take advantage of their naivety and fervent devotion. And hopefully, from time to time, they will be on the winning side of a virtuous cause.

Reflections

Rose and Harry

Epilogue

Throughout the first few years I spent reading and writing about my grandparents and the history in which they took part, I wondered whether there was any point to their story that's of relevance today—and I feared that there might be none. Who would care that two young men, members of the defunct Communist Party, risked their lives almost ninety years ago to fight for a lost cause in a foreign civil war, with one dying from a flesh wound while the other, a brilliant scholar, returned, married his dead comrade's widow, and proceeded to devote his career to sewing fur pelts in fealty to the U.S. Communist Party? The Party and the Stalinist government that controlled it are both long dead and gone, so why should anyone care?

But as current events at home and abroad have evolved in these few years since Melissa found the fateful Briefcase, I've come to realize that the two dimensions of fervent idealism illustrated by my family's story figure prominently in the world today. The first is the heroic idealism that drives people to dedicate their lives to worthy causes—to abandon the clear, comfortable path right in front of them and take the hard, risky, and sometimes treacherous road, with huge costs to themselves and their loved ones. The kind of heroic idealism that we've recently witnessed in Russia, as Alexei Navalny returned to his country, *knowing* that prison and almost certain death awaited him; and in Ukraine, as its citizens fight, and die, trying to save their democracy—and others from around the world travel to Ukraine to support them in their quest to forestall Russian aggression.[2]

Epilogue

Ruby and Harry took the hard road, venturing to Spain at least in significant part because they believed the fate of the world was teetering on a precipice—and they were right at the time. Unfortunately, the well-intended idealists who continued on in the Communist Party for decades, including Harry and Rose, were not. So the story of my grandparents is also a lesson in idealism gone astray—or, perhaps more accurately put, idealism lured astray. It's a reminder that while fervent idealism can motivate people to do good, selfless things, it can also blind them to reality, especially when the steering wheel is in the hands of someone adept at proselytizing, manipulating, and defrauding unsuspecting victims who continue to slavishly go along with the party line, ignoring glaring cautionary signals and suppressing their own doubts; impervious to facts.

As he looked back on the ashes of the U.S. Communist Party, George Charney repeatedly expressed his amazement at how gullible, supplicant, and blind to reality he and his fellow idealistic Communists had been: "How we, presumably intelligent people, persisted all these years in accepting this myth is beyond me."[3] Perhaps ironically, the history of the U.S. Communist Party is a sobering precedent that may help explain how so many passionate and intelligent people in America today have become captive to a fraudulent autocrat, blindly subscribing to myths that threaten our democracy. Having been repeatedly proselytized and seduced with false narratives, they summarily reject all contradictory evidence, just as George Charney and my grandparents dismissed facts before them as "inspired by anti-Soviet prejudice." It took twenty-five years, the death of Stalin, and the crucial blow struck by Khrushchev from within the Party to crack the shell that encapsulated the American Communists and awaken them from their trance. Our democracy may not have that long.

Beyond our domestic crisis, the state of the world is more worrisome than at any time since my childhood in the early 1960s during the Cold War, when we were ordered to hide under our desks during air raid drills. When I was eight, every kid in Ms. Alfano's third-grade class was required to make a diorama of a bomb shelter. During the Cuban Missile Crisis two years later, I asked my dad whether World War III was about to break out. I wonder what today's kids feel when they look at the scary world we're handing them.

During most of the first two years after Russia's invasion of Ukraine, as I worked on this book it appeared to me that the United States and Western European nations had largely learned the Spanish Civil War's costly lesson on the danger of appeasing an aggressive dictator. It now looks like I may have been wrong, as isolationism has once again reared its head in the United States. Although the parallels are obviously imperfect, as in 1936 we've watched a brutal dictator—this time Vladimir Putin—band together with other dictators to whom the United States' impassivity or vacillation will send signals of weakness and green lights. Like Ruby and Harry's Abraham Lincoln Brigade, the valiant Ukrainians attempting to withstand Putin's aggression are now massively outgunned. Without the continuing support it desperately needs, Ukraine, too, will be doomed to fail and dire consequences elsewhere could ensue. More than at any time since Ruby died in 1937, the fundamental lesson of the Spanish Civil War that FDR and other Western leaders learned only too late cries out to be remembered and heeded.

Acknowledgments

I owe an enormous debt of gratitude to a number of wonderful friends and family members who provided invaluable assistance, advice, and moral support along the way. Ted Fishman, a gifted writer as well as a beloved family member, read early drafts of the manuscript and served as a valuable mentor. In addition to bolstering my hope that my family's story was worth telling, Ted provided me with sage advice that pushed me to both think and research more deeply.

Three of my Tufts college friends played an enormous role in making this book a reality. Carl Carlsen shared the benefits of his experience teaching college English for decades and publishing his own works, by reading two early drafts of the manuscript and providing voluminous critiques that transformed the book. And no one has provided more valuable help and support for this project than my dear friend Annie Wilson. From her cattle ranch in the Flint Hills of Kansas, and in between writing curricula on the preservation of the prairie, leading her Tallgrass Express String Band, and writing and producing CD recordings of her songs, Annie brought her deep experience as a writing teacher to bear on my drafts. She read numerous drafts, discovered themes in my family's story that I had not recognized, and provided valuable substantive advice, stylistic edits, and perpetual moral support that helped me believe this was a worthwhile enterprise. Finally, Dale Graden, a third Tufts comrade and a professor of history at the University of Idaho, shared his extensive knowledge with respect to the Spanish Civil War and repeatedly pointed me to historical sources that I've heavily relied upon.

Two talented Hunter College students, Bernadette Mustacchio and Fergus Barragry, provided excellent historical research support with respect to various topics discussed in this book, including the Lipkaner Bessarabia Progressive Society, the demographics of the Lincoln Brigade, and Harry's furriers' union.

A note of thanks and a belated caution are in order with respect to the sources cited in this book. I've spent a lot of time over the last several years reading some of the leading works on the Spanish Civil War, the Scottsboro case, and the U.S. Communist Party, in order to cobble together the historical context for my family's story. Nevertheless, as is no doubt obvious, I am not a historian, and I have engaged in my unsystematic research only to discover, understand, and hopefully explain the forces that drove my forebears' idealistic passions, actions, and foibles. I'm indebted to the bona fide historians whose work made this one possible, including Paul Preston, Dan Carter, James Goodman, Fraser Ottanelli, Vivian Gornick, and Adam Hochschild, whose terrific book on the Americans who fought in the Spanish Civil War set me on this path in the first place. Two historians, in particular, deserve special thanks. First, Robert Rosenstone. Not only was his book on the Lincoln Brigade, originally written decades ago as a master's thesis, a major source for me, but Robert was good enough to spend considerable time corresponding and reading an early draft of the manuscript. Special thanks as well to Peter Carroll, who passed away as this book was going to print. Carroll was the most prolific authority on the Lincoln Brigade, and I relied upon his work extensively. And my thanks, too, to Sebastiaan Faber, noted author and professor of Hispanic studies at Oberlin, for his support, and for all he does to keep the history of the Lincoln Brigade alive and relevant.[4] Among other things, Sebastiaan introduced me to Chris

Brooks, the master of the Lincoln Brigade Archives, to whom I'm deeply grateful for generously taking the time to uncover the document that transformed my understanding of Harry, and located Ruby's actual resting place as well. I can only hope that the imperfect accounts of the Spanish Civil War, Scottsboro, and the U.S. Communist Party woven into my story based on the work of these outstanding historians have been of some interest to those not already knowledgeable about the subjects.

I'm indebted to four of my cousins who provided valuable assistance to this project. Beth Sommers, our family archivist and historian, repeatedly supplied important information to fill in missing links in our family history, and never lost patience with my incessant questions. Donald Leibner conducted the videotaped interviews of Rose and her sisters, and provided additional material, including about my great-grandfather Joseph Leibner's refrigerated fish car business and brush with the Department of Justice. And, of course, I'll be forever grateful to my cousin Carl Schwab, a lifelong hero of mine, who found and provided me with copies of the two letters Ruby wrote to Rose after being shot on account of a donkey, as well as the Lipkaner biography of Ruby. Carl passed away at the age of eighty-nine as this book was being finalized. The book is dedicated to him. And finally, I'm extremely grateful to my cousin Kim (Schwab) Simpson, Carl's daughter, who prepared the "scrapbook" on Irving Schwab as a present for her father decades ago. The material in the scrapbook uncovered by Kim's research was the source of most of what I was able to write about Irving's remarkable, unfortunately brief, career.

Andrew Jarvis, a good friend and a veteran of the publishing world, not only counseled me throughout the publishing process, but read several drafts of the manuscript and suggested what proved to be significant changes to the structure and content of the book. Andrew also recommended that I consider Whitefox, with whom he'd had experience in London, to publish the book. I'm glad he did.

I owe a huge debt of gratitude to Annabel Wright and the team at Whitefox she led. Annabel has provided sage advice concerning both the substance of the manuscript and every step along the road as we approached publication. Annabel's deep experience, impeccable judgment, and editorial recommendations were invaluable. Thanks, too, to Drew Cullingham, whose structural edit had a significant impact, and to Gemma Wain, for her thoughtful and utterly meticulous editing. Finally, Julia Koppitz provided invaluable counsel as she guided me through, and managed, the many steps entailed in transforming the manuscript into an actual, published book.

I could not have undertaken this project without the constant support of Shirley Gordon, who has worked alongside me for twenty years. Shirley produced and proofed every one of the myriad drafts of this book, pointing out my errors and inconsistencies along the way. Moreover, her contributions to this book represent a tiny fraction of the many ways in which I have benefited over the years from Shirley's amazing organizational and technical skills, her initiative, and her invariably optimistic attitude, which is contagious.

Finally, my wife Melissa, who kept me alive during my bout with cancer and assorted other medical adventures, and has blessed me with her steadfast, loving partnership and support for the past thirty-six years as we navigated the shoals of our careers and raised two remarkable sons. Melissa's extensive edits to multiple drafts of this book and, in particular, her affection for and insights about many of the people I've described, forced me to think harder and differently at numerous junctures. And, of course, she recovered the Briefcase.

Bibliography

Books

Avrich, Paul, *The Modern School Movement: Anarchism and Education in the United States*, Princeton, NJ: Princeton University Press, 1980; reprint edition, AK Press, 2006.

Bird, Kai, and Martin J. Sherwin, *American Prometheus: The Triumph and Tragedy of J. Robert,* Oppenheimer, New York: Vintage Books, 2005.

Carroll, Peter N., *The Odyssey of the Abraham Lincoln Brigade: Americans in the Spanish Civil War*, Stanford, CA: Stanford University Press, 1994.

Carroll, Peter N., *Sketches from Spain: Homage to the Abraham Lincoln Brigade*, Charlotte, NC: Main Street Rag Publishing, 2024.

Carroll, Peter, and James Fernandez (eds.), *Facing Fascism: New York and the Spanish Civil War*, New York: Museum of the City of New York/NYU Press, 2007.

Carter, Dan T., *Scottsboro: A Tragedy of the American South*, Baton Rouge, LA: Louisiana State University Press, 1969; revised edition, 2007.

Charney, George, *A Long Journey*, Toronto: Burns and McEachern Ltd., 1968.

Crossman, Richard (ed.), *The God That Failed*, New York: Columbia University Press, 2001.

Dollard, John, *Fear in Battle*, New Haven, CT: Yale University Press: 1943, https://doi.org/10.1037/10635-000.

Duberman, Martin Bauml, *Paul Robeson*, New York: Alfred A. Knopf, 1988.

Fast, Howard, *Peekskill U.S.A.: Inside the Infamous 1949 Riots*, New York: Open Road Integrated Media, 1951; eBook edition, 2011.

Gage, Beverly, *G-Man: J. Edgar Hoover and the Making of the American Century*, New York: Viking, 2022.

Goodman, James, *Stories of Scottsboro*, New York: Vintage Books, 1995.

Gornick, Vivien, *Romance of American Communism*, New York: Basic Books, 1977; revised edition, New York and London: Verso, 2020.

Hemingway, Ernest, *For Whom the Bell Tolls*, New York: Charles Scribner's Sons, 1940.

Hochschild, Adam, *Spain in Our Hearts: Americans in the Spanish Civil War, 1936–1939*, New York: Houghton Mifflin Harcourt, 2016.

Maddow, Rachel, *Prequel*, New York: Random House, 2023.

Orwell, George, *Homage to Catalonia*, London: Secker & Warburg, 1938.

Ottanelli, Fraser, *The Communist Party of the United States: From the Depression to World War II*, Newark, NJ: Rutgers University Press, 1991.

Peters, J., *The Communist Party: A Manual on Organization*, New York: Workers Library Publishers, July 1935; reprint edition, Proletarian Publishers, 1975.

Preston, Paul, *The Spanish Civil War: Reaction, Revolution, and Revenge*, New York and London: W.W. Norton & Co., 2006.

Richardson, R. Dan, *Comintern Army: The International Brigades and the Spanish Civil War*, Lexington, KY: University Press of Kentucky, 1982.

Rosenstone, Robert A., *Crusade of the Left: The Lincoln Battalion in the Spanish Civil War*, New York: Western Publishing Co., 1969; Pegasus, 2009.

Thomas, Hugh, *The Spanish Civil War*, revised edition, New York: Modern Library, 2001.

Articles, Journals, and Websites

Abraham Lincoln Brigade Archives, https://alba-valb.org.

Anderson, Eric G., *The Anarchist Classroom: A Test of Libertarian Education and Human Nature at the Modern School in New York and New Jersey, 1911–1953* (MA thesis), New York: City University of New York: 2018, https://academicworks.cuny.edu/qc_etds/5/.

"The Carp King," *American Business Survey*, August 1940.

Bibliography

"Darrow Declines to Defend Case," Newspapers.com, *Clarion-Ledger*, December 30, 1931, https://clarionledger.newspapers.com/article/clarion-ledger-darrow-declines-to-defend/146285408/.

"Darrow Drops Fight to Save Eight Negroes, Refusing to Enter Case With Communists," *New York Times*, December 30, 1931, https://www.nytimes.com/1931/12/30/archives/darrow-drops-fight-to-same-eight-negroes-refusing-to-enter-case.html.

"Darrow in Alabama to Aid Eight Negroes," *New York Times*, December 28, 1931, https://www.nytimes.com/1931/12/28/archives/darrow-in-alabama-to-aid-eight-negroes-he-and-hays-consult-counsel.html.

Faber, Sebastiaan, "Ukraine's Foreign Fighters Have Little in Common with Those Who Signed Up to Fight in Spanish Civil War," The Conversation, March 17, 2022, https://theconversation.com/ukraines-foreign-fighters-have-little-in-common-with-those-who-signed-up-to-fight-in-the-spanish-civil-war-178976.

The Volunteer, founded by the Veterans of the Abraham Lincoln Brigade.

Fur Trade Review, University of Minnesota, Vol. 54, No. 3, 1926.

"Gemilas Chesed," Jewish English Lexicon, https://jel.jewish-languages.org/words/2023#google_vignette.

Goodman, Marty, "Introduction to the *New Masses* Digital Archive on Marxists Internet Archive," Marxists.org, April 2019, https://www.marxists.org/history/usa/pubs/new-masses/intro.htm.

Graden, Dale T., "The Earth Endureth Forever: Hemingway in Spain," *The Volunteer*, June 10, 2016, https://albavolunteer.org/2016/06/the-earth-endureth-forever-ernest-hemingway-and-the-spanish-civil-war/.

"Herndon, Angelo," Notable Black American Men, Book II, Encyclopedia.com, May 15, 2024, https://www.encyclopedia.com/african-american-focus/news-wires-white-papers-and-books/herndon-angelo.

International Jewish Cemetery Project, "Lipcani," http://iajgscemetery.org/eastern-europe/moldova-inc-transnistria-region/lipcani.

International Labor Defense Records 1924–1946, Schomburg Center for Research in Black Culture, New York Public Library, https://archives.nypl.org/scm/20647.

Jewish Museum London, "Furrier's Hand Tools," https://jewishmuseum.org.uk/50-objects/1998-44-2/.

"Kenneth Hayes Miller," American Art Collaborative, http://browse.americanartcollaborative.org/actor/ulan/500025218.html.

"Kenneth Hayes Miller," Smithsonian American Art Museum, https://americanart.si.edu/artist/kenneth-hayes-miller-3331.

"Khrushchev's Secret Speech," February 26, 1956, Wilson Center, https://digitalarchive.wilsoncenter.org/document/khrushchevs-secret-speech-cult-personality-and-its-consequences-delivered-twentieth-party.

Khost, Alexander, "An Incomplete and Personal History of the Modern Schools," The Alliance for Self-Directed Education, March 1, 2018, https://www.self-directed.org/tp/history-of-modern-schools/.

Kramer, Hilton, "Art View," *New York Times*, March 11, 1979, https://www.nytimes.com/1979/03/11/archives/art-view-the-unhappy-fate-of-hayes-miller.html.

Lavi, Theodor, "Transnistria," *Encyclopaedia Judaica*. Encyclopedia.com, May 15, 2024, https://www.encyclopedia.com/religion/encyclopedias-almanacs-transcripts-and-maps/transnistria.

Leiter, Robert D., "The Fur Workers' Union," *ILR Review* Vol. 3, No. 2: Jan. 1950, https://www.jstor.org/stable/2518828; https://doi.org/10.2307/2518828.

"Lipcani," Wikipedia.com, https://en.wikipedia.org/wiki/Lipcani.

"Lipkany," *Encyclopaedia Judaica*, Encyclopedia.com, May 16, 2024, https://www.encyclopedia.com/religion/encyclopedias-almanacs-transcripts-and-maps/lipkany.

"Live Fish Monopoly Is Broken By Court," *New York Times*, July 3, 1926, https://www.nytimes.com/1926/07/03/archives/live-fish-monopoly-is-broken-by-court-group-did-2000000-business.html.

Lubasch, Arnold H., "7 Union Leaders Accused of Racket in Fur District," *New York Times*, March 28, 1973, https://www.nytimes.com/1973/03/28/

archives/7-union-leaders-accused-of-racket-in-fur-district-7-union-leaders.html.

Maddow, Rachel, *Ultra* podcast, https://www.msnbc.com/rachel-maddow-presents-ultra.

Pittman, John, "Book Review: A Man of Heroic Mold" (reviewing *All God's Dangers: The Life of Nate Shaw*), *Political Affairs: Journal of Marxist Thought and Analysis*, Vol. LV, No. 5, 1976.

Soyer, Daniel, "Between Two Worlds: The Jewish Landsmanshaftn and Questions of Immigrant Identity," *American Jewish History*, Vol. 76, No. 1, 1984, https://www.jstor.org/stable/23883236.

"SS *George Washington*," Wikipedia.com, https://en.wikipedia.org/wiki/SS_George_Washington.

Stead, Joe, "Peekskill Outrage: Sidney Poitier, Pete Seeger, Paul Robeson," YouTube clip, https://www.youtube.com/watch?v=1pgyACdT1rM.

Uhlman, J.R., *"A Bunch of Jews Defending Them Damned Ni__ers!": Radical Jews in the ILD's Scottsboro Campaign* (MA thesis), Australian National University, 1997, https://openresearch-repository.anu.edu.au/handle/1885/146138.

Wright, Richard, "I Tried to Be a Communist," *The Atlantic*, September 1944, https://www.theatlantic.com/magazine/archive/1944/08/richard-wright-communist/618821/.

Endnotes

Part I—Opening Windows

1. Adam Hochschild, *Spain in Our Hearts: Americans in the Spanish Civil War, 1936–1939* (New York: Houghton Mifflin, 2016*)*, 113–18.

2. Ibid., 45–6, 120, 132–4. According to Hochschild, in 1939 Roosevelt told his cabinet that his embargo on providing arms to the Republican army in Spain had been a "grave mistake." Ibid., 353.

3. Ibid., 96, 182–6.

4. Ibid., 126–7.

5. According to Hochschild, the *New York Times* ran more than 1,000 front-page headlines about the war in Spain. Ibid., xvi.

6. The Abraham Lincoln Brigade Archives, https://alba-valb.org/.

7. Ibid., https://alba-valb.org/volunteers/harry-nobel/.

8. The profile for Harry in the Archives indicates that he was sent to work in the Paris office in January 1937. The date appears to be inaccurate. Harry's profile states that he did not sail from the United States to Europe until February 20, 1937, and that he then fought in the battles of Jarama, Brunete, and Aragon. The likelihood that Harry was sent to work in the Paris office in January 1937 and then returned to the United States in time to depart for Europe again the next month is virtually nil. The correct date is likely January 1938.

9. Ibid., https://alba-valb.org/volunteers/rubin-schechter/.

10. It appears that the actual date of death was August 23, 1937, and that the Archives profile is incorrect in this respect. See note 134 infra.

11. Daniel Soyer, "Between Two Worlds: The Jewish Landsmanshaftn and Questions of Immigrant Identity," published in *American Jewish History*, vol. 76, no. 1 (1984), 6–7, https://www.jstor.org/stable/23883236.

12. Ibid.

13 Ibid., 17–18. According to the online Jewish English Lexicon database, *gmiles hesed* or *gemilas chesed*.

14 'Lipcani,' International Jewish Cemetery Project, http://iajgscemetery.org/eastern-europe/moldova-inc-transnistria-region/lipcani; 'Lipcani,' Wikipedia, https://en.wikipedia.org/wiki/Lipcani.

15 'Lipkany,' Encyclopedia.com, https://www.encyclopedia.com/religion/encyclopedias-almanacs-transcripts-and-maps/lipkany.

16 'Transnistria,' Encyclopedia.com, https://www.encyclopedia.com/places/commonwealth-independent-states-and-baltic-nations/cis-and-baltic-political-geography/trans-dniester-region#2587519998.

17 In 1927, Alex Schechter was nominated as third vice president of the American Fur Merchants Association: *Fur Trade Review*, vol. 54, no. 3 (1926), 128. The organization still exists in New York, described by Bloomberg as a "trade association of fur sellers dedicated to advocate for policy and regulations."

18 Robert D. Leiter, "The Fur Workers Union," *ILR Review*, vol. 3, no. 2 (Jan. 1950), 166–7, https://www.jstor.org/stable/2518828. According to the London Jewish Museum, furriery was a common trade for Jewish immigrants who settled in the UK from Eastern Europe, but they "tended to make cheaper imitations of more expensive furs" (https://jewishmuseum.org.uk/50-objects/1998-44-2/). During the eighteenth and nineteenth centuries, fur coats were popular luxury items in Europe but rare in this country. The industry was dominated by German immigrants until the turn of the century, when fur garments started to become popular here as a way to keep warm, and the industry took advantage of cheap Jewish laborers (Leiter, 166–8). The popularity of fur coats continued to grow, fueled by the prosperity following World War I, as more middle-class and even some working-class women began wearing fur coats. Hundreds of large and small businesses sprang up, concentrated in Manhattan's rectangular fur district, running from south to north between 26th and 30th Streets, and east to west between 6th to 8th Avenues. At the industry's height, over 80 percent of the fur coats manufactured in this country were made in this district, including by scrappy Jewish entrepreneurs like Ruby's father, Alex, who tended to focus on lower cost animal furs like rabbit, rather than the more luxurious mink (ibid., 164–8).

19 Ibid., 171. Leiter's article traces the history of the furriers' unions. After a brief period of independent existence, the Communist furriers' union, together with the Communists in the International Ladies Garment Workers Union, organized the Needle Trades Workers Industrial Union in 1928.

20 In the photo taken of Harry in Spain, I understood from my mother that the three additional men in the picture belonged to international brigades supplied by other countries, one of which was Yugoslavia.

21 A thumb piano is an African percussion instrument.

Part II—The Man in the Briefcase

1 "The Carp King," *American Business Survey*, August 1940, 25.

2 "Live Fish Monopoly Is Broken By Court," *New York Times,* July 3, 1926, https://www.nytimes.com/1926/07/03/archives/live-fish-monopoly-is-broken-by-court-group-did-2000000-business.html.

3 To complete the circle, my son Harris (named after Harry) is an antitrust lawyer working for the federal government.

4 Fraser Ottanelli, *The Communist Party of the United States: From the Depression to World War II* (Newark and London: Rutgers University Press, 1991), 30, and, generally, Chapter 2; Robert A. Rosenstone, *Crusade of the Left: The Lincoln Battalion in the Spanish Civil War* (Western Publishing Co, 1969; Pegasus, 2009).

5 Ottanelli, 28–36.

6 Ibid., 27–8.

7 Hochschild, 10.

8 Rosenstone, 72–4.

9 Ibid., 62–3.

10 Ibid., 60, 72; Ottanelli, 120–28.

11 Ottanelli, 40.

12 James Goodman, *Stories of Scottsboro* (New York: Vintage Books, 1994), 4–5; Dan T. Carter, *Scottsboro: A Tragedy of the American South* (Baton Rouge: Louisiana State University Press, 1969, 2007), 6.

13 Carter, 5.

14 Goodman, 25–6. According to Carter's earlier account, however, Ruby Bates told the deputy sheriff that she and Price had been raped by the nine boys when they were rounded up. Carter, 6.

15 Goodman, 26.

16 Ibid.

17 Carter, 19–23.

18 Ibid., 22; Goodman, 13 et seq.

19 Carter, 23.

20 Ibid., 26; Goodman, 13.

21 Carter, 27–8. According to Goodman's account, however, Bridges did testify that Bates's and Price's vaginas "were loaded with male sperm," Goodman, 14.

22 Carter, 29–30.

23 Ibid., 30–31; Goodman, 14.

24 Carter, 33–4; Goodman, 26. As Norris's testimony highlights, there was an obvious risk of adversity among the eight other defendants, and the notion that a single lawyer could represent all of them would be hard to imagine under today's legal ethics standards.

25 Carter, 35.

26 Ibid., 35–6.

27 Goodman, 42–3, 126, 131.

28 Carter, 37.

29 Ibid., 42.

30 Ibid., 43.

31 Ibid., 45–6; Goodman, 41.

32 Carter, 48; Goodman, 25.

33 Goodman, 49.

34 International Labor Defense records, Schomburg Center for Research in Black Culture, The New York Public Library, https://archives.nypl.org/scm/20647. Nicola Sacco and Bartolomeo Vanzetti were Italian immigrants and anarchists who were convicted of armed robbery and murder after a highly controversial trial that drew worldwide attention and protests. They were later executed.

35 Carter, 49; Goodman, 25.

36 Goodman, 32–8.

37 George Charney, *The Long Journey* (Toronto: Burns and McEachern Ltd., 1968), 247.

38 Rosenstone, 58–77; Hochschild, 9–10.

39 Peters, J., *The Communist Party: A Manual on Organization* (New York: Workers Library Publishers, July 1935; reprint edition, Proletarian Publishers, 1975), 4.

40 Ottanelli, 128; Rosenstone, 68 (explaining that the Communist Party membership grew most rapidly between 1935 and 1939 because of the stands that the Communists were taking on issues that were "right in the mainstream of society's beliefs and desires"); Kai Bird and Martin Sherwin, *American Prometheus: The Triumph and Tragedy of J. Robert Oppenheimer* (New York, Vintage Books, 2005), 115. According to Bird and Sherwin, in total during the 1930s about 250,000 Americans affiliated themselves with the Communist Party, although many only remained for a year. See also, Beverly Gage, *G-Man: J. Edgar Hoover and the Making of the American Century* (New York: Viking, 2022), 208–9 (explaining that although "formal membership never rose to more than 100,000, the communists' willingness to work with other groups made the party one of the practical and ideological centers of the Depression-era left").

41 Bird and Sherwin, *American Prometheus*, 114.

42 Ibid., 114–36.

43 Ibid., 135–42.

44 Ibid., 135–6.

45 In addition to Oppenheimer, other luminaries in this category included Aaron Copland, Paul Robeson, John Dos Passos, John Steinbeck, and Richard Wright. See Gage, 210.

46 My doubt is based largely on the fact that Oppenheimer remained an independent thinker who never altered his views to conform to the party line and expressed qualms about the totalitarian nature of the Stalinist regime, which would have been heresy at the time.' Bird and Sherwin, 136, 141. As the *New York Times* recently reported, since the release of the Oppenheimer movie in 2023, four historians have argued that various documents show that Oppenheimer was a member of a "secret Berkeley unit" of the Party and that Oppenheimer had perjured himself at the hearing in which he denied having been an actual Party member. Oppenheimer's biographer, Kai Bird, sharply disagrees and accuses the proponents of "pushing their own little crusade." https://www.nytimes.com/2024/10/08/science/oppenheimer-communism-history-nuclear-bomb.html

47 That the training was scheduled for all day Saturday and Sunday, for four weeks, was indicative of the fact that membership in the Communist Party was an all-consuming commitment that was too burdensome for some members, who dropped out within a year or two. See Bird and Sherwin, 115.

Part III—The Soldier

1   Paul Preston, *The Spanish Civil War: Reaction, Revolution, and Revenge* (New York/London: W.W. Norton & Co., 2006), 5, 17.

2   Ibid., 39 et seq.

3   Ibid., 96–8.

4   Ibid., 115–16.

5   Ibid., 153–4.

6   Ibid., 136; Hochschild, 30.

7   Preston, 135–43, 161.

8   Ibid., 137–8, 141.

9   Ibid., 157; Hugh Thomas, *The Spanish Civil War* (New York: Modern Library, 2001 ed.), 374–5, 379 (noting that Germany signed the French declaration on August 24, 1936).

10 Thomas, 444–5; Carroll, 59–62. Carroll writes that American policy was neutral in name only, and that like other Western powers, Roosevelt's administration was hostile to Spain's leftist government, which was viewed as a threat to America's economic interests. On January 6, 1937, Congress passed a resolution formally banning arms shipments to Spain. Thomas, 558.

11 Preston, 145–9; Thomas, 379–81: 428–9. Thomas's exhaustive history of the war contains a detailed explanation of Stalin's conflicting motivations and actions. For example, at the same time that the U.S.S.R. was pledging not to send arms to Spain, Stalin was keeping his options open and approving exports of war material to the Republican government. Thomas also details how other parties to the Non-Intervention Agreement were similarly duplicitous in implementing the pact, which proved to be a sham. See ibid., 374 et seq.

12 Preston, 159.

13 Preston, 150; Thomas, 432–3. As Thomas chronicles, by November 1, 1936, Russia also had 500 personnel in Spain, including field officers, pilots, tank specialists, and flying instructors.

14 Thomas, 448–9.

15 Preston, 161.

16 Ibid., 145; Hochschild, 353.

17 Preston, 106–8.

18 Ibid., 133.

19 Ibid., 267–71; Rosenstone, 150; Hochschild, 175–7.

20 Hochschild, 43–6.

21 See Thomas, 505–25.

22 Preston, 252–65; Rosenstone, 150; Hochschild, 182–7.

23 Preston, 256–61.

24 Hochschild, 104; Peter N. Carroll, *Sketches from Spain: Homage to the Abraham Lincoln Brigade* (Main Street Rag Publishing, 2024), 7.

25 Rosenstone, 112–19; Carroll, 71–5; Peter Carroll and James Fernandez, eds., *Facing Fascism: New York and the Spanish Civil War* (New York: Museum of the City of New York and NYU Press, 2007), 80.

26 Ottanelli, 175; Rosenstone, 98. There are different estimates of the number of American volunteers. Some put the number at 2,500–2,800. See, Carroll, 14; Hochschild, xvi (also noting that approximately 750 of those volunteers died there); *Facing Fascism*, 1.

27 Hochschild, 79.

28 Ibid., 101; Thomas, 557; Rosenstone, 32 (according to Thomas and Rosenstone, there were ninety-six American volunteers on the *Normandie*); Carroll, 14.

29 Carroll, 6.

30 Rosenstone, 185; Hochschild, 229.

31 Hochschild, 100; *Facing Fascism*, 72 (between a fifth and a third of the 3,000 Americans who fought in Spain were either born in New York City or were living there when they volunteered; between 800 and 1,000 men and women left the city to serve in Spain).

32 Rosenstone, 104.

33 Hochschild, 100 (reporting that the average age was twenty-nine); Rosenstone, 111 (reporting that 70 percent were between twenty-one and twenty-eight years old).

34 Carroll, 16.

35 Ibid.

36 Ibid.

37 "Jewish Volunteers in the Spanish Civil War," Abraham Lincoln Brigade Archives, https://alba-valb.org/resource/jewish-volunteers-in-the-spanish-civil-war/; Rosenstone, 110; Carroll, 18.

38 "Jewish Volunteers in the Spanish Civil War."

39 Ibid.

40 Carroll, 126. Among the letters I found in the Briefcase were a few written to Tom Mooney by Irving Schwab's wife (and Ruby's sister), my Aunt Bessie, whom I did know well. They revealed that she, too, had been working for the Communist Party and advocating on behalf of Mooney. See also Hochschild, 103, indicating the Communist Party chose Abraham Lincoln's name for the first American brigade to dispel any notion that it wasn't American.

41 Carroll, 37, 71–5, 126.

42 Carroll, 98–9; Hochschild, 114; Rosenstone, 36–48.

43 Hochschild, 114; Rosenstone, 44.

44 Thomas, 577–8.

45 "FAQs," Abraham Lincoln Brigade Archives, https://alba-valb.org/who-we-are/faqs/; by one estimate, almost half of the American volunteers were dead. Ottanelli, 176; *Facing Fascism*, 15.

46 Hochschild, 134.

47 Rosenstone, 94.

48 Carroll, 66, 124.

49 "SS *Washington*," Wikipedia, https://en.wikipedia.org/wiki/SS_Washington.

50 Rosenstone, 124–6; R. Dan Richardson, *Comintern Army: The International Brigades and the Spanish Civil War* (Lexington, KY: University Press of Kentucky, 1982), 40–41.

51 Hochschild, 132.

52 Ibid., 132–3; Ottanelli, 175–6.

53 Rosenstone, 129–32; Carroll, 124–6.

54 Ruby's letter, dated March 28, reflected that he had arrived in Spain before April 2. Although I originally thought his profile in the Lincoln Brigade Archives was wrong, it's likely that the archives recorded a volunteer's arrival in Spain as of the date on which he reached the headquarters of the International Brigade at Albacete, referred to in Ruby's letter.

55   Ruby was apparently not the only Lincoln volunteer in Spain thirsting for letters from back home. See *Facing Fascism*, 82 ("The Lincolns' constant appeals for genuine American cigarettes were only outnumbered by their demands for more letters. They devoured and shared with each other news of family and friends, the 'local dirt'....This feeling of continued involvement with struggles at home, of being part of a much wider movement, allowed them to proffer advice and chide their correspondents on to greater efforts, as well as underpinning their own commitment to the fight.")

56   Marty Goodman, "Introduction to the *New Masses* Digital Archive on Marxists Internet Archive" (April 2019), https://www.marxists.org/history/usa/pubs/new-masses/intro.htm.

57   Ibid.

58   Richardson, 72–7; Rosenstone, 154–5; Carroll, 95–6, 144.

59   Richardson, 136–49.

60   Carroll, 140.

61   Paul Avrich, *The Modern School Movement, Anarchism and Education in the United States* (Princeton, NJ: Princeton University Press, 1980; AK Press 2006 edition), iii; Eric Anderson, *The Anarchist Classroom: A Test of Libertarian Education and Human Nature at the Modern School in New York and New Jersey, 1911–1953* (CUNY Queens College MA thesis), 3–4, https://academicworks.cuny.edu/qc_etds/5/. There were twenty-two Modern Schools opened in the United States, more than any other country. Ibid., 29–31, 49.

62   Avrich, 4–5, 18–20.

63   According to Paul Avrich, the leading historian on the Modern School movement, the Dicks were "European revolutionaries, materialist, Ferrerist, and pro-Soviet." Ibid., 321. Regardless of their personal political beliefs, the Dicks apparently pursued a strictly libertarian, non-political, approach to educating children. Jim Dick reportedly insisted that while teachers could answer questions about revolution, they "were not to push radical ideas on the students," and he warned against the harm of foisting political propaganda on the children. Ibid., 76–7.

64 Ibid., 344-45.

65 Ibid., 345.

66 Ibid. Also see Alexander Khost, *An Incomplete and Personal History of the Modern Schools* (2018), https://www.self-directed.org/tp/history-of-modern-schools/.

67 My mother's report was also at odds with Paul Avrich's account of the Dicks' philosophy and the reports of other Lakewood alums. On the other hand, although my mother has proved to be an unreliable reporter in a number of instances, Melissa, hardly a gullible person, found her to be very credible as to this one. Moreover, some commentators have asserted that Avrich was more an overly generous advocate for the Modern Schools than an objective reporter. See Anderson, 5. So, it's possible that the Modern Schools' "no punishment" mantra—or, at least, the Dicks' rhetoric—was just propaganda and that the Dicks were hypocrites. It's also possible, however, that my mother—hurt, and seething with resentment that her parents had abandoned her—misremembered being hit with a switch as a five- or six-year-old when she talked to Melissa a half-century later.

68 My mother lived with her grandparents until she was about fourteen or fifteen, when Rose and Harry—who married after Harry returned from the army following World War II—brought her back to Queens, apparently at his instance. In the meantime, Lakewood continued in operation until 1958. When it closed, it was the last surviving Modern School in the United States. See Avrich, 50. As Anderson recounts in *The Anarchist Classroom*, 79–91, the Modern School movement ultimately failed for a number of reasons. It continued to be plagued by the conflict between its communist and libertarian factions. And significantly, the Modern School movement was a victim of its success in attacking the traditionally rigid, authoritarian approach to education. Some of the Modern Schools' practices were adopted, and co-opted, by the progressive education movement as well as the Montessori schools. Thus, by the 1940s parents seeking a libertarian education had other options, while many parents wanted a more formal education for their children. And Anderson has opined that, most importantly, the demise of the Modern Schools was due to the changes in American society with which the Modern Schools failed to keep up. Ibid., 90–91.

69 Preston, 275.

70 Thomas, 689–90; Preston, 275.

71 Preston (at 275) puts the number of Republican troops at 50,000; Hochschild (at 223) has the total at 70,000.

72 Thomas, 690.

73 Ibid., 690–91.

74 Ibid.; Preston, 275.

75 Thomas, 691–2.

76 Ibid., 692.

77 Preston, 275; Thomas, 694; Rosenstone, 183.

78 Rosenstone, 183.

79 Ibid., 183–8.

80 Preston, 275; Thomas, 691; Rosenstone, 186–8.

81 Rosenstone, 183; Hochschild, 225.

82 Thomas, 691, 694.

83 It's not clear whether the soldiers pictured in the film included members of the American brigade or were either all Spanish soldiers or from other International Brigades. It's also very possible that they were intermingled. In his August 12 letter detailing how he came to be wounded on account of the mule, Ruby wrote that a Spanish comrade came to his aid on the battlefield after he was hit. According to Hochschild, due to the embargo on Western arms sales to the Republican government, most of the weapons the Americans had were antiquated Russian models, consistent with those in the film. Hochschild, 118–20.

84 According to Thomas, the Nationalists took control of all but the cemetery on June 24. Thomas, 694.

85 Ibid., 694; Rosenstone, 188.

86 Thomas, 694–95.

87 Ibid. As Carroll recounts, the two American battalions had been "chopped in half," and were thereafter merged into a single command, officially known as the Lincoln-Washington, but commonly known as the Lincoln Brigade. Carroll, 142.

88 Ernest Hemingway, *For Whom the Bell Tolls* (Simon & Schuster Inc., New York, 1940), 232. Hemingway spent extended periods of time in Spain, beginning in the 1920s, during the civil war, and then in later years as well. He wrote more about the Spanish Civil War than any other single topic, as chronicled in Professor Dale Graden's "'The Earth Endureth Forever': Hemingway in Spain," https://albavolunteer.org/2016/06/the-earth-endureth-forever-ernest-hemingway-and-the-spanish-civil-war/. Although Lincoln veterans who survived the war looked forward to the publication of *For Whom the Bell Tolls,* many of them, along with other Communists, lambasted Hemingway because of the novel's vivid description of a fictional episode involving atrocities committed by the Republican forces, and its negative portrayal of André Marty, the Communist leader in Spain. In a furor that lasted for over a decade, Hemingway was accused of giving aid to "humanity's worst enemies" and criticized for presenting "an unforgivable distortion of the meaning of the struggle in Spain." See Carroll, 237 et seq., 316; also *Sketches from Spain*, 96 (writing of Milton Wolf: "Angered by the book's portrayal of Communists, Wolf's brigade attacked the author. He wrote a personal letter calling Hemingway a 'tourist' ... Wolf's anger never cooled").

89 Carroll, 116–17, 251. John Dollard's study, *Fear in Battle,* was published in 1943.

90 Preston, 275.

91 Rosenstone, 186–8; Carroll, 147–8.

92 Minnie's letter reflects that, more than two weeks after Ruby sent his July 25 letter to Rose telling her that he had been wounded, Rose either had not yet received it or had not yet broken the news to the family. That question was resolved by the letter Rose wrote to Ruby on August 19 (returned to her after his death) in which she noted that she had only received his July 25 letter two days earlier, on August 17.

93 The entire section of the letter containing Ruby's conversation with the donkey is quoted at pTK supra.

94 Minnie's August 10 letter indicated that Ruby had been promoted to Secretary of the combined Washington and Lincoln Brigades after the two battalions were combined. ("Congratulations on your graduation to Secretary of both battalions. I guess there's something in that.")

95 As the Lipkaner biography of Ruby indicated, his mother could only read Yiddish (which Ruby sometimes referred to as "Jewish"); his father read both Yiddish and Hebrew.

96 I believe the Mary referred to in this letter was married to Ruby's friend Sidney, who was also in Spain and wrote the July 18 letter discussed earlier.

Part IV—Death

1 Rosenstone, 196–7; Carroll, 154 et seq.

2 Carroll, 154.

3 Rosenstone, 202–5.

4 Ibid., 205.

5 Ibid., 211. See also Carroll, 156–8.

6 Rosenstone, 213, quoting Hemingway, *The Spanish War*, 34.

7 Rosenstone, 233 et seq.; Carroll, 160–62.

8 Preston, 276; Carroll, 162.

9 Rosenstone, 276–86; Carroll, 171–6, 189.

10 See Hilton Kramer, "Art View," *New York Times*, March 11, 1979, https://www.nytimes.com/1979/03/11/archives/art-view-the-unhappy-fate-of-hayes-miller.html; Smithsonian American Art Museum, "Kenneth Hayes Miller," https://americanart.si.edu/artist/kenneth-hayes-miller-3331; American Art Collaborative, "Kenneth Hayes Miller," http://browse.americanartcollaborative.org/actor/ulan/500025218.html.

Part V—Those Who Lived On

1. Ottanelli, 44–5. Many who joined the Party found the demands made on their time too onerous and dropped out; only the most dedicated, such as my grandparents and Irving, remained on board for an extended period. See also Carroll, 13; Rosenstone, 76–7.

2. Ottanelli, 55–6.

3. Ibid., 65–75.

4. Ibid., 83 et seq.

5. Ibid., 83.

6. Carroll, 75.

7. Ottanelli, 111–15.

8. Ibid., 124–5.

9. Carroll, 49; Ottanelli, 164–5.

10. Ottanelli, 128.

11. Richardson, 15; Rosenstone, vii.

12. Richardson, 31–2; Thomas, 440.

13. Richardson, 31; see also *Facing Fascism*, 64–5, noting the U.S. Communist Party's involvement in fundraising, recruiting, and the campaign against the extension of neutrality legislation to Spain ("Communist leader Earl Browder warned that unless the United States changed its policy and 'clasps hands with the peace-loving people of the world' to stop fascism, 'bombs on Madrid' would be a prelude to 'bombs on New York and San Francisco'").

14. *Facing Fascism*, 31–7; Carroll, 64–8. Carroll asserts that contrary to claims made by anti-communists, no official in the Communist Party ever ordered anyone to go to Spain.

15. Richardson, 38; Ottanelli, xx; Carroll, 67 (referring to the World Tourist Travel Agency, which reportedly handled bookings for Communist leaders).

16. Richardson, 15.

17 Ottanelli, 182; Charney, 123–4.

18 Ottanelli, 182–3; Carroll, 226–7.

19 Carroll, 248–52.

20 See, e.g., Gage, 209–10 (The Communist Party "also engaged the cause of Black civil rights, on the premise that race was a pernicious social construct developed to divide the working class. At a time when few white-run organizations took any interest in civil rights issues, communists invested time and energy—and often risked their lives—in emerging fights against lynching, Jim Crow segregation, and the economic oppression of Southern sharecroppers.")

21 Goodman, 57.

22 Carter, 52–3, 62–3; Goodman, 32–4.

23 Goodman, 32.

24 Ibid., 28–9. Irving Schwab was one of the ILD's spokesmen. Goodman recounts a speech Irving gave in 1931 in which he spoke about a worldwide tour to help the Scottsboro Boys. Ibid., 279–80.

25 Goodman, 36; Carter, 73.

26 Goodman, 82–4.

27 Ibid., 97–100; Goodman, 37.

28 Carter, 99–101. Chamlee was a Chattanooga lawyer and a former solicitor general of Hamilton County, Tennessee. Goodman, 32, 43.

29 Carter, 101–2; Goodman, 37–8. The drama concerning Darrow's aborted entry into the case, followed by his exit, was the subject of articles in the *New York Times*, one of which mentioned Irving's participation on the ILD team. "Darrow in Alabama to Aid Eight Negroes," *New York Times*, December 28, 1931; "Darrow Drops Fight to Save Eight Negroes, Refusing to Enter Case With Communists," *New York Times*, December 20, 1931; "Darrow and Hays Turn Down Offers," *Clarion Ledger*, December 29, 1931.

30 Carter, 182–4 (also suggesting that Irving was part of the trial team, and quoting him as saying "I had just about as soon try the cases here"

after Judge Hawkins granted the change in venue from Scottsboro to Decatur), 192 et seq.

31 Ibid., 146.

32 According to Carter, the shepherd was the sister of an ILD lawyer. Ibid., fn. 95, at 233. I wonder, however, whether the shepherd was my Aunt Bessie, Irving's wife. As confirmed by a letter contained in the Briefcase that she wrote to Tom Mooney—the prominent Communist incarcerated at San Quentin for whom the Washington Battalion was originally named—Bessie was working for the ILD in New York. Samuel Leibowitz violently objected to bringing Bates to New York. Bates, herself, claimed she came north with a friend. Goodman, 196.

33 Carter, 232–4; Goodman, 140–3.

34 Carter, 240.

35 Ibid., 213–16. The second doctor, Marvin Lynch, was also slated to testify but was unwilling to do so for fear that his career would be destroyed. However, Lynch requested to meet privately with the judge, and told him that, based on his examination, he didn't believe the girls had been raped. He said that when he told the two women he believed they were lying and knew they hadn't been raped "they just laughed at me."

36 Goodman, 153.

37 Carter, 265–9; Goodman, 176–82.

38 If there was any lingering doubt about the outcome of the trials, Callahan's instructions to the jury at the close of the evidence erased it. As one striking example, the judge instructed the jury: "Where the woman charged to have been raped, as in this case, is a white woman there is a very strong presumption under the law that she would not and did not yield voluntarily to intercourse with the defendant, a Negro" (Goodman, 227). Callahan blocked Leibowitz at every turn, including by barring him from cross-examining Victoria Price concerning her sexual activity on the day prior to the alleged rape. The evidence in Patterson's earlier trial had established that on the night before boarding the train, Price had intercourse with a white man she knew named Jack Tiller. That would have accounted for the small amount of non-motile semen Dr. Bridges found in her vagina when he

examined Price after she claimed to have been raped by all nine of the Scottsboro Boys. Goodman, 212 et seq; Carter, 274 et seq.

39 Ibid., 238–40.

40 Carter, 322; Goodman, 249.

41 Carter, 347; Goodman, 257.

42 Goodman, 304-07. Clarence Norris was convicted and sentenced to death; Andy Wright was convicted and sentenced to ninety-nine years; and Charlie Weems was convicted and sentenced to seventy-five years.

43 Ibid., 308. Lawson stated that given that Eugene Williams and Roy Wright had been twelve and thirteen years old at the time of the alleged rape, justice had been served by their having spent the last six years in prison—provided they left Alabama and never returned.

44 216 Norris and Andy Wright were paroled the following year, although both were later returned to prison for parole violations. Powell was not paroled until 1946—fifteen years after the first sham trial, and Patterson was never granted parole but escaped from the Kilby prison in 1948. Clarence Norris, the last surviving Scottsboro Boy, was pardoned in 1976. After the state of Michigan refused to extradite Patterson, in 1950 the state of Alabama agreed to drop its quest to extradite him. Ibid., 376–81; 393 (for a full chronology of the Scottsboro saga).

45 Goodman chronicles the tragic lives of each of the nine Scottsboro Boys, including the horrific treatment they endured while incarcerated and their troubles after they were finally released. See, Part IV, 337 et seq.

46 Charney, 22–4.

47 Ibid., 84–5.

48 Ibid., 25–7.

49 Ibid., 26–8.

50 Ibid., 28–30.

51 Vivien Gornick, *The Romance of American Communism* (London/New York: Verso, 1977), 219–20.

52 Charney, 29.

53 Gornick, xvi.

54 Ibid., 37.

55 Ibid., 76.

56 Ibid., 115–16.

57 Charney, 47.

58 Gornick, 130–8, 144.

59 Charney, 123–5 (emphasis added).

60 Ibid., 116.

61 Ibid., 182.

62 Gornick, 176. Author Richard Wright wrote of one such sham trial in his 1944 *Atlantic* article, "I Tried to Be a Communist": "Toward evening the direct charges against Ross were made, not by the leaders of the party, but by Ross's friends, those who know him best! It was crushing. Ross wilted. His emotions could not withstand the weight of the moral pressure … The moment came for Ross to defend himself … He stood, trembling; he tried to talk and his words would not come." *The Atlantic* (September 1944), 54. This was part 2 of the article; part 1 appeared in the August 1944 edition.

63 Charney, 184, 196.

64 Gornick, 176–8.

65 Charney, 183–4.

66 See note 62, supra.

67 Richard Crossman, ed., *The God That Failed* (New York: Columbia University Press, 2001 edition), vii.

68 Charney, 190–1.

69 Ibid., 204–7.

70 Ibid., 247–8.

71 *The Communist Party Manual on Organization*, 4.

72 Ibid., 7. The author of the *Manual* was J. Peters, who was a Soviet spy active in the leadership of the U.S. Party.

73 Ibid., 9.

74 Ibid., 11.

75 Ibid., 14.

76 Ibid., 15–16.

77 J.R. Uhlman, *A Bunch of Jews Defending Them Damned Ni__ers* (1997), 15–16, https://openresearch-repository.anu.edu.au/handle/1885/146138.

78 *The Communist Party Manual on Organization*, 16.

79 Ibid., 23.

80 Ibid.

81 Ibid., 26.

82 Ibid., 26–7.

83 Ibid., 116.

84 Ibid., 30–32.

85 Ibid., 32–3.

86 Ibid., 37.

87 Ibid., 43.

88 Ibid., 70.

89 Ibid., 89.

90 Ibid., 91–92.

91 Ibid., 104–5.

92 Ibid., 105.

93 Ibid., 108.

94 Ibid., 112.

95 Ibid., 124.

96 Ottanelli, 123–5; Hochschild, 135.

97 Ottanelli, 124–5.

98 Gornick, xvii; Rosenstone, 63–9.

99 *Manual*, 8, 124.

100 See Rachel Maddow, *Prequel: An American Fight Against Fascism* (New York: Random House, 2023); and Maddow's *Ultra* podcast, https://www.msnbc.com/rachel-maddow-presents-ultra.

101 Gage, 324; *Facing Fascism*, 174 (noting that in 1940 the FBI ransacked the VALB's national office in New York).

102 Gage, 321.

103 Ibid., 345–46. According to Gage, as a result of the Venona decryption program, the FBI "identified 349 people in the United States connected in one way or another to Soviet espionage, whether as information contacts or as fully committed underground agents." Gage concluded: "Taken as a whole, the Venona decryptions lend substance to Hoover's claims that Soviet espionage was a genuine problem in the 1940s, not just a figment of the anticommunist imagination."

104 Ibid., 346, 372–7. According to Gage, although Venona documented the espionage activities of Julius Rosenberg, the evidence as to Ethel was more ambiguous, and the Venona evidence pertaining to the information Julius provided to the Soviets "was somewhat less dramatic and consequential than the Rosenbergs' popular image as master atomic spies would suggest." The existence of the Venona decryption program, and much of the evidence it produced, was not publicly disclosed until the 1990s, after Hoover's death.

105 Ibid., 455–7.

106 Charney, 29-30.

107 https://digitalarchive.wilsoncenter.org/document/khrushchevs-secret-speech-cult-personality-and-its-consequences-delivered-twentieth-party.

108 Gornick, 156.

109 Ibid., 200–201; *Sketches from Spain*, 90 (poem by Peter Carroll chronicling that George Watt quit the Party when Stalin was rebuked:

Endnotes

"the most traumatic episode of my life. With real regrets, he warned of blind faith in any movement, no matter how worthy the cause."

110 Charney, 249–50.

111 Ibid., 253.

112 Gornick, 10. There are varying estimates of the number of defections. See Carroll, 345–6 (reporting that membership, which had been as high as 75,000 in 1945, dropped from 17,000 in 1956 to 5,000 by the following year).

113 Gage, 455–6. Hoover engaged in what Beverly Gage describes as "by far the most notorious program of Hoover's career" in an effort to destroy the remnants of the Communist Party after Khrushchev's 1956 speech. His COINTELPRO program employed two tactics to manipulate, misinform, and disrupt the Party. The first involved the use of anonymous letters sent to Party members or press contacts, to highlight unflattering matters concerning the Party. Hoover would use this same weapon against Martin Luther King (ibid., 607–8). The second tactic deployed against the Communists involved the use of informants to spread rumors and stoke division within the Party.

114 Rose and Harry were not alone in embracing the Italian Communist Party in the wake of Khrushchev's Secret Speech. Another American Communist reported: "For me, the rise of the Italian Communist Party is the earth renewed ... No matter what the Italians do or do not accomplish within the next twenty or thirty years, they will provide the link between the Stalinist past and the unknowable socialist future. And that is of vital importance. Inestimable importance." Gornick, 242.

115 Charney, 280.

116 Ibid., 260.

117 Ibid., 277.

118 Ibid., 312.

119 Ibid., 315.

120 Ibid., 322.

121 Ibid., 324–26.

122 Gornick, 24–5. See also Carroll, 345 et seq.

123 Carroll, 146; *Sketches from Spain*, 30.

124 Carroll, 213.

125 Rosenstone, 363. See also Carroll, 343, 378.

126 Rosenstone, 346; Carroll, 250–2.

127 Dated August 8, 1937, a one-paragraph nondescript excerpt relating to Ruby noted: "He is most responsible and reliable and has done leading work in the CP of the United States in the capacity of Section Organizer and Education director." It went on to say that "he was wounded in the recent action at the Madrid front [i.e., at Brunete] and is now in the hospital at Murcia." So this document was the source of the entry in Ruby's profile indicating that he was hospitalized and died in Murcia. Until receiving this document and some further assistance from Chris Brooks, I had believed that the profile was wrong and that Ruby had been hospitalized in Madrid. The records Brooks provided showed that I had been mistaken. See note 134, infra.

128 Brooks proceeded to give me the following detailed explanation of how the Lincoln Brigade Archives had catalogued the Soviet records: "The IB [International Brigades] Records were placed within Fond 545 Comintern Archives, the overarching collection that contains the records of the International Brigades. Fond 545 is further divided into six Opis—Series or Record Group. Each Opis contains multiple Delos or Files. Each individual document is assigned a Listy or document number. The six opisi are:

Опись (Opis 1) Документы Военного комиссариата интербригад (Documents of the Military Commissariat and International Brigade.)

Опись 2. (Opis 2) Документы Центральной военной администрации интербрига (International Brigades Base documents and Documents of the Central Military Administration of the International Brigade.)

Опись 3. (Opis 3) Документы 35 и 45 дивизий, 10-15, 129 интербригад и соединений республиканской армии Испании (Documents of the 35th and 45th Divisions, X-XV, and CXXIX International Brigades and squadrons of the Republican Army of Spain.)

Опись 4. (Opis 4) Документы интернированных бойцов и командиров интербриг (Documents of the interned soldiers and commanders of the International Brigade in the concentration camps of France and North Africa.)

Опись 5. (Opis 5) Фотографические документы интербригад республиканской армии Испании (Photographic documents of the international brigade of the Republican army of Spain.) Note: Opis 5 is currently not online.

Опись 6. (Opis 6) Списки, личные дела бойцов и командиров интербригад (Lists and personal files of soldiers and commanders of the international brigade.)

129 *Manual*, 112.

130 Gornick, 145.

131 After extoling Harry's ability as a soldier, the assessment of Harry that Chris Brooks had uncovered went on to assess Harry's character, political credentials, and potential future in the Party upon his return to the United States:

> With a bit more initiative, he could develop into good leader. Good for organizational work, accepts responsibility.... Is being recommended for work in Paris apparatus because of dependability and organizational ability. Recommend special political education upon return to States.

It's not clear whether Harry was ever elevated to a leadership position in the Party.

132 "7 Union Leaders Accused of Racket in Fur District," *New York Times*, March 28, 1973, https://www.nytimes.com/1973/03/28/archives/7-union-leaders-accused-of-racket-in-fur-district-7-union-leaders.html.

133 Preston, 261.

134 One reason for my skepticism is that my grandmother's report that "two guys from the Brigade who were given leave and went to see him in the hospital" doesn't square neatly with what I belatedly came to learn about where Ruby was hospitalized, died, and is buried. Courtesy of the Lincoln Brigade archivist, Chris Brooks, as this book was about to be typeset I received a record documenting that Ruby was hospitalized in Murcia, over 250 miles from where his brigade comrades were likely

located, rendering it doubtful that they visited him. More importantly, the record reflected that Ruby's remains were exhumed and transferred twice after he was buried on August 24, 1937—first, on December 12, 1939, to a "judicial ditch," and then again in 1989 to "Dignified Tomb Zone 2 No 99 and No 100." https://www.fosasmemoriahistoricamurcia.com/personas/rubin-schechter/? (English translation). A memorial lists Ruby (with his last name misspelled) as among more than 100 veterans of the International Brigades buried in Murcia. Notably, the record I received from Brooks states that Ruby died on August 23, 1937, and was buried on August 24. His profile in the Lincoln Brigades Archives states that he died on August 24. I suspect that the profile is wrong and that the correct date of death was August 23—which would be consistent with references to the date of death in other documents (including Rose's letter to Ernest Meyer, supra).

135 Carroll, 281–83, 293.

136 Ibid., 268; Gage, 321 et seq. (discussing Hoover's surveillance campaign targeting the Communist Party and suspected Communists); *Facing Fascism*, 174 (the FBI ransacked the VALB's national office), and 176–7 ("The late 1940s brought a concerted assault on the Communist ties and 'fellow travelling' of Lincoln veterans…. The taint of Republican Spain became *prima facia* evidence of subversion and disloyalty.")

137 Carroll, 293–310.

138 It is true that Hoover devoted special attention to suspected Communists in Hollywood. Gage, 323. As Gage recounts, when Hollywood movies began to appear praising the Soviet war effort, Hoover became obsessed with the writers, directors, actors, and artists suspected of propagating pro-Soviet ideas. The Bureau's investigation produced long lists of Party members and sympathizers associated with Hollywood.

139 Carroll, 288–90, 296–8; *Sketches from Spain*, 56 ("He worked tirelessly for the cause, despite threats of subpoenas. A good part of the time, he told his dad, I have two cars and two FBI college boys on my tail"), and 57 ("The witch hunters kept an eye on that outfit, the FBI at his door every Monday morning").

140 Bird and Sherwin, 540 et seq.

141 See Gage, 393–4. Gage reports that as part of the Responsibilities Program, beginning in 1951 the FBI provided state and local authorities with information about left-leaning professors, librarians, and defense workers. The program expanded quickly, and by the following year the FBI was notifying governors and university presidents about faculty members and staff employed in state university systems. By May 1952, two months after I was born, the FBI was reporting on secondary school teachers. By 1955, when the program closed, the FBI had secretly disseminated information on more than 900 people, most of them teachers, librarians, professors, and university administrators. More than half of those people were fired or left their jobs. I suspect that my uncle may have been a victim of this campaign, which was conducted largely without public notice, in contrast to the highly publicized spectacle conducted by Joe McCarthy, with whom Hoover had an often contentious relationship (ibid., Chapter 33 and 425–36).

142 Charney, 209–24.

143 Carroll, 362, 369.

144 Howard Fast, *Peekskill U.S.A.: Inside the Infamous 1949 Riots* (New York: Open Road Integrated Media, 2011 edition; originally published in 1951).

145 Martin Bauml Duberman, *Paul Robeson* (New York: Alfred A. Knopf, 1988), 364–5.

146 Fast, 25–6.

147 Duberman, 365; Fast, 47.

148 Duberman, 367; Fast, 60 et seq.

149 Duberman, 368.

150 Ibid.; Fast, 74–76.

151 Fast, 77–79.

152 Duberman, 369; Fast, 81.

153 Duberman, 369–70; Fast, 81–83.

154 Duberman, 369; Fast, 86.

155 Fast, 86.

156 Ibid., 89.

157 Ibid., 132–3.

158 "Peekskill Outrage," https://www.youtube.com/watch?v=1pgyACdT1rM (video about the Peekskill riot and Robeson, narrated by Sidney Poitier and Pete Seeger).

159 "The Real 'Nate Shaw'," *Political Affairs: Journal of Marxist Thought and Analysis* (May 1976), 59.

160 Although Irving was involved in the Herndon case, he did not serve as trial counsel. The ILD hired two local African American lawyers to try the case, apparently the first time African American lawyers served as lead counsel in a civil rights case in the South. See https://www.encyclopedia.com/african-american-focus/news-wires-white-papers-and-books/herndon-angelo.

161 Gornick, 25.

Reflections, Epilogue, and Acknowledgments

1 See also *Facing Fascism*, 180 (noting that in addition to continually protesting against U.S. support for Franco, Lincoln veterans' advocacy extended to other causes, including protesting the "whites only" policy in Levittown, Long Island, marching in solidarity with the Selma civil rights protest, and marching in opposition to the Vietnam War, South African apartheid, and Ronald Reavgan's South American policy).

2 It is tempting to draw parallels between the volunteers who traveled to Spain to join the International Brigades in 1936, and those venturing to Ukraine to support the fight against Putin's aggression today. And we have friends, and the idealistic children of friends, who have done so, working alongside Ukraine's medical and relief teams. Nevertheless, as Sebastian Faber explains in an astute, recent analysis, some who have joined in the actual fighting, if not many, of them—including combat veterans—have little in common with the left-leaning volunteers like my grandfathers who left home to fight in Spain. https://theconversation.com/ukraines-foreign-fighters-have-little-in-common-with-those-who-signed-up-to-fight-in-the-spanish-civil-war-178976.

3 Charney, 116.

4   Sebastiaan Faber and Peter Carroll have served as the editors of *The Volunteer*, which was founded in 1937, the year of Ruby's death, by Lincoln Brigade veterans. It is published by the Abraham Lincoln Brigade Archives (ALBA). *The Volunteer* publishes both a print edition, of which, until his recent passing, Peter Carroll served as the editor, and an online edition (https://albavolunteer.org/) for which Sebastiaan Faber, until recently, served as the editor.

Milton Keynes UK
Ingram Content Group UK Ltd.
UKHW040331031224
452051UK00014B/370/J